THOUGHT AND NATURE

Thought and Nature

STUDIES IN RATIONALIST PHILOSOPHY

ARTHUR W. COLLINS

UNIVERSITY OF NOTRE DAME PRESS
NOTRE DAME, INDIANA 46556

Apart from minor changes, chapters II, IV, V, and VI of this
book appeared in *The St. John's Review*, volume 31, number 1;
volume 32, number 1; and volume 34, numbers 1 and 2; between 1979 and 1983.

Library of Congress Cataloging in Publication Data

Collins, Arthur W.
    Thought and nature.

    Includes index.
    1. Rationalism. 2. Empiricism. 3. Philosophy,
Modern—17th century. 4. Philosophy, Modern—18th
century. I. Title.
B833.C65   1985   149'.7   84-40823
ISBN 0-268-01856-1

Manufactured in the United States of America

For
LEO RADITSA

Contents

Preface   ix

I. Introduction: Rationalism and Empiricism   1

II. The Scientific Background of Descartes' Dualism   26
  1. *Introduction*   *26*
  2. *Descartes' argument*   *27*
  3. *The scientific background*   *35*
  4. *Conclusions*   *51*

III. The Metaphysical Elements of Spinoza's
Philosophy of Mind   61
  1. *The objectives of this study*   *61*
  2. *The concept of substance*   *62*
  3. *Appearance and reality*   *66*
  4. *Causality and intelligibility*   *71*
  5. *The rejection of dualism*   *77*
  6. *The apparatus of substance and attributes*   *81*
  7. *The infinity of attributes*   *86*
  8. *Aristotle and Spinoza*   *95*
  9. *The order of ideas*   *98*
  10. *Mind and physiology*   *101*
  11. *The problem of objects for ideas*   *107*
  12. *Representation and knowledge of the external*   *111*

IV. The Unity of Leibniz's Thought on Contingency,
Possibility, and Freedom   123
  1. *The defects of Cartesian physics*   *123*
  2. *Nature itself*   *130*
  3. *Analyticity*   *139*
  4. *Possibility and possible worlds*   *157*
  5. *Freedom*   *166*

V. Kant's Empiricism   180

VI. Ambiguities in Kant's Treatment of Space   198
    1. *Introduction*   198
    2. *Outer sense and idealism*   200
    3. *Transcendental aesthetic*   204
    4. *The construction of spatial objects*   209
    5. *Sensation and the objectivity of outer sense*   214
    6. *Primary and secondary qualities*   222
    7. *The spatial and the temporal*   226
    8. *A sketch for the consistent Kantian*   236

Index   245

Preface

Although the chapters of this book were written as self-contained studies and can be read independently of one another, they are also intended to form a connected whole. Apart from the fact that the chapters constitute a chronologically organized treatment of the great rationalist philosophers, the most prominent connecting element is the emphasis on the philosophy of mind. Indeed, my own study of rationalism developed out of my efforts, over a number of years, addressed to the concepts of conciousness, perception, and belief. My experience convinces me that we cannot fully understand our own philosophical ideas and problems, or understand and assess our own intuitive sense of the options from which philosophical solutions may be chosen, without the study of the history of philosophy. All the studies contain expositions of points of contact between contemporary discussions and the ideas of the seventeenth- and eighteenth-century rationalists, and there are many sidelong glances at the empiricist philosophers in relation to present-day philosophical problems and arguments.

It is universally agreed that Descartes' thinking has had the greatest and the most enduring influence on the development of modern philosophy. Descartes' philosophy of mind has decisively shaped epistemology and metaphysics and determined the agenda of problems characteristic of European philosophy up to the present. Nowadays Descartes' thinking is typically studied with little or no reference to the scientific objectives and constraints which guided the development of his ideas and which those ideas, in large part, express. This is partly a consequence of Descartes' own presentation of his ideas in the *Meditations*, where his views are developed as though from an abstract and rather arbitrarily adopted method of doubt. The *Meditations* has become the epitome of Descartes for the modern student. Chapter II places Descartes' famous dualism and the arguments that defend that dualism in the setting of scientific ideas from which Cartesian dualism originated.

Approaches to Leibniz's thought have been handicapped, ironically, by the prestigious but untenable interpretations of his twentieth-century rediscoverers: Bertrand Russell and Louis Couturat. In particular, they agree in imposing on Leibniz a hopeless commitment to the idea that all truth is analytic, a view which obliterates human freedom and contingency. Chapter IV treats Leibniz on contingency, possibility, and freedom in order to counteract the widespread influence of these interpreters.

Whereas interpreters of Leibniz have read an insensitive and unattractive thesis into his writings, interpreters of Spinoza have found profound insights and an ingratiating modernity. The considerable contemporary praise for Spinoza does not correspond to any great influence exerted by his ideas on his successors. There are, to be sure, important belated influences of Spinoza on nineteenth-century philosophers, but he does not play a role in the development of European thought comparable to that of Descartes and Leibniz. Chapter III explains the serious and unresolvable difficulties of his metaphysics and philosophy of mind against which the claim that he prefigures Freud or contemporary mind-brain identity theory ought to be judged. The dominance of medieval and Greek patterns of thought and the lack of influence of developing scientific ideas on Spinoza are also explored.

Chapters V and VI are expressions of admiration for Kant and of the conviction that his ideas hold much that is of value for us, especially in the philosophy of mind. The theme of "refutation of idealism" underlies both chapters, and this is, in my view, the heart of Kant's best and not-fully-assimilated contribution to philosophy. I am sure that all admirers of Kant find their enthusiasm tempered by the exceptional obscurity and inconsistency of his work. It may be that we should be grateful even for these universally recognized characteristics of Kant's writings that cost students of his thought so much time and energy. Kant, after all, is a great reconciler, not only of opposed arguments like those of Newton and Leibniz on space and time, but of whole traditions such as empiricism and rationalism. The preponderance of philosophers, more pessimistic about the prospect for reconciliation, suffer from a premature need to resolve ambiguities and to eliminate what appear to be inconsistent strains in their thinking. Many philosophers seem to feel the need to stand up and be counted, for example, as a nominalist or a Platonist, as a dualist or a mind-brain identity theorist, as a scientific realist or an anti-foundationalist. Kant tolerates inconsistent strains and unresolved ambiguities to an extraordinary degree. This is not a mystical bent or a love for a thriving but murky pond full of unsorted and suggestive thoughts. Kant simply sees very compelling lines of thought that have opposed tendencies, and he is unwilling to give any of them up merely to straighten things out and leave himself with a presentable roster of opinions. He develops what seems valuable and postpones (sometimes ignores) the confrontations in the hope that things that seem opposed will fit together in the end. He always seems to have ideas that make this more than a bare hope. I am convinced that Kant's profundity is achieved in part by his willingness to discard and then to oppose any important line of thought only because it does not seem to cohere well with other points on which he has committed himself. All too often philosophers tidy up their arguments and systems like political ideologists clarifying the party line. Kant is never tempted by this at all. Is not his rejection of this approach quite visible in the broadest outlines of Kant's thinking? He divided reality into two sorts, empirical and transcendental, rather than discard one or the other of two attractive but discordant doctrines: determinism and freedom, for example. In Chapter VI I take Kant to task for adopting this expedient, but I also approve the underlying set of mind that leads him to it.

Many friends and colleagues have helped and encouraged me in various ways in the preparation of this book. Leo Raditsa asked me to write chapters II, IV, V, and VI for the *St. John's Review*, of which he was the editor. Those chapters have also benefited from his criticisms and suggestions. Charles Landesman read and commented helpfully on all of the chapters. Harry Frankfurt gave me useful criticisms and advice for the chapter on Descartes. Finally, Maurice Mandelbaum encouraged me to publish these studies as a book and helped to arrange the publication.

Arthur W. Collins

New York City
March 1985

Introduction: Rationalism and Empiricism

At the beginning of the *Meditations* Descartes explains that any "secure and lasting result in science" requires assurance that what merely seems to be true will not, in the end, prove false, as so many beliefs inherited from childhood have proved false. Plausibility, conviction, even very great conviction, may conceal error, so Descartes says that he, and by that he means also we, "must withhold our assent no less carefully from what is not plainly certain and indubitable than from what is obviously false."[1] Of course, we cannot examine all of our beliefs one at a time, but we are able to see a possibility of error in all the beliefs of great classes sharing the same foundation, and "when the foundation is undermined the superstructure will collapse of itself." Most of our beliefs about the world "are got either from the senses or by means of the senses."[2] But beliefs that rest on the evidence of the senses are certainly not indubitable. Thus, the primary effect of the famous method of doubt is the elimination of the sensory as part of any satisfactory foundation for knowledge and for scientific knowledge in particular. If a foundation for utterly reliable belief is going to be found at all, it will not be an empirical foundation.

The general contours of rationalist philosophy and the opposition of rationalism and empiricism are already indicated in these first lines of the *Meditations*. Foundations for knowledge must lie in truths that we possess and can recognize as true without having to acquire them in experiences of the world. These truths will turn out to include, in addition to the truths of logic and mathematics, those that derive from analysis of our own concepts and, most important, the *cogito* and the class of truths deriving from the *cogito* that constitute our knowledge of the contents of our own conscious minds.

The common thread connecting subjective certainties, conceptual analyses, theorems of mathematics, and truths of formal logic is the clarity and distinctness of our ideas in framing and entertaining these propositions. Clear and distinct ideas are the basis of truths accessible to intuition, which, together with deduction from intuited premises, exhausts the resources for knowledge in the recipe of the *Regulae*.[3] Of course, in the *Meditations* even beliefs involving only clear and distinct ideas are subjected to skeptical examination, and the hypothesis of the deceiving demon temporarily undermines some of them, such as the arithmetical proposition that $2 + 3 = 5$. Perhaps Descartes means that this high-water mark of skepticism undermines the claims of every belief and covers all those involving clear and distinct ideas as well as all empirical beliefs. Wherever he draws the line here, the point is that these truths built out of clear and distinct ideas eventually pass the test and attain standing as indubitable premises ready to serve as foundations for lasting results in science.

In contrast, beliefs dependent upon the senses are not set aside provisionally until a further procedure reinstates those that, though at first suspect, turn out to be true. There is a sense in which no beliefs requiring sensory evidence ever turn out to be true. They are not merely dubitable beliefs. They are all actually false. Sensory beliefs are unclear and confused representations, and, as such, their unsatisfactory status is permanent. Their lack of distinctness consists in the fact that they do not discriminate features of the representation from features of the extramental reality they purport to represent. There is no unclear and confused reality which these ideas might correctly represent. Therefore, from the beginning Descartes repudiates beliefs based on sense experience and seeks foundations for all knowledge only among propositions whose truth is recognized by reason.

There is justice in this bald account, and it is easily documented, not only by appeal to the writings of Descartes but also from the writings of Spinoza and Leibniz. At the same time it is a profoundly inadequate account. This is obvious as soon as we reflect that Descartes and Leibniz were themselves scientists, and Spinoza was a maker of instruments who was in touch with scientific work and sketched a theory of motion and of physiology in his *Ethics*. None of these thinkers could have entirely failed to understand the role of experiment and empirical observation in the discovery of scientific truths about the details of the world in which they were all keenly interested.[4] In recounting his understandings in physiology and optics Descartes describes his own experiments and observations and recommends that they be repeated by the reader.[5] He uses evidence, for example, from his dissections of the heart and eye of animals as an indispensable part of his explanation of the circulation of the blood and of visual perception. It is not credible to suppose that Descartes thinks of his reasoning here as deduction from indubitable premises all of which are certified by reason alone. In any case, Descartes' thinking and that of the other rationalists attain minimal plausibility only by allowing a reasonable scope to empirical information in the fabric of human knowledge.

Rationalists, after all, do not present a preposterous account of our knowledge of reality, but it would be preposterous to suppose that one could find out the determinate, detailed constitution of the world by some deductive process starting from premises from which every bit of empirical information is excluded in favor of nonempirical truths attested to by pure reason. Everyone knows, and quite obviously all the rationalist philosophers know, that the particulars of the world are only known to those who examine the world.

Is this a question of inconsistency in the rationalist program? Leibniz and Spinoza follow Descartes in constructing criteria for the recognition of truths that apply to the ideas and concepts upon which we reflect and not to matters alleged about external reality as perceived. And yet any superficial examination of all three writers shows that they do not limit their premises in practice in accordance with these austere criteria, but freely appeal to both common and specialized knowledge of the world that is got by empirical means. For instance, the rationalist Leibniz, arguing against the views of the empiricist science of Newton, in the correspondence with Samuel Clarke, uses empiricist principles, and not criteria of clarity, distinctness, or adequacy of ideas, in opposing the Newtonian doctrine of absolute space. Such a conception of space should be set aside, Leibniz thinks, because its existence or nonexistence would make no difference to the total of experiences, so that the hypothesis is empty.[6] Again, Leibniz criticizes Descartes' mechanical laws for their failure to cohere with the observable facts, and Leibniz rightly assumes that Descartes intends his laws of impact to hold for the impacts of bodies that we observe. The theory of intuition and deduction of the *Regulae*, and the promise of reduction to absolute certainties of the First Meditation, are apparently inconsistent with Descartes' acceptance of the obligation to present theories that cohere with the observed facts. But Descartes' would be a ridiculous science if he really rejected this obligation altogether. Had he promoted such a science, he should have shown no interest at all in empirical investigation of the rainbow, the magnet, the refraction of light, or the circulation of the blood. But, of course, he studied all of these phenomena, and he plainly counted it a virtue of his metaphysical understanding of the world that he was able to offer explanations for all of them which *save the phenomena.*

At the end of the *Discourse on Method* Descartes comments with considerable sophistication on such explanations, many of which were published in the accompanying essays on optics and meteorology. He defends his use of "suppositions" and tells us

> For it is my view as to the connection of my conclusions that, just as the last are proved by the first, which are their causes, so the first may in turn be proved by the last, which are their effects. [And this is not circular reasoning] . . . for the effects are for the most part known with certainty by experience so that the causes from which I have deduced them must, indeed, be themselves proved by means of [the effects].[7]

By the effects "known with certainty by experience" Descartes surely refers to observable facts. These certainties are not framed in terms purified of every reliance on the senses and merely inspected for their clarity and distinctness. He is asserting that his accounts are what we call hypotheticodeductive explanations of known empirical facts in the course of which confirmation accrues to the hypotheses—and these are Descartes' "suppositions" which are needed premises in the deductions.

There are numerous passages in Descartes' writings where the same kind of sentiment is reasserted, even though it is so out of keeping with the impoverished rationalist foundation for science he has announced.[8] To an extent this does represent an incoherence and an unresolved tension in Descartes' thought. At the same time there are themes that tend toward the reconciliation of the austere exclusion in principle and the reasonable acceptance in practice of empirical investigation and empirical fact. Before considering reconciliation, I would like to consider two further areas in which his sensitivity to empirical discoveries is a crucial element in the construction of Descartes' rationalism.

Descartes knows that the intellectual crises of his world have been precipitated by empirical experiment, observation with telescopes, and precise measurement of what is accessible to the senses. A vast suspicion of the pronouncements of philosophers and scientists, an anxious real skepticism, and a shattering failure of confidence lie behind the academic exercise of doubt in the *Meditations*. Common and natural beliefs that had seemed secure through two thousand years were rather suddenly overthrown by new scientific findings. And the old beliefs that plainly had to be discarded were not superstitious dogmas but the considered opinions of unbiased intelligent thinkers, with Aristotle at the head of them, who started from a moderate and reasonably critical acceptance of the world as sense experience reveals it. The immutability of celestial things, the circular motions of the heavens, and the geocentric solar system revolving around a stationary earth at the center of things were defended by the authority of church dogmatists, but they were also features of reality that seemed to be revealed to perceptual inspection. Aristotle's physics, based on the view that the several forms of matter seek their proper place, was also an empirical generalization founded on facts that seemed readily apparent to the senses. His theory of inertia—force must be expended to keep a body in motion at constant velocity—coheres with the world of everyday experience, while the modern replacement appears to defy what we observe. The inquisitors examining Galileo's views were not just dogmatic representatives of vested interests: they were also heirs of a powerful and sensible intellectual tradition founded on the intelligent interpretation of empirical information. Conversely, scientific thinkers of the generations of Galileo and Descartes were obliged to recognize that their own views, even though they were based on experiment and observation, entailed a critique of Aristotelian empiricism and a systematic suspicion of perception. What appears to be the case to the senses represents, at best, a problem. Sensuous appearances are misleading and must be reconciled with the findings of a science based on the mathematical interpretation of nature.

This amounted to an intellectual crisis, because rejection of scientific conceptions long accepted was not just a matter of the inadequacy of a miscellany of opinions of physicists. As Descartes understands, observational astronomy and the new mechanical physics threaten the entire scholastic-Aristotelian view of what the physical world is. The new science bids to remove man from the center of the universe and to destroy the theatrical interpretation of physical reality as a stage on which the drama of human salvation or damnation is played out. Descartes' insistence on mechanics in the explanation of observed motions will overthrow the ubiquitous scholastic teleology that found in every detail of the world divine intentions and comforting relations to human existence and destiny. Descartes takes a large step toward seeing the world, as we have gradually come to see it, as a vast, mostly unknown, system of things and forces, which is neutral to our existence and aspirations, and in which we have neither central position nor role of great consequence.

In a way Descartes' egocentric subjectivism is itself a recognition of and a remedy for the loss of physical centrality in the universe by man. His psychology effects a radical restoration of man to the center of things by identifying that center, not with the physical point occupied by the earth, but with the psychological center, the unique point of view of one person's consciousness. By the terms of the new Cartesian centrality, the admirable and wonderful self-reliance of the individual—the bold independence of a single consciousness as the center of a system of meaning, intention, and knowledge—is set over against *the rest of the universe*, which becomes the "external world" that balances the subjective inner world by some miraculous equation. In Leibniz's version this equation is spelled out in the claim that the entire universe—past, present, and future—is mirrored in the mental representation of every monad, though this representation is seldom either conscious or distinct. In the absolute self-reliance of the Cartesian conscious mind at the focal point of its world we find the core of the modern conception of the individual and the initiation of romanticism.

Finally, it is empirical investigation and observation and, ultimately, perceptual acquaintance with the physical and physiological processes involved in perception that underlie Descartes' analysis of the inadequacy of perceptual belief. Descartes understands that the transmission of light, sound, and pressure involves nothing mental and cognitive. These are causal and mechanical matters. Mental apprehension, conscious awareness, is not to be found either in the external stages of these causal processes or in the stages of the same processes that unfold within the body. The inner stages are the physiological processes by means of which the physical stimulation of the organs of perception is transmitted to the brain and finally to the mind. The perceptual experience is or involves an inner mental object of awareness, and, once it is so understood, the obvious question of its reliability as a representation of something outer is generated. This understanding of the physics and physiology of sense perception greatly reinforces the suspicion of the senses Descartes derives from the fact that they sometimes deceive us. The scientific description explains just how it can happen that the senses sometimes lead us into false beliefs. Defective transmissions will generate inappropriate inner objects of perceptual consciousness. The scientific picture also explains how the senses are systematically misleading with respect to the general conception of reality to which they give rise. The physiological story ideally supports the theory of secondary qualities according to which sensuous features like color belong only to the inner representation and not to any outer reality represented. The secondary qualities are merely subjective responses to stimuli from outer objects which themselves lack sensuous character altogether.

The reliance on the empirical in constructing the rationalist rejection of empirical foundations is not strictly inconsistent. Bertrand Russell once pointed out that such a procedure uses the valid pattern of argument that the scholastic logicians called the *consequentia mirabilis*. By accepting the data of the senses we establish that those data are unacceptable. If commonsense perceptual belief is true, it leads us to scientific knowledge, which shows us that commonsense perceptual belief is false. Therefore, it is false. But this reconstruction of the argument is certainly not in the spirit of the rationalist critique of the senses. From a formal point of view Russell's reconstruction does not allow us to rescue the mediating scientific understanding, whereas it is plain that the rationalists mean that the story of the stimulation of the sense organs, the transmission of nerve impulses, and the causal production of an inner object of perceptual consciousness is a true story. There is, indeed, an element of inconsistency in Descartes' attitude toward the empirical, and it is never satisfactorily resolved. But we make out, in his thought, hints of a resolution and the direction that a resolution must take. It is easiest to approach this question looking back from the views of later thinkers in this tradition, and especially the views of Leibniz and Kant.

Leibniz says, very much as Descartes does, that sense perception is intrinsically faulty as a source of knowledge of reality. Perception is "confused thought" in which a blurred aggregated image is the surrogate for the infinite detail of monadic reality. At the same time, as we noted, Leibniz is a scientist, and an empirical scientist. Like Descartes', Leibniz's analysis of the deficiency of the senses is rooted in an empirical understanding of how the senses work. But in Leibniz's thinking explicit provision for this seeming inconsistency is offered in his recognition of two levels of discourse about reality. Perceptual experience generates one level, the realm of phenomena. Although entirely inadequate as an index of true being, which is all monads, thinking about phenomena is by no means wasted thinking. On the whole, phenomena are *bene fundata*, or well-founded, and, as such, they are the subject matter of scientific investigation and prediction, even though they fail to represent things as they really are.

According to Leibniz's division of subject matters, space and time only characterize things at the level of phenomena. Discourse about the whole perceived world of spatiotemporal reality lacks the credentials demanded by ultimate metaphysical foundations, but it is indispensable for the conduct of life and for the practice and understanding that makes up natural science. The eternal reality of simple monads can be described only in nonempirical terms. Metaphysical knowledge has priority in the sense that in order to know what phenomena are we must understand them relative to a knowledge of substances which make up the system of monads. Leibniz never offers a unified system in which the discourse of perceptual science is placed in any definite logical relations with the theory of monads. Often his discussions of force, of hierarchies of monads, of dominant monads in animals, and of human consciousness (as a monad) suggest that some such logical relations ought to be forthcoming, so that, for example, empirical physics might be placed on a foundation in the theory of monads. The hopes encouraged by these discussions are always disappointed, and, on the whole, it seems to me that Leibniz does not think these two levels of discourse could ever be united.

There is a similar, though far less clearly developed, theme in Spinoza's thinking. The level of thought that relies on sense perception and imagination characterizes realities in terms of sensuous features, in terms of part and whole relationships, in terms of discriminable individuals, and in terms of time and duration, while none of these terms have footing in the characterization of the ultimate reality of substance as grasped by reason. But Spinoza simply takes the empirical to be the common level of thought which is inadequate and confused. He does not connect perception with a valuable phenomenal level of thought, nor does he identify natural science as the study of reality under empirical description. This difference is partly to be attributed to the fact that Spinoza is far less involved with the actual development of science than are the other major rationalist philosophers. In consequence he is less attentive to the demands of science, less appreciative of the methods of science, and less concerned that his system provide a conceptual place for empirical investigation.

Leibniz's distinction of phenomenal and metaphysical levels of thought is greatly strengthened and clarified by Kant. The world of sense perception is the phenomenal world. As for Leibniz, so too for Kant, the phenomenal reality, and no other, is spatiotemporal. The inadequate phenomenal representation and the adequate metaphysical account of Leibniz become two realities in Kant's thinking, and his work is marked by a restless shifting of the balance between mind-dependent empirical reality, which is the subject matter of all science, and the transcendental and unknowable reality of things as they are in themselves. In Kant's thinking the usual rationalist condemnation of the imagination as the origin of confusion and inadequacy in phenomenal representations gives way to a constructive role for the imagination in the necessary synthesis of the materials of sense that makes of them an intuitable object of perception and understanding. As the phenomenal gains in value and significance, so the Leibnizian metaphysical representation shrinks in Kant's system, becoming the ineliminable but sterile idea of nonspatiotemporal noumenal reality about which we can never know anything. As an evidence of its ancestry in the development of rationalist thought, Kant continues to designate the transcendental world of things as they are in themselves "the intelligible world," although it yields nothing at all to our intelligence.

Let us return to Descartes' thought, keeping in mind the provisions made for empirical knowledge in the subsequent rationalist tradition. The need and the preliminary preparations for such provisions are visible in Descartes, although they are not developed. To see this, we should draw attention first to the difference between the subjective knowledge of one's own mental life guaranteed by the *cogito* and all the other rational resources for human knowledge that survive the trial by radical doubt. Only the subjective truths bring with them any knowledge of existence whatsoever. Mathematical and logical truths, and conceptual analyses of substance, essence, causality, and so on, are collectively devoid of any existential implication. No claim about what actually exists in the universe, particular or general, comes from these rationally accessible truths. Existence enters Descartes' thinking in two ways: the *cogito* directly establishes the existence of the thinking subject, and the existence of God is established in various ways, all of which appeal to the concept of God which the thinking subject finds in his conscious mind. No concept other than that of God supports an existential statement by itself. Knowledge of the existence of God reduces to the subjective knowledge derived from the *cogito*, according to the causal argument of the Third Meditation. It is possible that the same could be said of the Cartesian version of the ontological argument for God's existence in the Fifth Meditation, although this is not clear. Descartes sometimes appears to worry about the doctrinal acceptability of this ordering of knowledge and tries to restate matters so that knowledge of God comes first, but it is fair to say that self-knowledge is the foundation of all knowledge of existence in his epistemology. This is simply the advantage and also the burden of the egocentric starting point that the *cogito* provides.

Emphasis on the *cogito* does not mean that self-knowledge is limited to the recognition of my own existence as a thinking thing. In the Second Meditation Descartes establishes the existence of the thinker: "I am, I exist, that is certain."[9] Then he proceeds immediately to a vast expansion of the foundation of secure subjective truths. All the contents of the mind, the doubts, thoughts, emotions, and acts of will, considered in themselves as constituents of my mental life, are apprehended as part of my existence as a thinking thing, and my knowledge of these constituents in all their detail is as secure as my knowledge of my own existence. In fact, Descartes makes it clear that my knowledge of my own existence, as a thinking thing, is my knowledge of the contents of my mind.

> Even if I am all the while asleep; even if my creator does all he can
> to deceive me; how can any of these things be less a fact than my own

existence? Is any of these something distinct from my consciousness?
Can any of them be called a separate thing from myself?[10]

Most important for our interests, my perceptual experiences belong
to this sphere of secure knowledge of the inner. These are the "many
things" that I perceive "coming as it were from the senses."[11]

In these early passages in the *Meditations* Descartes thoroughly
reconstructs the traditional philosophical and commonsense understandings of perceptual experience. The objects with which we become acquainted in such experiences are no longer material objects
outside us in the world. In Descartes' reorganization all of that outer
world has become a matter of hypothesis and argument. What I
really know in perception is a certain class of my own ideas. With the
rest of the content of my consciousness, my knowledge of these ideas
"coming as it were from the senses" is perfectly secure. The insecurity
is transferred to the question of the relation between the wholly
known inner objects and the wholly unknown outer realities which
we suppose to have caused the existence of our perceptual ideas and
which we suppose those ideas to represent.

As we have noted, all knowledge of determinate existence in the
world is, according to Descartes, secured through knowledge of the
existence of the thinking subject and the mental contents of which
it is composed. When it comes to perception, this means that the
perceptual ideas that I have, the immediate objects of my perceptual
consciousness, make up an indubitably existing, albeit a purely mental, subject matter. Perception has to be reinterpreted, deleting from
it the usual idea that it gives us acquaintance with extramental realities. All extramental existences are things of which complex inferences might give us some knowledge but the mere occurrence of
perceptual experiences certainly cannot. As Descartes expresses this
radical reinterpretation of perceptual consciousness and the objects of
perception, following the discussion of the piece of wax in the Second
Meditation,

> But it must be observed that perception of the wax is not sight, not
> touch, not imagination; nor was it ever so, though it formerly seemed
> to be; it is a purely mental contemplation, which may be either im-
> perfect and confused, as it originally was, or clear and distinct, as it
> now is, according to my degree of attentiveness to what it consists in.[12]

When Descartes says that perception of a piece of wax is not sight or touch, he does not mean to deny that there is visual and tactual perception. What is intended is brought out in the assertion that such perception is really a "mental contemplation" (*inspectio*). The mind does not reach out into the outer world of extended things. Perceptual acquaintance is not acquaintance with things outside of the mind. Vision and touch are commonly understood, as Descartes knows, to include cognitive contact with the outer perceived object. That is what Descartes means to deny. Descartes preserves a secure datum in perception, but in the process he obliterates the cognitive connection with the external and the nonmental.

Insofar as perceptual ideas are simply among the things found in the mind by the conscious subject, these ideas are completely cut off from any scientific representation of the physical world. The clarity and distinctness of perceptual ideas, which Descartes says is attained when we are sufficiently attentive to them, is achieved precisely by separating them from our habitual propensity to take such ideas to be external realities or dependable news of external realities. The same motif is reinforced in the Fourth Meditation when Descartes maintains that the unbounded *will* is the faculty to which human error is to be traced. There is no possibility of error in the mere contemplation of ideas as we find them in the mind. The intellectual step by which we take ideas to be representations of reality beyond themselves is effected by the will, and the risk of error thus created can be eliminated by inhibiting the will. The familiar traditional and commonsense idea of perceptual consciousness of the outer is the product of the adventurous activity of the will. When we have controlled it, we describe the objects of which we are aware in terms that fit them as we find them. They are objects with sensuous properties deployed in space. As we have already mentioned, the sensuous characters of perceptual ideas consist of purely subjective secondary qualities which we confusedly project onto external causes when the will has not been controlled. But the geometrical character of the ideas we apprehend is eventually, in the Sixth Meditation, discovered to be a faithful representation of a geometrical reality outside us. Descartes' argument for the existence of a material world amounts to an argument to show that our ideas of extended sensuous objects actually correspond to an existing order of extended things outside the mind, although the sensuous character of the ideas is not found in the outer

objects. To an extent this argument parallels the proof for the existence of God that Descartes gives in the Third Meditation. We
would not have the ideas of extended realities outside us that we do
have were it not for the actual existence of such an extended reality.
The parallel has to be qualified by the fact that the argument only
succeeds, Descartes believes, in the context of extended things because we can invoke the fact that we are creatures of a good God who
would not burden us with an irresistible disposition to refer our
perceptual ideas to an order of extended realities outside the mind
if there were no such realities.

After this proof Descartes presents ideas that come as close as
anything in his writing to an endorsement of a phenomenal level of
discourse. The production of perceptual ideas is now ascribed to
nature, as organized by God's ordinances, and the question of the
value of perception is explored as an investigation of "what nature
teaches us" through the generation of our perceptual experiences.
The general thought that we have a bodily nature in an environment
of other bodies, and the thought that contact with some of these en-
vironing bodies is harmful, and contact with others, beneficial, are
now promoted to the rank of truths. There is a fresh discussion of the
deformations and illusions of the senses but now in the atmosphere
of the assumption that perceptual ideas are not wholly without re-
deeming value. We are equipped with the disposition to experience
pleasure and pain so that we can learn to maximize the helpful stimu-
lations and minimize the harmful. In comparable discussions elsewhere[13] Descartes explains that the errors that we make in miscon-
struing perceptual experience as direct information about the outer
world can be understood as part of the functioning of a protective
mechanism which enhances our capacity to learn from experience in
childhood before our capacity to use reason critically and reflectively
has matured. This ultimate explanation is hinted at in the initial
recognition of "the multitude of errors that I had accepted as true *in
my earliest years*" in the opening sentence of the *Meditations*. One
could say that the seed from which the full flowering of phenomenalism in Leibniz and Kant grows is this Cartesian recognition of the
usefulness of confused perceptual thinking in childhood.

Descartes' famous slogan "My physics is nothing but geometry"
has to be qualified by the existential claim founded on experience in
the Sixth Meditation. He has already argued in the fifth that geom-

etry, the science of the extended, is not empirical. But the existence of a subject matter for that science requires appeal to experience in Descartes' reasoning.

Although the role of thinking about the perceptual realm is enormously developed in the later rationalist tradition, the fundamental Cartesian idea that rejects perceptual contact with mind-independent reality is retained. Leibniz assigns a much larger, clearer, and more satisfying role to empirical thinking. Kant disparages the claims to nonempirical knowledge of reality, even as his system divides reality so as to leave a conspicuous place for the subject matter of such invalid claims. Both Leibniz and Kant impose a further important reorganization on Descartes' format for understanding the world. For them the phenomenal is not identified with the given. Descartes contrasts the security of what is immediately accessible to consciousness with conjectural outer objects ill-represented by ideas. *Phenomena bene fundata* include more than those Cartesian representations that have been tested, screened, reinforced, and corrected by intelligent processes. The phenomenal includes everything at the perceptual level, and that means all these representations and their spatiotemporal objects. Descartes thinks that the rightly characterized extramental object is a spatiotemporal object. For both Leibniz and Kant spatiotemporality is but a representational device imposed by the mind, and the idea of a spatiotemporal realm is the idea of phenomenal reality. In Spinoza's far more obscure system, spatiality characterizes substance or reality, while temporality has no credentials in the metaphysically ultimate account.

Insofar as Kant adheres to phenomenalism, insofar as he is faithful to the force of the word "appearance" ("Erscheinung"), he retains the essentially Cartesian distinction. This is so in spite of the fact that it is one of Kant's major objectives to set aside this Cartesian-idealist program once and for all. Perhaps this is Kant's most profound and best idea in philosophy. Much of the difficulty of the *Critique of Pure Reason* derives from the incompleteness and vacillation in Kant's effort to achieve a nonrationalist philosophy.

We may call the root element of Cartesian rationalism the internalization of the object of consciousness. It does mark a complete and irreparable break with empiricism, but only with the empiricism of Aristotle and the scholastic tradition in which Aristotle's empiricism is incorporated. Although the classical Greek philosophers and the medievals know that sense perception depends upon causal processes within and outside the body, they do not make the object of perceptual consciousness an inner object. The inner phases and constituents of the physiology of perception are not objects of consciousness for these old traditions. There are many different ancient and medieval theories of perception. The status of the inner elements in perceptual processes is not the same for all of these theories, and it is often not at all clear what the status of inner goings-on is. But none of them approach the Cartesian internalization of all objects of consciousness. It is for this reason that the solipsistic skeptical agenda of philosophical problems, which is characteristic of modern philosophy as a whole, has no natural place at all in the environment of Greek or medieval thinking.

Plato, like Descartes, rejects the senses as a source of secure knowledge of the world. But Plato does not base this rejection on the thought that the very existence of a physical order of objects of perception outside us is uncertain since all that we know for sure is the inner realm of our own perceptual ideas. For Plato perception does inform us of the existence and character of the external things that we see, here, and touch. Perception generally affords us "true belief" about just that realm of perceivable outer material things. Those external realities, and not something in the mind, are the objects of perceptual apprehension. The trouble with perception, in Plato's opinion, is precisely that *it is* an apprehension of outer material reality which constitutes an unstable flux of "becoming." Perception does not put us in touch with anything fundamental or permanent. Consciousness of an ever-shifting sensible surface is not an intellectual grasp of reality of sufficient penetration to deserve to be called knowledge.

If we ask, "How does Plato justify assertions about a material order of things on the basis of the evidence of immediate experience?" we find no answer at all because, for all his criticism of empiricism, Plato never doubts that perceivable things in the material world are the objects of our perceptual consciousness. There is no gap requiring a bridge of inferences between perceptual experience and outer objects. In the same way we do not find any Aristotelian theory of the external world, erected on an evidential base of inner perceptual ideas, because such a theory can only be projected by a philosopher who has followed Descartes into the egocentric subjectivism of which he is the creator. "There are these conscious states," we post-

Cartesian philosophers say, thinking of our own conscious states, "but with what confidence can we pronounce on any existences outside of and independent of our consciousness?" The classical Greek traditions and the prevailing scholastic-Aristotelian empiricism do not have any view on this standard modern question because they take it for granted that in perception we are acquainted with the outer world and not with our own mental states. Many an earlier philosopher reflected on the implications of dreaming and perceptual aberration, but none drew the Cartesian conclusion that the immediate objects of perceptual consciousness are all inner mental things.

When we come to consider philosophy after Descartes, the stark contrast and opposition between rationalism and empiricism withers away. It would not be unreasonable to say that modern empiricism is just an outgrowth of Cartesian rationalism. The philosophy of the classical British empiricists Locke, Berkeley, and Hume is literally unthinkable without the Cartesian philosophy of mind and the special epistemological outlook that comes with it. In important ways the empiricist development after Descartes is more faithful to large elements of Descartes' program than is the later tradition of continental rationalism. Neither Spinoza nor Leibniz is enthusiastic about a systematic method of doubt in philosophy. Leibniz expressly asserts that systematic doubt can be too radical, since nothing at all will be able to stop the catastrophic landslide of uncertainty that is set in motion by devices such as the deceiving demon hypothesis.[14] In contrast, it is in empiricist philosophy, and especially in twentieth-century works such as those of empiricists like Bertrand Russell, C. I. Lewis, A. J. Ayer, and Roderick Chisholm, that the idea of pressing beliefs to a foundation that is insulated against every possibility of error is preserved.

This is a natural consequence of the empiricists' acceptance of Descartes' internalization of the objects of perceptual consciousness. Such inner mental objects are known in empiricist thought as "sense impressions" or "sense data" or "appearances" or "states of being appeared to." On the whole, modern empiricists conform to the broad pattern of the Sixth Meditation in moving from solid data about inner objects of consciousness to claims about external reality. Empiricism has generally agreed with Leibniz that science deals, in the first instance, with phenomena which are representations in our minds. Modern empiricism largely accepts the idea of a preliminary science needed to secure the subject matter of physics and biology by establishing that there is an external physical world for such sciences to study. Of course, the realists among empiricist metaphysicians will not identify the spatiotemporal objects of inner representations as mind-dependent phenomena, which is what Leibniz and Kant take such objects to be. And empiricists are likely to be either inhospitable to or pessimistic about the speculations at the metaphysical level which are so important to the rationalist. But the project and the raw materials for science are viewed in much the same way by rationalists and empiricists after Descartes. Locke, who singled out Descartes as the only contemporary thinker for whom he could express admiration, conceived of science limited to the investigation of perceptually accessible nominal essences, while metaphysically real essences remain forever unknown. Although this conception is itself unstable in Locke's thought, it is similar to Leibniz's phenomenalism and to the Kantian contrast between the empirically knowable world and the permanently inaccessible world of things as they are in themselves.

Empiricist theories of scientific knowledge founded on perceptual experience generally take one or the other of two fundamental forms. Both forms stem from the full acceptance of the Cartesian interpretation of the object of consciousness and the Cartesian epistemological program. First, there are theories that regard the inner data of perceptual consciousness as the facts for which science proposes explanatory hypotheses. References to external physical things only figure in the theoretical hypotheses which are confirmed, in the hypotheticodeductive fashion, by their success in explaining the occurrence of, the character of, and the patterns among mental perceptual experiences. According to such a theory we believe that there are physical objects, including our own bodies, and we believe that such bodies are in complex causal relationships, because such beliefs best account for our subjective conscious experience. The second kind of empiricist theory holds out no hope for the intelligibility, much less the confirmability, of such hypotheses. Since our experience is entirely limited to mental objects, we can have no conception at all to go with the assertion that there are any other kinds of things. In voicing any hypotheses about extramental material things we literally do not know what we are talking about. The meaningless positing of such entities can hardly offer us satisfying explanations of anything. Faced with this severe constraint, the strict phenomenalist must reduce the terminology of the outer and physical to the phenomenal discourse that fits what we do know. That means reduction to the inner materials that determine the horizons of intelligibility for us. Such thinking engenders views like the theory summed up in Russell's well-known dictum "Physical objects are logical constructs out of sense data."

There are a great many variants of these two types of empiricist theory of knowledge of the external world. The point is that, different as the theories are, they all share the Cartesian internalization of the object of perceptual consciousness. In this respect modern empiricism has much more in common with rationalism than with the classical empiricism of Aristotle retained in the perspective of the scholastic philosophers.

The broad affinity of post-Cartesian rationalism and empiricism was understood in the eighteenth century by both Kant and Thomas Reid. Reid goes beyond appreciation of the common acceptance of the internalization thesis in rationalism and empiricism, and ascribes the same view indiscriminately to ancient and modern philosophy. He even interprets Plato's "myth of the cave" as asserting that we do not encounter outer objects in sense perception. Thus,

> All the philosophers from Plato to Hume agree in this, that we do not perceive external objects immediately, and that the immediate object of perception must be some image present to the mind.[15]

In spite of his untenable interpretation of Plato and other inadmissible extrapolations to classical philosophy, Reid is generally sensitive to the special role of Descartes in the generation of the modern epistemological outlook. Kant assembles the modern rationalists and empiricists under the general heading "idealist" philosophers just because they all internalize the object of consciousness and leave us aware only of our own ideas. Among these idealists Kant distinguishes those who, like Berkeley, deny the existence of extramental material objects altogether from those who, like Descartes and Hume, believe that demonstrable or confirmable hypotheses can assure us of the existence of the nonmental world. The former are the "dogmatic" idealists, and the latter the "problematic" idealists, in Kant's classification. They are both to be defeated by Kant's "Refutation of Idealism."

From the end of the eighteenth until the beginning of the twentieth century this rationalist foundation of both the great modern traditions of philosophy remained in the background. Nineteenth-century idealists were concerned to undercut the terms in which the contrast between the subjective inner and the objective outer can be expressed. But this project gradually lost momentum and, among English-speaking philosophers in any case, finally disappeared when Russell and Moore rejected idealism. All the while Cartesian roots lay deep but unattended in empiricist philosophies like that of J. S. Mill as well as in the philosophical outlook of Russell and Moore themselves.

Recent decades have seen a vigorous reemergence of these seventeenth-century themes. Mach, Russell, Carnap, and Ayer offer metaphysical and epistemological programs in the tradition of Locke and Descartes. Heidegger and Dewey understand their own projects in terms of fundamental opposition to Cartesian dualism and egocentric subjectivism. Waves of pragmatists, new realists, commonsense philosophers, ordinary-language philosophers, Wittgensteinians, conceptual geographers, behaviorists, and materialists of every stripe have tried to overthrow the Cartesian philosophy of mind that sets the schedule of philosophical problems. Cartesianism is "the official doctrine" that Gilbert Ryle tries to displace at last. J. L. Austin uses a combination of ridicule and common sense in the effort to banish the resurgent phenomenalist empiricism of Ayer and others. Wilfred Sellars repudiates "The Myth of the Given," which is the secure Cartesian perceptual idea, and W. V. Quine's "Two Dogma's of Empiricism" are, first, the "analytic," or conceptual truths, and, second, the incorrigible perceptual data, which together make up the Cartesian foundation. Richard Rorty records all of this opposition in *Philosophy and the Mirror of Nature*. He sums it up as a struggle against the demand for objective knowledge itself, and he announces with enthusiasm the demise of philosophy as it has been known as a consequence of the failure of rationalist foundationalism.

The scope and variety of recent opposition, and the felt need for this opposition, attest to the tenacity of rationalist ideas in modern philosophy. It commonly happens that opponents of the rationalist program unwittingly adopt one decisive form of the Cartesian scheme of things while trying to attack another form. As a result their articulated understandings collapse into a version of, rather than a repudiation of, the internalization thesis. This even happens in the context of philosophical behaviorism.

The behaviorist vigorously rejects dualism, nonmaterial mind-stuff, and the introspectible inner world or private theater of consciousness which is, according to the Cartesian system, the incorrigible source of information concerning the individual's own mental states. But the behaviorist assumptions about the substitutes required for the discarded mental states betray a deep and unacknowledged influence of Cartesian subjectivism. Thus, for example, the behaviorist does not present the objects of the outer world as the subject matter of a subject's statements of belief. In the behaviorist's account a belief is a behavioral disposition of a believer. Thus, when a person tells us that he holds a certain belief, he tells us something about himself and makes no claim about the outer world. In this the behaviorist has accepted the Cartesian identification of a subject's belief as constituted by some fact about him. The behaviorist differs merely on the nature of the fact that constitutes a subject's belief. The behaviorist even tries to deal with the special authority with which a subject can pronounce on the content of his own mind which, when treated by Descartes, becomes the doctrine of the incorrigible immediate mental object. The advantage that a subject has in stating his own belief rests on the fact that the believer is always present when he behaves himself, while others are but intermittent observers of the manifestations of the dispositions which are beliefs. As Ryle puts this behaviorist claim:

> Lest any reader feels despondency at the thought of being deprived of his twofold Privileged Access to his supposed inner self, I may add the consolatory undertaking that on the account of self-knowledge that I shall give, knowledge of what there is to be known about other people is restored to approximate parity with self-knowledge.[16]

The point that I mean to emphasize is that Ryle continues to accept the Cartesian contention that the knowledge displayed in stating my beliefs, including perceptual beliefs, is *self-knowledge*. On the behaviorist understanding to which Ryle is subscribing here, I am able to say that I believe what I do only because I know something about myself and not because I am in contact with the world and my expressions of belief are statements about the world. The Cartesian mind composed of mental states of the individual becomes a behaviorist mind composed of dispositions of the individual. The rationalist egocentrism reappears in a stunted and exotic form which is not noticed only because the behaviorist, profoundly convinced of the subjective orientation of all psychological statements, does not pay very close attention to just what he is saying. When I ascribe a belief to someone else, of course, my ascription depends on my knowledge of that other person's behavioral dispositions, including verbal dispositions. Following the "parity" of self-knowledge and knowledge of others that Ryle announces, my ability to say what I believe myself is based on my knowledge of my own dispositions, including verbal dispositions. But this is a grotesque suggestion. "I have heard him say as much on many occasions" is just right as backing for "He believes that such and such," but "I have heard myself say as much on many occasions" is just bizarre. But if beliefs were dispositions of believers and if Ryle were right in saying

> The sorts of things I can find out about myself are the same as the sorts of things I can find out about other people, and the methods of finding them out are much the same . . . ,[17]

then this bizarre statement would be a straightforward expression of the foundation of my knowledge of my own belief. Although behaviorism often pays the excessive price of seeming to deny obvious facts about sensations and pains and mental images in its opposition to dualism, it has not fully broken with the Cartesian tradition that provides an egocentric subject matter for all mental discourse. The conceptual disaster in behaviorist analysis of first-person psychological statements is a consequence of this hidden Cartesian assumption.

In contemporary philosophy of mind, behaviorism has been vanquished, but Cartesian thinking reappears, even more forcefully, in the efforts of materialists over the past twenty years. This is the period in which the ambitions of artificial intelligence and Turing machine analysis have flourished. Ever more complex and sophisticated versions of the mind-brain identity theory have been propounded. Philosophers have tried to be in real touch with the complexities of neurophysiological science. The striking thing about all these materialist philosophers is how very much of the Cartesian understanding of the mind they begin by accepting. There is a range of immediate experience, and this comprises the individual's acquaintance with his own thoughts, desires, emotions, intentions, feelings, beliefs, perceptual experiences, and so on. These are all inner states of the individual just as Descartes said. The only mistake Descartes made, from the viewpoint of these contemporary materialists, is not the identification of all these mental things as inner realities, but simply the metaphysical status to which Descartes allocated them in insisting on a non-material mind. From the outset modern materialist philosophy of mind is a materialist Cartesianism. The subject matter of first-person psychological statements is something inner to which the speaker has a special access. But the inner mental thing is something in his head rather than something in his ethereal mind. The well-known mind-brain theorist J. J. C. Smart makes this point self-consciously and with particular force.

> . . . [We] can see that our talk about immediate experience is neutral between materialism and dualism. It reports our internal goings-on as like or unlike what internally goes on in typical situations, but the dualist would construe these goings-on as goings-on in an immaterial substance, whereas the materialist would construe these goings-on as taking place inside our skulls.[18]

It seems to me that recent materialist philosophy of mind has actually been harmed by an illusion that it is the "scientific" theory, an illusion encouraged by restating what is at heart a very naive speculation in the terminology of neuron-firings and computer programs. The Cartesian element in materialist theories readily gives rise to absurdities that are quite analogous to those we have mentioned in the context of behaviorism. Where the conceptual defects of the inner mental objects of the Cartesian story relied on the atmosphere of mystery that surrounds the very concept of the ethereal mind, the defects of the materialist version rely on endless wonders and possibilities with which we are ready to credit brains and computers.

I believe that there is no prospect at all for these theories. The trouble with the Cartesian mind is not the stuff of which it is made. The Cartesian account will not be made acceptable by merely changing the metaphysical classification to which mental constituents are assigned. Wittgenstein and Ryle offered profound but indecisive critique of the inner-world interpretation of conscious mentality more than a generation ago. Ryle tended to slip into an incoherent behaviorism that simply denies the facts. Wittgenstein's method of presentation, his hostility to philosophical theory, his resistance to the mode of assertion in philosophy, his preference for stimulating fragments and rhetorical questions, and, finally, the fact that his reflections are inconclusive even in his own eyes mean that we cannot find a satisfactory alternative to the Cartesian concept of mind in Wittgenstein's work.

In the last decade Saul Kripke has presented arguments that will dash the hopes of materialist philosophers of mind if they gain general acceptance. These arguments are the subject of current controversy. Maybe they are not correct. The remarkable fact of the matter is that Kripke, like the materialists he rebuts, fully accepts the preliminary Cartesian understanding of the objects of consciousness without significant investigation or reflection. He argues that these mental items cannot be successfully identified with neural realities. But Kripke's discussion starts and ends within the Cartesian framework of internal objects, the metaphysical status of which is presumably at issue. As is so often the case with twentieth-century debates in the philosophy of mind, all participants accept the underlying Cartesian premise.

If the revolution in philosophy that Descartes introduced must be set aside, as so many contemporary philosophers believe, and as I believe; if dualism is an irrevocably mysterious metaphysics; and if the idealist epistemology that follows the internalization of all objects of consciousness is inherently barren, then the roots of Cartesian thinking have to be very much more fully understood than they are understood in current discussions. Behaviorism and all the forms of the mind-brain identity theory stand no chance of success because none of them starts from a satisfactory appreciation of the character, the power, and the manysidedness of the rationalist philosophy. On the contrary, among today's anti-Cartesians, fundamental Cartesian principles are accepted unreflectingly, as if they were not philosophical at all, but just the facts of the matter. Kripke's argument really shows the shallowness of the purported opposition to Cartesian dualism in contemporary materialist thinking. Kant's thinking cuts more deeply than does most twentieth-century opposition to the rationalist egocentric-subjective perspective. When he is refuting idealism, Kant reject's, not the particular substance of which dualists want to make the mind, but rather the very idea of a philosophical starting point consisting of a conscious subject aware exclusively of the contents of his own mind. In the spirit of this criticism, from which Kant often diverges, the objects of consciousness, the immediate objects and not inferred objects, must be outer material things which are not dependent upon the mind that apprehends them. Kant's arguments for this view are very far from being clear and much further from being conclusive. They do constitute a real opposition to the Cartesian platform in comparison with which contemporary materialism and recent behaviorism are embarrassingly superficial. For a better understanding of the extraordinary grip of the rationalist point of view, no study is more valuable to us than that of the rationalist philosophers themselves.

NOTES

The following abbreviations are used in these notes:

AT I-XI   C. Adam and P. Tannery, *Oeuvres de Descartes*, Nouvelle presentation, Paris, 1964.

HR I-II   E.S. Haldane and G.R.T. Ross, *The Philosophical Works of Descartes*, London, 1911.

AG   E. Anscombe and P. Geach, *Descartes: Philosophical Writings* London, 1964.

L   Loemker, Leroy, *Leibniz: Philosophical Papers and Letters*, second edition, Dordrecht, 1969.

1. AG 61.
2. AG 61.
3. See Rule III, HR II, 5-8; AT X, 366-70. The summary statement on AT 368 seems to contain a misprint. Descartes says that of all mental operations only two are secure against all possibility of error: "admittunturque tantùm duae, intuitus scilicet & inductio." In the immediately following discussion deduction, and not induction, is identified as "hic alium adjunximus cogniscendi modum," and the rest of the work consistently pairs intuition and deduction.
4. For a full discussion of this issue see Garber, D., "Science and Certainty in Descartes," in Hooker, M., ed., *Descartes: Critical and Interpretive Essays*, Baltimore, 1978, 114-51.
5. For example, see *Discourse on Method*, V, vi.
6. Leibniz says, for example, "motion does not indeed depend upon being observed, but it does depend upon being possible to be observed." Leibniz's fifth letter, Alexander, H.G., *The Leibniz-Clarke Correspondence*, Manchester, 1956, 74. The translation is Clarke's.
7. AG 55-56.

8. Perhaps the most conspicuous is *Principles of Philosophy*, IV, CCIV.

9. "Ego sum, ego existo, certum est," AT VII, 27; this is as close as Descartes comes in the *Meditations* to the formula "Cogito ergo sum" traditionally associated with his thought.

10. AG 70-71.

11. "multa etiam tanquam a sensibus venienta," AT VII, 28.

12. AG 73.

13. HR II, 254.

14. "And if this doubt could once be justly raised, it would be straightway insuperable," L, 385.

15. *Essays on the Intellectual Powers of Man*, Cambridge, Mass., 1969, 124.

16. *The Concept of Mind*, London, 1949, 155.

17. Ibid.

18. "Materialism," *Journal of Philosophy*, 60, 1963, 162.

II

The Scientific Background of Descartes' Dualism

1. Introduction

Dualism is the thesis that all the finite individual things that exist in the universe are either minds or bodies. Bodies are material things whose principle and defining feature is extension or the filling of space, and minds are nonmaterial things, and their principle and defining feature is thinking or being conscious. The most important aspect of Descartes' dualism is its characterization of a human being as a composite entity. In an individual man mind and body are closely associated. In some sense they are united. However, they cannot lose their distinctness as two separate substances, that is, as two entities each of which endures through time, undergoes its own changes, and thus accumulates its own history. Changes the mind undergoes are changes in thought and consciousness, and the history of a mind is a sequence of mental states, mental contents, and mental activities. The body undergoes physical changes and has a physical history, the history of a material object. The crucial claim of dualism is that the body is not the thing that thinks in a man. The fundamental nature of body is being extended, and this contrasts with and excludes being conscious.

Descartes' philosophical arguments for this dualism are most fully rendered in his *Meditations on First Philosophy*. It is worth reminding ourselves that this work bears the subtitle "In which the existence of God and the distinction between Mind and Body are demonstrated."[1] The same arguments are prefigured briefly and partially in part four of the *Discourse on Method*. They are recast in part one of the *Principles of Philosophy*, and they appear elsewhere in Descartes' writings.

Although Cartesian dualism still exerts an immense influence in philosophy, Descartes' arguments for his dualism, from their earliest presentation, have been found wholly inadequate by most readers. Even those who accept or share his dualist convictions have found his defense of them quite unsatisfactory. The inadequate arguments represent an effort to frame definitive demonstrations for convictions that were deeply held by Descartes and that were understandably compelling to him. But the thinking which actually led Descartes to these convictions is remote from the matters that figure in the official proofs of his late metaphysical works.

2. Descartes' Argument

The *Meditations* can be divided into two unequal parts at the end of the second day's thinking. Under this division the first part contains the initial encouragement of systematic and radical doubt, culminating in the two general skeptical hypotheses: the dream hypothesis and the deceiving demon hypothesis. This first part also contains the *cogito* argument by which doubt is at last halted in the unshakeable self-knowledge of the thinking subject. It concludes with the recognition in the latter part of the Second Meditation that the immediate contents of consciousness, construed only as "ideas" in the mind, all share the indubitability of the *cogito*. At this point the existence of the thinking subject and the existence and content of all his ideas are guaranteed. Preparation has been made for the survey and classification of ideas in the Third Meditation. Everything but this sphere of consciousness remains in doubt. The existence of a material order and of the thinking subject's own body remain to be argued for. Even the simplest mathematical propositions have yet to attain standing as truths.

To this day every philosophical intelligence feels the power of this representation of the subjective starting point for philosophical thinking. Although modern philosophers owe so much to the phenomenological starting point discovered in the first two Meditations, almost nothing in subsequent thought has been influenced by arguments and claims found in the second part of the work. But the whole of Descartes' official defense of dualism is found in this second part.

In the Third Meditation Descartes turns to God in devising an escape from the threatening prison of solipsistic consciousness. Few have followed him in his view that the idea of God is the first for which we are able to know a corresponding existence. Of empiricist philosophies only Berkeley's accords comparable prominence to theological premises in moving from the flux of immediate experience to a more stable independent reality. Empiricism has generally rejected the uses of theology on which Descartes relies.

The function of Descartes' theology in the Third Meditation is precisely to prepare the ground for the proof of the existence of material things. The causal argument, there mounted, claims that the existence of God is implied as a needed causal antecedent both by the existence of an idea of God and by the subject's possession of that idea. This reasoning is supplemented in the Fifth Meditation by Descartes' version of the "ontological argument" for God's existence. The intervening discussion concerns the nature of human error and establishes the compatibility of man's imperfection with the conclusion reached in the Third Meditation: man's creator is an infinite and perfect God. This is Descartes' highly intellectualized version of the traditional problem of evil. His solution emphasizes human freedom and places responsibility for human deficiencies on men themselves, while God is asserted to have made men capable of correcting all the errors to which they are susceptible.

This reconciliation of divine perfection and human inadequacy is not original. Saint Augustine presented much the same argument, although he vigorously rejected optimistic attitudes concerning man's power to correct his shortcomings. Augustine adverts to the freedom of man in order to deny God's responsibility for human vices. In his proof of the existence of a material world and its distinctness from the mental, Descartes exploits an aspect of the argument never contemplated by Augustine: If God is absolved from responsibility for human failings *only* because man is free and, thus, responsible for himself, then, insofar as man is not free, it should follow that God is responsible for him. As we shall see, it is just this contrapositive entailment of an earlier solution to the problem of evil that Descartes invokes in moving from our ineluctable belief in the existence of a material world to the justification of that belief.

The very same pattern—exploitation of an old argument for new ends—recurs in the use of the ontological argument in the Fifth Meditation. This argument is best known in the eleventh-century formulation of Anselm of Canterbury and in the framework of its later rejection by Thomas Aquinas. Descartes has proved the existence of God in the Third Meditation. Is another proof added as reinforcement? No, in the Fifth Meditation the material world is Descartes' real objective. The ontological argument serves to focus the discussion on the concept of essences that Descartes requires in his subsequent reasoning. The discussion consists in an extended comparison of our idea of God and our ideas of material things. Both are construed as formulations of essences. For our purposes we can think of an essence as a cluster of characteristics that define an entity of a certain type. In the case of extended things such as triangles the investigation of essence provides answers to the question What must an existing thing outside the mind be like if it is to be a triangle? Then theorems about triangles are said to be entailments of the essence of triangles. Such propositions, formulating geometrical knowledge, do not assert the existence of anything. In the example considered by Descartes knowledge of essence yields only an entirely secure but hypothetical statement: If there is actually a triangle somewhere, then it has an angle-sum of two right angles. A parallel examination of the essence of God as indicated by our idea of God reveals, according to Descartes, that the proposition "God exists" is entailed by this idea, just as the angle-sum theorem is entailed by the idea of a triangle. Descartes' interest in the ontological argument really lies in the contrast it affords between the essence of God that sustains an existence claim and the essence of matter that does not.

In the last Meditation the existence of material things is proved *via* complicated appeals to the known essence of material things and the now-known existence and character of God. Because his power is infinite, God could have given us the ideas that we have of material things in our geometrical thinking and in perceptual experience even though there were no such material things outside our thought. He could have planted ideas of external things directly in our consciousness, or he could have induced them through some intermediate reality, sufficient for the production of those ideas, but entirely unlike a material world. Such possibilities, however, would be inconsistent with God's infinite goodness. For we have an irresistible disposition to refer our perceptual ideas to material things outside us. If no such material things were in fact the source of those ideas, our disposition would be a systematic misinterpretation of our experience *that we could never correct*. Just here Descartes employs the optimistic principle introduced in the Fourth Meditation: God enables us to correct any errors to which we are susceptible. This justifies the proposition that there is a material world which is the source of our perceptual experiences and which is the nonmental subject matter of which geometrical truths are true.

The dualism which is the final objective of the *Meditations* now requires only the proposition that bodies and minds, both of which are known to exist, are also distinct existences. Descartes argues that, though it may be that every mind is an embodied mind, minds could exist without bodies and God could have made our conscious minds just as they are without equipping us with bodies at all. He seems to regard this appeal to God's power as a needed premise for the distinctness of minds and bodies. This is likely to be confusing to his readers. After all, if the essence of triangles is to be three-sided, and of pentagons, to be five-sided, then, obviously, existing triangles cannot be existing pentagons. But Descartes writes as though he takes seriously the possibility that the thing that is conscious might be a corporeal thing, even though its essence is consciousness, while the essence of corporeal things is extension, and even though these are distinct essences. We notice that the essence "being conscious" does not obviously exclude the essence "being extended" on logical grounds, as three sidedness and five-sidedness exclude one another. But this difference is not the only foundation for Descartes' conviction that further reasoning is needed.

Prevailing scholastic-Aristotelian conceptions explicated the relationship between mind and body with the help of a ubiquitous form-matter distinction. Applied to human existence, the soul is taken by this tradition to be the form of the body, so that the animated body is a single substance, and not a composite of soul and body, each possessing an independent substantial existence. In light of this doctrine the immortality of the soul and its survival of the dissolution of the body in death became special problems for scholastic philosophers.

In addition to this tradition Descartes takes into consideration commonsense intuitions which make it difficult to think of a person as a mere association of a spiritual being and some inert clay. In the famous phrase he allows that "I am not present in my body merely as a pilot is present in his ship,"[2] and he draws attention to pains, which are *experienced* and not merely *observed* as a pilot might observe events damaging to his vessel. This intimacy with the corporeal nature of one's own body arises "from the mind's being united to and, as it were, mixed up with the body." In a letter to his sometime disciple Regius, Descartes says that an angel inhabiting a body would perceive impinging motions but would not feel sensations as we do.[3] An angel would be like a pilot in a ship.

In this letter Descartes expresses a confusing vacillation between the accepted scholastic view that a man is an *ens per se* (a substantial unity) and the view that a man is an *ens per accidens* (a composite being) which an angel inhabiting a body would be. Descartes' vacillation is partly due to his desire not to offend other religious thinkers and authorities needlessly. He recommends qualified endorsement of the prevailing view to Regius as a matter of prudence. But his intellectual uncertainty is also apparent. Descartes never reaches a satisfactory understanding of the "mixing" of mind and body in human existence.

Descartes' demonstration of dualism amounts to these propositions: (1) We have indubitable knowledge of the existence of ourselves as thinking beings and of the content of our conscious thought and experience. (2) The idea of an infinite, perfect, and independent being, which is the idea of God, is found among our conscious thoughts. (3) We know that God must exist as the required cause of the idea of God. (4) Some of our ideas are clear and distinct, and propositions involving clear and distinct ideas can be known to be true. (The seeming mutual dependence of this and the previous proposition is the foundation of the common charge that Descartes' reasoning is circular.) (5) Mathematical truths are prominent among those certified by their clarity and distinctness. (6) Perceptual ideas of sensuous qualities are confused ideas of things external to our minds. (7) Geometry is clear and distinct thinking about extended things, without the confused sensuous aspect, but with an essential imaginative component that connects geometry with perception. (8) The goodness of God assures us that there is an external world corresponding to and causing our perceptual ideas, and that this reality exemplifies the truths of mathematics in the form in which they are presented in geometry, but not as represented in perceptual experience. (9) From our ideas alone we know that the essence of mind is consciousness and the essence of body is extension, and that these are distinct essences. (10) The power of God certifies the real distinctness of existing minds and bodies, though the thinking subject's mind is intimately connected with his body in a way that is not entirely intelligible. (11) The distinctness of minds and bodies is confirmed by the reflection that a mind is an indivisible thing: for example, there is no such thing as half a mind. Bodies are all essentially divisible.

The striking thing about reactions of Descartes' early readers to this argument for dualism is that so much of it is ignored. The standard response to Descartes, one might say, has been to accept his dualism and to pay little attention to his demonstration of its correctness. The authors of "Objections" published with the *Meditations* write as though Descartes has based his dualism on the first two Meditations alone. In criticisms addressed to the Second Meditation, Hobbes and Gassendi, authors of the third and fifth set of Objections respectively, both complain that Descartes has only assumed that the mind is not corporeal.[4] In replying, Descartes points out that he did not claim to have proved the incorporeal status of the mind until the Sixth Meditation. In the earlier context, where these materialists find an unsupported assumption of dualism, Descartes merely notes that he can imagine that there are no material things at all, though he is at the same time conscious of his own existence. He cannot imagine that there are not minds, for his own consciousness is incompatible with *that* supposition. Then he says:

> But perhaps it is the case that these very things which I suppose to be nonentities [that is, bodies imagined not to exist], and which are not properly known to me, are yet in reality not different from the "I" of which I am aware. I do not know and will not dispute the point.[5]

At this point he does not dispute the view that the thinking thing may be corporeal. It may be the body that thinks.

It is not only predictably critical materialists who respond as though Descartes had rested his dualism on the first two Meditations. The preponderance of readers incline to look for, and to find, in the first part of the text a more direct, less ornate argument for the nonmaterial status of the mind. Then they find this simpler argument inadequate, but it is not an argument that Descartes has presented.

The "diverse theologians and philosophers" whose views Mersenne assembled as the second set of Objections say:

> Up to this point [the Second Meditation] you know that you are a being that thinks; but you do not know what this thinking thing is. What if it were a body which by its various motions and encounters produces that which we call thought? For granted that you rejected the claim of every sort of body, you may have been deceived in this, because you did not rule out yourself, who are a body. For how will you prove that a body cannot think, or that its bodily motions are not thought itself?[6]

Even the judicious Antoine Arnauld either ignores or rejects out of hand the whole elaborate argument we have summarized. In his, the fourth set of Objections, Arnauld says:

> I can discover no passage in the whole work capable of effecting this proof, save the proposition laid down at the outset: I can deny that there is any body or that any extended thing exists, but yet it is certain that I exist so long as I make this denial, hence, I am a thing that thinks and not a body, and the body does not pertain to the knowledge of myself. But the only result I can see this to give, is that a certain knowledge of myself be obtained without knowledge of the body. But it is not yet quite clear to me that this knowledge is complete and adequate, so as to make me sure that I am not in error in excluding the body from my essence.[7]

It is true that Descartes does not give any fuller reason for his contention that the essences of mind and body are distinct than the clear and distinct separability of these ideas in our thought. We can suppose all bodies nonexistent, but we cannot suppose all minds nonexistent. However, this is not Descartes' argument for dualism. He invokes theological premises three times in moving from this thought-experiment to the conclusion that the mind is not material. The existence of God is needed to assure me of the truth of what I think clearly and distinctly: by ruling out the deceiving-demon hypothesis. The goodness of God is appealed to in assuring me that my propensity to refer perceptual ideas to an outer material reality is justified. Finally, the power of God is cited to certify the distinction between minds and bodies, however intertwined their real instances. Even Descartes' friendliest critics such as Father Gibieuf and Princess Elizabeth do not find his reason for the distinction between

mind and body satisfactory, and in their hesitations they pay no attention to theological niceties. Gibieuf thinks that the claim to have
established the real essence of mind may have been accomplished by
an illegitimate abstraction.[8] Elizabeth's response is generous but still
skeptical. Her attention is quite properly focused on the desperate
problem of mind-body interaction that is imposed by the acceptance
of dualism. She writes to Descartes:

> The senses teach me *that* the soul moves the body but neither they nor
> the imagination nor the intellect teaches me *how*. Perhaps there are
> properties of the soul unknown to us which will overturn the convic-
> tion of the soul's nonextension which I acquired from the excellent
> arguments of your Meditations.[9]

These critical reactions are at least partly a consequence of the
order of the argument in the *Meditations*. We start with assurances
about the mind and mental contents. The question at the beginning
of the Third Meditation is What *else* exists? What is there *in addition*
to this mental reality? And the answers: God and the material world
naturally seem to be an articulation of *further* realities outside the
mind. There is an awkward turn of thought in the reflection that the
mind itself might be a constituent of this *further* material reality.
Managing the awkward turn of thought, readers come to imagine
that it has eluded Descartes and that he rests his dualism on the
natural presumption of the otherness of body that derives simply
from the skeptical subjective starting point. When we correct this
misinterpretation, however, we are left only with Descartes' unconvincing theological arguments.

Descartes' demonstration of dualism is, then, inadequate. Empiricists have generally eschewed any religious foundation for metaphysics, and even the firm believers among Descartes' first readers
and critics found little to convince them in his theological premises.
This is understandable. However great our faith, how could we pre-
sume to have so fine a grasp of the implications of the goodness and
power of God as to rest upon it our confidence that outer reality does
fit our spatial intuitions and does not fit our perceptual experiences?
The response to Descartes' argument shows that his premises are less
attractive than his conclusions. We cannot avoid asking, Are there
not other reasons for his acceptance of a dualism that, in itself, has
seemed correct to so many philosophers?

3. The Scientific Background

In the *Meditations* we are invited to consider the securely known conscious mind and then to ask, Could this consciousness turn out to be a corporeal thing? Could it be the body that thinks? It is instructive to consider a parallel question that is not represented in the *Meditations* at all. Suppose that we could, somehow, start from a secure knowledge of material things and then ask, Could these material things themselves manifest intellectual activities and consciousness? Could it be minds that are extended? No such question can arise in the *Meditations* because, following the skeptical method, "the mind is more easily known than the body."[10] These unfamiliar questions, however, would far better reflect the order of discovery in Descartes' own attainment of a dualist metaphysics than the artfully organized questions and answers of the *Meditations*. He is convinced that matter cannot possibly think long before he attempts to prove that mind cannot be extended. It is his scientific thought about the material world, unencumbered by systematic metaphysics, that is the source of Descartes' conviction that mind and matter are distinct essences and distinct existences.

The metaphysical doctrines for which he is famous did not receive any formulation in Descartes' writings and played no part in his thought for many years after he had begun systematic study of the physical world. It is easy to read the philosophy of the *Meditations* and the *Principles of Philosophy* back into Descartes' earlier thought as expressed in his youthful scientific writings, in *Le Monde*, and in the *Rules for the Direction of the Mind*. Étienne Gilson's studies of Descartes have done much to correct this error.[11] In the *Discourse on Method* Descartes tells us that after he had resolved on a life of search for truth and had begun to construct scientific explanations on the model of mathematical understanding

> . . . nine years elapsed before I had yet taken any position concerning the difficulties commonly disputed among the learned or begun to search for the principles of any philosophy more certain than the common variety [*plus certaine que la vulgaire*].[12]

Descartes identifies the success of his physical researches with the gradual elimination from his own thinking of a prevailing tendency to ascribe intellectual functions to mere physical things and

events. Aristotelian physical explanations fail, in his opinion, just
because they confuse mental and physical things and they ascribe
mental powers and functions to matter. These are the scholastic accounts in terms of *substantial forms* and *real qualities* that Descartes
attacks in letters to other thinkers. Writing to de Launay he says:

> The earliest judgments which we made in our childhood and the com-
> mon philosophy later, have accustomed us to attribute to the body
> many things which belong to the soul, and to attribute to the soul
> many things which belong only to the body. So people commonly
> mingle the two ideas of body and soul when they construct the ideas
> of real qualities and substantial forms which I think should be al-
> together rejected.[13]

And to Princess Elizabeth:

> . . . . we have hitherto confounded the notion of the soul's power to
> act on the body with the power one body has to act on another. We
> attributed both powers not to the soul, whose nature we did not yet
> know, but to the various qualities of the body such as weight, heat,
> etc. We imagined these qualities to be real, that is to say to have an
> existence distinct from that of bodies, and so to be substances,
> although we called them qualities.[14]

Descartes overcame these confusions by developing a conception of
material things that excludes mind. In his replies to the sixth set of
Objections, offered by anonymous theologians and philosophers,
Descartes says that his own reasons set out in the *Meditations* for the
view "that the human mind was really distinct from the body and was
more easily known than it" were not fully persuasive, even to him,
when he first thought of them. He was like an astronomer who could
not stop thinking of the earth as larger than the sun after possessing
demonstrations that it is much smaller. Then Descartes says that to
reinforce his assent, he "proceeded further,"[15] keeping his ideas
straight until

> I observed that nothing at all belonged to the nature or essence of
> body except that it was a thing with length, breadth and depth, ad-
> mitting of various shapes and various motions. [Such shapes cannot
> exist apart from the bodies that have them, and, in contrast,] . . . col-
> ors, odors, savors, and the rest of such things, were merely sensations
> existing in my thought, and differing no less from bodies than pain

differs from the shape and motion of the instrument which inflicts it. Finally, I saw that gravity, hardness, the power of heating, of attracting and of purging, and all other qualities which we experience in bodies consisted solely in motion or its absence, and in the configuration and situation of their parts.[16]

One aspect of dualism emerges here from the concept of the subjectivity of the sensuous. Descartes reports his appreciation of the fact that a shape cannot exist separately from the body shaped, while color does not exist in the shaped body and, therefore, must exist in some other substance. So a nonmaterial mind is implied here as the locus of secondary qualities which have some reality somewhere but cannot be referred to the physical world. It is often said that the mind for Descartes is a receptacle for sensuous characteristics which have been removed from bodies. There is justice in this interpretation. The last clause in the quoted passage, however, leads to a deeper reason for the thesis that the mind is nonmaterial.

"Gravity, hardness, the power of heating" and other "qualities" are prominent in Descartes' examples of spurious scholastic explanations that purport to know about the substantial forms of things and the real qualities they contain. Descartes thinks of his own attainment of a far superior conception of physical objects and events as conditioned by the rejection of these concepts. The scholastic explanations Descartes discards are those often ridiculed for their vacuousness by later critics: burning wood heats because the wood contains the power of heating; opium induces sleep because of its soporific virtue. This charge of vacuousness is not Descartes' objection at all. He finds the scholastic explanations defective because they import a psychological dimension into the physical order where explanation should only be mechanical. Qualities and substantial forms are psychologically intelligible determinants of change. They are like souls.

Writing to Mersenne in 1643, Descartes says that there are two principles that need to be established:

The first is that I do not believe that there are in nature any real qualities, attached to substances and separable from them by divine power like so many little souls in their bodies. [Claims involving such qualities make assertions that we do not understand, and] . . . the philosophers invented these real qualities only because they did not think they could otherwise explain all the phenomena of nature; but I find on the contrary, that these phenomena are better explained without them.

The second principle is that whatever is or exists remains always in the state in which it is, unless some ulterior cause changes it. . . . [17]

The first principle excludes the psychological from physics. The second rejects intrinsic causality, and it is the foundation of Descartes' law of inertia.[18]

The two principles of physics Descartes expounds to Mersenne are closely connected, and both focus on the repudiation of mental functions in accounts of physical change. Real qualities and substantial forms were conceived by the scholastics as self-contained causes of motion, in the general sense in which both qualitative changes and movements were called motions. If every change of state (and motion is itself a *state* for Descartes) must have some "ulterior" cause, that is, external cause, as the second principle requires, then there will be no self-induced motions to be ascribed to the real qualities and forms that are rejected by the first principle. But we still have to ask why it is that Descartes construed the prevailing explanations as psychological and why he says they amount to projecting "little souls" into material things.

The concept of substantial forms rests on Aristotle's distinction between form and matter. Any existing entity must be composed of something, and that matter of which it is composed must have some organization or other making it the particular thing it is, for the same matter has the potential to figure in the constitution of many different particular objects. So Aristotle thinks of matter as *potentiality* which is realized in a particular being by form, or *actuality*. This pair of metaphysical concepts reflects a Platonic influence, and it was much exploited by medieval thinkers. Unlike Plato, Aristotle usually says that forms do not exist by themselves, apart from any matter, any more than matter exists by itself without being anything in particular, that is, without any form at all.[19] The real qualities and substantial forms of scholastic science are derived from this basic concept of form and matter. To understand them we should appeal to a further Aristotelian distinction between natural objects and artificial collocations, and to the Aristotelian emphasis on organisms as the paradigm illustration of existing substances.

A natural entity for Aristotle is precisely one that contains within itself the causal foundation for its own development and behavior.[20] It is the possession of such self-realizing potential that makes something into a substantial unity in the fullest sense.[21] For Aristotle this concept is the foundation of the difference between artifacts and self-reproducing things that are not made by men.[22] The intrinsically caused motion that is best illustrated by reproduction marks an entity as a natural object. Reproduction leads us immediately to the emphasis on organisms that is characteristic of Aristotle.

We should note, however, especially because it is directly relevant to Descartes' thinking, that natural objects manifesting natural motions are not confined by Aristotle nor the scholastic tradition to living things. The downward motion of heavy things toward the center of the universe is a natural motion according to Aristotle. This coheres with common sense in that one does not have to do anything to a heavy thing to induce its fall except remove obstacles.[23] One does not have to remove obstacles and then push the heavy thing downward. It is, then, as though the push comes from within as part of the nature of the heavy thing which will be manifested in self-induced changes when inhibiting forces are removed. In the same way light things recede from the center, and, generally, the four elements have their proper places in the universe, which is where they tend to go. The empirically observed universe has a layered structure, earth mostly at the center, water for the most part next closest, and so on. This seems obvious confirmation of the conception of natural motion since it appears that things have mostly gone where they belong.[24] And Aristotle has a theory of the transmutation of elements from heavy to light and from light to heavy which could account intelligently for the fact that a permanent stasis is not reached.[25] Within the setting of this theory of natural motion, to say that a body is heavy is just to say that it contains within itself a causal factor that originates motion toward the center. As we shall see, Descartes' contention that scholastic physical explanations psychologize inanimate material things is especially clearly articulated in connection with weight and gravitational motion.[26]

In Aristotelian thought the motions and changes that a thing can induce in itself in virtue of its formal nature are all construed as realizing an innate potentiality for attaining an objective. Such objectives are ascribed to the objects that are able to move themselves. The power to initiate motion is thus an intrinsic directedness. The motions which result from this indwelling causal initiative are, therefore, susceptible to teleological explanations citing final causes. The natural motion that the contained quality *gravity* induces is a *directed* motion toward the place the heavy object seeks to occupy.

This finalism connects the inanimate physical world with essentially biological understanding. Gravitational motion is assimilated to the pattern of explanation that seems so natural for motions like those involved in respiration, which have a legible goal in the welfare of the breathing animal. So the paradigm of a substance is a living organism. The Aristotelian doctrine articulating four types of explanatory question, usually called the theory of four causes, can be thought of as an implicit definition of an individual substance. For a thing that is a true substantial unity each of the four questions, including the question that calls for a purpose or objective, has an answer. Physicists as well as biologists investigate final causes of phenomena. Although in some cases the efficient, final, and material causes collapse into a single factor for Aristotle, finality is never absent from nature.[27]

The various souls that Aristotle finds in plants, animals, and men are among the forms capable of initiating motions with obvious natural objectives. The organization of complex organisms is intelligible in terms of hierarchies of such forms. In *De Anima* the rational soul is the highest form of the body making up a man. It is "the first actuality of the body," a doctrine taken over by Thomas and other scholastics.[28] Aristotle considers the possible separate existence of souls, which seems to be excluded by his form-matter conception of individual things. "Suppose the eye were an animal, sight would have been its soul. . . ."[29] A sightless eye could exist as a material object with a lower form, though not really as an eye, while sight could not exist at all without some material embodiment. In a passage that has reverberations in the *Meditations* Aristotle goes on to say:

> From this it indubitably follows that the soul is inseparable from its body, or at any rate that certain parts of it are (if it has parts)—for the actuality of some of them is nothing but the actuality of their bodily parts. Yet some may be separable because they are not the actualities of any bodies at all. Further we have no light on the problem of whether the soul may not be the actuality of the body in the sense in which the sailor is the actuality of the ship.[30]

I want to emphasize that in Aristotle's thinking, souls are like the qualities gravity, heat, and attraction in that they are originative causes of motion and change. Intrinsic causal agency is found in gravitational fall, in the growth of plants, in the locomotion of animals, and in consciously directed human actions. Behavior-directing factors which are mental by Descartes' criterion are, for Aristotle, sophisticated versions of the same inner determination of motion that is manifested by heavy objects.

The Aristotelian model of explanation, invoking forms as causes of motion, was accepted by the scholastic thinkers to whom Descartes reacts.[31] In scholastic terminology forms are qualified as *substantial* not because they are thought to be independent substances. Substantial form contrasts with *accidental* form. The substantial form of a thing comprises its essential nature. Accidental forms have the same status as intrinsic causes of change, although possession of them is inessential:

> . . . [T]he substantial form differs from the accidental form in this, that the accidental form does not make a thing to be absolutely, but to be such, as heat does not make a thing to be absolutely but only to be hot.[32]

An existing thing could lack an accidental form that it has and yet remain what it is. Accidental forms include the real qualities that Descartes repudiates.

These Aristotelian-scholastic views are the occasion for Descartes' contention that forms and qualities are like "little souls" in material objects. The conscious rational soul of man, in this tradition, is the substantial form of man. It accomplishes in a consciously articulated way the initiation of movement toward ends just as substantial forms and qualities in inanimate objects initiate directed changes in phenomena like combustion and the fall of heavy bodies. The heat generated in combustion, as Descartes reads scholastic accounts, is the realization of a contained goal-like potential in the wood. For Descartes the production of heat is not the goal of a material object. Nor is burning a self-caused action in which a piece of wood can engage. Nothing happens but the turbulent motion of minute particles, progressively disturbing the stabler structure of the unburned wood. Heat is merely a subjective feature of our perception of these particle motions, which are not directed from within the particles that move.

In *La Traité de la Lumière*, tactfully summing up his rejection of scholastic explanations of combustion, Descartes says:

> Though another may imagine, if he wishes, that there is in this wood the Form of fire, the Quality heat, and the Action which burns it, as entirely distinct constituents, for my part, since I am afraid of error if I posit anything more than what I see must be there, I content myself with conceiving in it only the movement of its parts.[33]

The burning wood manifests only externally caused motions of particles. The realization of self-contained potentialities and the attainment of objectives, which do characterize actions of minds, are absent in combustion.

In the Fourth Meditation Descartes says that he finds "final causes to be wholly useless in physics,"[34] for the reason that the purposes of an infinite Divinity are largely opaque to men. But his scientific investigations have given him a more fundamental reason for excluding finalism. He actually finds teleological explanations defective even in cases where our assessment of purposes and ends is quite correct.

> This rule—that we should never argue from ends—should be carefully heeded. For . . . the knowledge of a thing's purpose never leads us to knowledge of the thing itself: its nature remains just as obscure to us. Indeed, this constant practice of arguing from ends is Aristotle's greatest fault.[35]

For example, when we rightly understand that the heart beats in order to circulate the blood, we do not thereby know anything at all about what makes it beat as it does. We still need a causal explanation that purpose does not provide or even suggest.

Descartes' most instructive criticisms of mental concepts in physics concern weight and gravitational motion. He portrays the evolution of his own thought about gravity as a gradual emancipation from a universal propensity to mind-matter confusions traceable to childhood interpretations of experience:

> . . . I noticed that from infancy I had passed various judgements about physical things, for example, judgements which contributed much to the preservation of the life I was then entering; and I had afterwards retained the same opinions which I had before conceived touching these things. . . . [And although the mind was at the time]

conscious of its own nature and possessed of an idea of thought as well as extension, nevertheless, having no intellectual knowledge, though at the same time it had an imagination of something, it took them both to be one and the same and referred all its notions of intellectual matters to the body.[36]

The primitive theory of childhood springs from the intimate connection between phenomena and the conditions for our survival as organisms. Sensations of pleasure and pain succeed in the function of assuring survival precisely through our inclination to identify pleasurable and painful sensations with the outer objects that stimulate them. As a consequence of this biologically useful merging of physical cause and mental effect we naturally develop a mentalistic conception of physical reality.

Reconstructing his own intellectual biography, Descartes explains how the scholastic-Aristotelian explanation of the fall of heavy bodies springs from this childhood imputation of "intellectual matters to the body." Gravity, conceived as a real quality, is the self-contained cause of motion in a heavy thing. This quality is a soul-like constituent, in the first instance, because it cannot be located inside the heavy thing as a part can be, just as the conscious mind of a man initiates his movements but is not locatable in some particular place within his body. The soul is able to focus all its causal efficacy at a single point, and so, too, the formal quality "gravity" can exercise its causal force at a point. In the case of the efficacy of the soul at a point Descartes means that in the transition from intention to behavior a single part of the body can be moved in a particular way while the rest is unaffected. The heavy body seems to mimic this in that wherever a rope is attached, all of the contained gravity acts at that one point "as if the gravity resided in the part along which the rope touched and was not diffused through the others."[37]

Descartes' physics, however, rejects the concept of gravity as a space-filling quality of body that can act at a point. Effectiveness at any selected point remains the right idea when we are thinking about the operation of minds in bodies that do have minds: "Indeed it is in no other way that I now understand mind to be coextensive with the body, the whole in the whole and the whole in any of its parts."[38]

Descartes finds the most telling evidence of a confused assignment of mental functions to matter in the alleged directedness of gravitational movement.

The chief sign that my idea of gravity was derived from that which I
had of the mind, is that I thought that gravity carried bodies toward
the center of the earth as if it contained some knowledge of this center
within it. For it could not act as it did without knowledge, nor can
there be any knowledge except in the mind. At the same time I attributed also to gravity certain things which cannot be understood to
apply to the mind in the same sense; as, e.g., that it is divisible,
measurable, etc.[39]

In other words, the internal source of motion must be understood within the scholastic explanation not only as an agency capable
of inducing movements that express the whole power of the inner
cause at any one point in the body but also the inner agency must
know where the center is from the place the heavy body happens to
occupy. Given a spherical universe, heavy bodies may reside in any
direction whatever from the center. It follows that the same quality,
gravity, is able to induce motions in one body in any direction whatever. A body will move in a certain direction along a straight line
through the center of the universe if it is on one side of the center,
and it will move in exactly the opposite direction along that same line
if it is on the other side. How does this inner determinant manage
to cause diametrically opposed motions? The supposition that it does
requires that the inner causal factor be able to discriminate from one
another the positions a body may occupy relative to the center. By
analogy, a bird's nest is its natural place, and a bird is able to and
does move toward that nest if the obstacles are not too great. But this
ability would be quite unintelligible if we were not willing to ascribe
to the bird something like knowledge of the location of the nest. It
would be unintelligible just because the ability imputed is a plastic
disposition that issues in variously directed flight, depending on the
relative positions of bird and nest. It is not a brute tendency to move
in some set way. Thus, the theory of natural place and natural motion, widely accepted by such prominent scholastic scientists as John
Buridan and Albert of Saxony, does interpret gravity on a pattern
suitable for animal and human behavior that exhibits discrimination
and intelligence.[40]

In the last analysis, Descartes assigns even the intelligent perfor-
mances of birds and all other nonrational living things to the world
of mindless mechanical interactions. A man knows where his home
is, and his knowledge together with his conscious control of his own

movement does indeed explain his homecoming at the end of the day. The explanatory schema here, however, is grossly misapplied, Descartes believes, in accounts of free fall, and it is misapplied in accounts of the behavior of brutes as well.

The uncompromising segregation of human actions which do support psychological explanations and animal behavior which does not is simply the consistent working out of the implications of the rejection of mental factors in elementary phenomena such as gravitational fall. The essence of mind is consciousness. Where there is no consciousness, mind-like functions have no footing in scientific explanation. The deeply rooted inclination that we possess to read psychological activities into nature is most obvious in our thinking about animals that share so much with us from the point of view of physiology. Even this almost irresistible psychologizing is the elaboration of the confused thinking of childhood wherein the inner conscious affective and sensuous representation is hopelessly mixed up with the outer things that are both the causes and the objects of the ideas that we have in perception. Descartes adheres firmly to the view that physiology is just mechanical physics applied to intricate structures and elaborately organized functions that are found on a very small scale in living things.

Contemporary materialist philosophers of mind rely on the complexity of the brain and the nervous system to lend plausibility to their hypothesis that neural events may be identical with conscious experiences and thoughts. No simple working of levers and gears could produce a feeling. But, perhaps, somehow, the billions of nerve cells, each with its delicate electrical activity, interconnected in hierarchical networks, containing a world of feedback mechanisms, graspable as a maze of information channels, controls, dampers, and amplifiers — perhaps mere physical activity at this level, still dimly, partially, and provisionally understood, can amount to conscious thought.

Descartes is unattracted by this kind of speculation. He was deeply impressed by physiology, and his visionary program for a physiological psychology in *The Passions of the Soul* is in the spirit of contemporary neurophysiology even though the details of Descartes' neural science are now but picturesque misconceptions. He is never tempted, however, by the hypothesis of mind-brain identity. Complex physical events are only physical events.

This intuitive conviction that the intricacy of the physical cannot

convert it into consciousness was well expressed by Leibniz. In the
Monadology he suggests that the microscopic size of things in the
nervous system gives a spurious aura of feasibility to materialism. But
if the mind-machine were enlarged to the size of a mill, we could
enter it and would "find only parts which work upon one another,
and never anything by which to explain a perception [that is, a conscious experience.]"[41]

Descartes' rejection of materialist conceptions of mind rests on
his conviction that his own gains in understanding have been possible
only because he has eliminated a mental aspect from even the subtlest physical activities. *La Description du Corps Humain* begins with
the theme of self-knowledge. Man's understanding of himself should
extend to anatomy and physiology and not only to the moral dimensions of human existence. From this self-study Descartes envisions
unlimited practical results for medicine in the cure and prevention of
disease, and even the retarding of old age. But these results will be
forthcoming

> . . . only if we have studied enough to understand the nature of our
> own body and do not attribute in any way to the mind the functions
> which depend only on the body and on the disposition of its organs.[42]

Again Descartes cites patterns of thought developed in childhood as
an obstacle to understanding. We know we have conscious control of
some bodily movements, and, therefore, we incline to ascribe a mental principle to all the others. Ignorance of anatomical structure and
the mechanics of physiology permits us to extend the psychological
explanatory idiom to the motions of the heart, the arteries, and di-
gestive organs, "though these, containing no thought, are only bodily
movements."[43] One body is moved by another, not by anything non-
bodily. Where we do not consciously experience the dependence of
movement on the mind, we should not ascribe it to the mind.

> . . . [A]nd even the movements that are called voluntary proceed
> principally from the disposition of the organs, since they cannot be ex-
> cited without those bodily dispositions, whatever volitions we may
> have, even though it is the mind that determines them.[44]

The physiology of bodily movements, then, reveals that even for movements under the control of the will physical effects must have physical causes. Here the question of a final reconciliation of a thorough-

going mechanical viewpoint with mental control is left open.

La Description will try to explain, Descartes says, "the machine of our body" and to show that we have no more reason to ascribe its physiological workings to a soul than we have to impute a soul to a clock.[45] A clock plainly has no soul, although its inner workings and outer behavior are elaborately organized in ways that reflect the intelligence of its maker and the human objectives in its use. These relationships to conscious mental activities are not, in the case of a clock, the occasion for a confused imputation of thinking to the mechanism itself. But it is just this confusion to which we are susceptible when we think about the workings of an animal's body or our own.

Descartes' lifelong interest in automata,[46] clever products of engineers devised for the amusement of kings, provides him with another telling analogy with which to expose the error of mentalistic explanations in physiology. Automata seem to react to stimuli, to have goals, and, generally, to move as though directed by a contained intellect. A naive spectator will actually believe that a mechanically operating automaton is guided by some kind of conscious appreciation of the environment, and that it manifests a will of its own and thought-out responses. When we understand that such things are accomplished by cleverly rigged magnets, or gears, or hydraulic valves, the illusion of mental control vanishes.[47] Descartes believes that the appearance of a mental element in the natural *machines* that are animal and human bodies is just as much an illusion, although it is much more difficult to dispel.

The finest and most consistent expression of a mechanical conception of human physical existence extending to *all* of the inner and outer manifestations of mind appears at the end of the posthumously published fragments of Le Monde. Descartes has exploited throughout the book a curious rhetorical device that is both prudential and intellectually liberating. He expressly offers, not an explanatory picture of our "world" and the human race to which we actually belong, but, instead, the complete science of an imaginary world located somewhere in the reaches of extension far from our skies.[48] Suns and planets are formed by an evolutionary process commencing from an initial chaos from which everything develops in strict obedience to permanent laws of motion. Living things and the analogs of men, in this imagined world, come into existence in the same way. In the

Traité de L'homme these are "men of clay whom God has made to be as like us as possible."[49] Descartes does ascribe a mental constitution to these "men." Like us, they have ideas, appetites, passions, and memories. The physical aspect of their existence is *absolutely* mechanical and wholly explicable without any appeal to a mental constitution. Insofar as Descartes believes that we are in fact such men, he ascribes to us, here, a complete physiology *without mind-body interaction*.

> I would like you to suppose that all the functions I have attributed to this machine, such as the digestion of food, the pulse in the heart and arteries, the nourishment and growth of the members, wakefulness and sleep; the reception of light, of sounds, of odors, of heat and similar qualities, by the external organs of sense; the impression of ideas from them on the organ of common sense[50] and of imagination, the retention or engraving of these ideas in the memory; the interior movements of appetites and of passions; and finally the exterior movements of all the members, which are so well suited both to the action of objects presented to the senses and to inner passions, that they imitate as perfectly as possible those of a true man: I say I would like you to consider that these functions follow entirely naturally in this machine, from the mere disposition of its organs, neither more nor less than the movements of a clock or other automaton follow from the disposition of its counter weights and wheels; so that there can be no reason at all to conceive in it any other vegetative soul, nor sensitive soul, nor any other principle of movement and of life than its blood and its spirits, excited by the heat of the fire which burns continually in its heart, and which is of no other nature than all the fires which burn in inanimate bodies.[51]

Of course, Descartes does not mean that the workings of the human body do not show any indisputable marks of mind and intelligence at all. God is responsible for the constitution of men, and his workmanship manifests a standard of creative intelligence that no engineer can approach. The human body reflects, therefore, the mind of God, but in the creation of the body-machine God has utilized only extended particles interacting according to fixed laws. From this point of view all of the motions of the human body, molar and microscopic, including all those that go into voluntary actions, have their sufficient physical causes. Only this exceptionless principle could justify the corresponding claim that no motions of the "men" of *Le Monde* require explanations that invoke a mental function.

Descartes drew back from this wholly mechanical man. He mars the consistency of his insight by allowing a unique locus of mind-body interaction in the pineal gland. In this tiny gland the animal spirits, which are the most rarefied bloodlike constituent of the nervous system, are affected by the mind. Descartes invokes the fragile support of the fact that the pineal gland is not double and is, to that extent, a plausible site for a central integration of the functions of the many dual parts of the sensory system and brain.[52] The animal spirits are only *deflected* by mental influence, according to Descartes' account, so that the total quantity of motion of physical things can remain constant.

Had Descartes retained the rigorously consistent view he formulated at the end of *Le Monde*, he might have been led to abandon the concept of a substantial mind altogether. The idea of deflection of the animal spirits requires a quasi-physical influence and leads at once to a "paramechanical" conception of mind.[53] And the interaction creates a fundamentally unintelligible leakage from the self-sufficient sphere of physical activity. Mental deflection of particles, however subtle they may be, violates a crucial feature of a mechanical system like that which Descartes' physical universe is supposed to comprise. This is expressed by later science as violation of the conservation of energy. If nonphysical agencies can cause any movement or deflection at all, that movement or deflection could, for example, compress a spring or raise a weight, thus causing an increase in total energy. Defects in his understanding of force leave Descartes without an appropriate concept of energy in terms of which he might have grasped this criticism. However, his limitation of the supposed influence of the mind to deflections that leave "the quantity of motion" unchanged reveal Descartes' own qualms concerning the compatibility of conservation and mind-body interaction. His clear grasp of inertia, requiring uniform motion *in a straight line*, should have but did not reinforce those qualms considerably.

But for the pineal gland Descartes' dualism would have a very different force. The tendency of his total scientific effort is the elimination of mental direction as a factor in explanations of physical changes and motions. Beliefs, acts of will, desires, and intentions do not move parts of the body any more than an inner quality, gravity, moves a heavy thing, or inner self-realizing heat creates changes in a piece of wood. Of course, we are left with the fact that men do act, execute their intentions, and gratify their desires.

The uncompromised vision at the end of the *Traité de L'homme* rejects the idea that the relationship between psychological explanations of human behavior and physical explanations of the motion of bodily parts can be expressed as any kind of interaction between substances. Beliefs, desires, and the like, figuring in psychological accounts, are not physical causes, and only physical causes can move material objects. All motions, even of "the blood and the spirits," have sufficient physical causes, although we do not have a complete account of these physiological events. "No other principle of movement" is required, not in the case of a man's body any more than in the case of an automaton.

For myself, apart from the outmoded scientific details, I think this view of bodily motions is correct. The right way of capturing intellectually the relationship of mental concepts and physical events is at present the subject of scientific investigation and of unsettled philosophical reflection. At present a materialist philosophy of mind that identifies beliefs and desires with neural states and processes is dominant. Like the theory of the pineal gland, this contemporary materialism assigns a causal role to mental things. For Descartes' paramechanical events materialism substitutes a frankly physicalist interpretation of mental functioning. The theory gets undeserved support from association with the sophisticated physiology and anatomy that has replaced Descartes' curious conceptions of the facts. As far as I can see, materialists have not offered anything at all to make it intelligible that a physical occurrence in the brain can be a belief, or a desire, or a thought.[54]

There is a strange irony in the mechanical perspective on the body expressed in *Le Monde*. It is as though we start wanting to know how a certain miracle occurs, the miracle of mental control of movements in the physical world. How does a desire and a belief move a hand? We know that muscles, not thoughts, move hands. Nervous impulses, not desires, move muscles. The ironic explanation of the miracle that Descartes reaches, at least on this occasion, is that the miracle does not occur. Beliefs and desires and other mental things simply cannot be attached to motions as their causes. The same irony appears in Descartes' account of the miracle of vision. How do we manage to get a conscious picture of the external world through the organs of sense? In the *Optics* Descartes explains what happens when we see, invoking as a helpful analogy a blind man feeling his way with a stick! Descartes particularly wants to reject the idea that "intentional species," which scholastic philosophers took to be tiny images, leap into the eye and somehow migrate to an inner center of conscious reception. He interprets the transmission of light as a kind of pressure which does not involve the entrance of anything into the eye,[55] just as pressures in the blind man's stick do not involve a flow of things through the stick and then into the hand. This is the thinking that lies behind the Second Meditation when Descartes says:

> But it must be observed that perception of the wax is not sight, not touch, not imagination; nor was it ever so though it formerly seemed to be; it is a purely mental contemplation.[56]

In other words, the miracle of real contact with outer reality does not occur at all. So vision is like blindness, and mental control is really automatism.

These understandings would be grotesque but for their profound appreciation of the idea that elements in our discourse about conscious experience are not to be identified with stages in physiological processes. The positive thesis that Descartes adopts is unsatisfactory. Because he thinks of the mind as a second substance with its own independent footing in reality, he is left with a "two-worlds" view and the quagmire of unintelligible interaction that leads to bizarre Occasionalism or idealist elimination of the physical world altogether. Although he rightly rejects confused interpretation of mental discourse that assigns it physical referents, Descartes precipitates these difficulties because he posits an inevitably mysterious nonphysical mind.

4. Conclusions

The question remains: Why did Descartes construct the metaphysical proofs presented in the *Meditations* which reflect the true foundations of his thinking so inadequately? There is a strand of reserve and secrecy in Descartes' writing. As a young man, Descartes described himself with some aptness as entering on the stage of public life masked like an actor, so that his audience will not see his true state of mind.[57] He intentionally published his geometry in a form difficult to follow lest others, grasping his discoveries too easily, claim to have possessed them already. He was always concerned about the reception of his scientific innovations by religious authorities. He withheld the publication of *Le Monde* upon hearing of the condemnation of Galileo by the Inquisition. He always organized his presentations as prudently as he could. His life and letters show an exceptional desire for privacy and avoidance of embroiling controversy. Leibniz and others complain that he conceals the sources of his ideas which often contain unacknowledged influence of the writings of others. The first concern of Descartes as a writer is not the artless expression of his personal thought.

Descartes, however, certainly did believe that the many-sided insights of scientific works needed a coherent metaphysical foundation to replace the discarded Aristotelianism. The theological turn of his arguments rests on sincere religious commitment. Furthermore, the metaphysical arguments do involve as their first stage the articulation of the subjective point of view, which has great power and from which the metaphysical arguments are mounted with a certain naturalness. It is worth emphasizing that this systematic subjectivism is not part of the context of scientific investigation for Descartes. Egocentric skepticism is absent from the methodology of the *Rules*. There is no hint of the method of doubt or of the phenomenological resolution of doubt by the *cogito* argument in the scientific work presenting the findings that motivate Descartes' dualism.

Finally, the metaphysical demonstrations constitute a conservative and backward-looking project for Descartes relative to the progressive content of his scientific thought. The crucial arguments are reconstructions and new employments of ideas taken over from existing traditions. Starting from the *cogito* argument, the *Meditations* are full of Saint Augustine. The ontological argument is Anselm's. In discussing causes that contain the reality of their effects "eminently" *versus* "formally," Descartes is employing traditional scholastic distinctions.[58] The concepts of essence and existence, as Descartes employs them, are taken over from Saint Thomas and Aristotle. None of this battery of terms, concepts, and arguments appear in the scientific contexts that really motivate Descartes' dualism.

We can see the late metaphysical works as a restatement in

which Descartes tries to connect his radical conclusions to existing traditions of thought. This understanding does not confer any greater merit on the tortured theology of the official proofs of dualism. I should say that the influence of dualism, which is certainly not due to these arguments, rests, first, on the appeal of the subjective starting point of the *Meditations* and, second, on a rough, widespread, frequently unstated appreciation of the tendency of Descartes' scientific thinking which I have tried to describe here.

The philosophical issues to which Descartes' dualism is addressed are still at the center of metaphysics and epistemology. In contrast, the relevance of Cartesian science diminished rapidly following the appearance of Newton's superior theories. Descartes has retained prestige as a mathematician, although his mathematical work is read chiefly by historians. But Descartes' metaphysical writings have always been studied, and they have exerted a decisive influence on modern thought, especially through Berkeley, Locke, and Hume. It is Cartesian metaphysics, separated from the context of scientific thought, that has influenced empiricism.

In assessing Descartes' dualism we should restore its scientific setting. We should also ignore the deficiencies of his outmoded conceptions. This does not mean only that we should overlook Descartes' beliefs that a fire burns in the heart and that animal spirits are a rarified form of blood. More important, we have to ignore his limited conception of physical objects and his reduction of physical events to motions and impacts among particles. Even his idea of causality ill fits contemporary physics wherein causal relations are expressed in equations that do not break up reality into discrete consecutive events. Let us just imagine all of Descartes' old-fashioned ideas replaced by some up-to-date conception of the physical world. We want a conception that is free of psychological and teleological ideas. We do use such a conception of physical reality in our thinking, and it corresponds to, in fact it is the heir of, Descartes' mechanical universe of extended particles.

Given such a conception of the physical world, I believe that Descartes is right to exclude explanations that introduce nonphysical factors as causes of physical events. He is also right to refuse a materialist reduction of the mind to the body. The joint assertion of mechanism and rejection of mind-brain identity can appear paradoxical. The seeming difficulty is clear. If mental things like beliefs and desires are not physical causes, and if only such causes can account for physical changes and motions, then what is the connection between beliefs and desires and human actions to which beliefs and desires are patently relevant? Under the pressure of this question Descartes allowed an exception to his otherwise rigorous mechanism, a unique channel connecting two metaphysically incommensurable worlds, namely, the pineal gland. This is a mistake. The mistake is engendered by a substance-conception of mind. Descartes patterns his thinking about mental concepts on material things and events, as though, by somehow subtracting materiality, we arrive at *nonmaterial* things and events. This kind of thinking is encouraged by the methodological outlook of the *Meditations*. We are more or less forced to conceive of the mental as a realm of things and events. The phenomenological perspective seems to certify the reality of mental goings-on and then raises the question, What is all this? By this we mean: What is the metaphysical status of mental things, the existence of which is assured? When the materialist identification is rejected, mental things and events necessarily appear to be *another kind of reality*. Then the problem of interaction is generated, and Descartes' compromise, so destructive of his principle insight, is motivated.

We have to ask, What is a conception of mentality that does not generate a second realm of things and then lead to the hopeless problem of interaction? This question from Descartes' perspective is, What are we to make of the phenomenology of the Second Meditation if we neither identify mental things with neural things nor posit any substantial *res cogitans*? It is helpful here to focus on *truth* where Descartes focuses on *reality*. The thinking subject, tentatively repudiating all empirical knowledge, finds that his own beliefs and desires, as such, are not jeopardized. Though the outer world may all be illusion, he believes, for example, that he is in a room with an open fire, and he desires to warm himself. Belief and desire are thus insulated from empirical skepticism. Descartes reads this, in the idiom of realities, as demonstrating the existence of certain things (ideas in the mind) or the occurrence of certain events (thinking). Though there may be no firelit room, my believing-that-there-is is something that does exist, and my desiring does occur. Abandoning this mode of expression, we can retain the insights of the subjective point of view by saying that "I believe I am in a firelit room" and "I want to warm myself by the fire" are *true*, and these truths are independent of the existence of the room and the fire. Though these subjective reports are true, what their truth implies about realities is not obvious. In particular, it is not obvious that believing and desiring are things that are present in men, or go on in men.

Elsewhere I have argued that any account of belief that identifies believing with an inner something, whether material or nonmaterial, cannot be correct.[59] At the least, reflection on mental concepts creates serious questions about the unargued-for interpretation of these concepts in terms of inner realities, that is, the interpretation that Descartes shares with contemporary mind-brain materialism. If this interpretation is set aside, we can try to overcome the illusion that mental states must be identified with brain states lest they be identified with states of some unscientific and intrinsically mysterious nonmaterial mind. This illusion is one of the pillars of mind-brain materialism.

In the "Conversation with Burman" Descartes is close to the kind of understanding I recommend here. Explanations that state the purpose for which things take place do not give a causal account even if the claim about purpose is correct.[60] Applied to psychology, Descartes' insight amounts to this: We ask a man why he has done something, fired a gun, for example. The answer tells us that he desired something (to scare the birds away from his field) and that he believed something (that firing the gun would scare away the birds). So a combination of a desire and a belief explains the action by displaying the purpose of the behavior explained. If Descartes is right, however, this leaves untouched all physical questions of the form What caused this object to move? And is it not clear that Descartes is right? Assuming the correctness of the psychological explanation, we know the man's intention and the point of his behavior. But none of this sheds light on causes of the movement of his finger on the trigger, any more than it sheds light on causes of the movement of the bullet in the gun barrel.

There is something naive in the idea that a man's believings and wantings are states and events inside him that are capable of moving parts of his body, as contracting muscles can move fingers and expanding gases can move bullets. It would be preposterous to say that "wanting to scare birds" might directly cause the motion of a bullet. Nor could wanting something directly cause the motion of a finger. As Descartes puts it, motions of fingers depend on "the disposition of the organs," which means that there are physical events and conditions in the nerves and muscles which explain the motion of the finger. These physical causes are certainly not what is referred to as "wanting to scare birds." When we are subject to materialist inspiration, we are tempted to place the causal efficacy of mental things further along in remote neural stretches of the sequence of physical events. "Wanting to scare birds" then becomes a posited neural cause, the immediate effect of which also has to be posited. A vague sense of the fabulous complexity of the brain helps us to imagine that this transaction that would be preposterous out in the open is easily accomplished in the nervous system. But, in fact, "wanting to scare birds" does not belong anywhere in a sequence of causally intelligible motions of things. Nor are wantings spiritual occurrences. We must formulate the truth-conditions for "He wanted to scare the birds" without making *wanting* into any occurrence at all.

The difference between the Cartesian theory of the pineal gland and the materialist theory is that the materialist asserts that the relevant mental things are themselves physical states and events. He does this precisely to make them eligible as causes of motions while saving the principle: physical motions must have physical causes. That is the principle that Descartes adopts and also compromises. But the trouble with mental things as candidate causes is not just their vexed metaphysical standing. From the point of view of physics "knowledge of a thing's purpose never leads to knowledge of the thing itself."[61] Here, knowledge of the thing itself means knowledge of the causes of physical changes. Beliefs and desires explain actions in terms of purposes and goals. As Descartes believed, these explanations, even if they are correct, leave all questions of physics unanswered.

NOTES

Translations are from the English-language versions cited in these notes. Wherever there is no English reference the translations are mine. No references are given for well-known themes of the *Meditations* except where passages are quoted. For my general understanding of Descartes I am much indebted to Étienne Gilson.

The following abbreviations are used in these notes:

AT I-XI   C. Adam and P. Tannery, *Oeuvres de Descartes*, Nouvelle pres-
          entation, Paris, 1964.
HR I-II   E. S. Haldane and G. R. T. Ross, *The Philosophical Works of
          Descartes,* London, 1911.
AG   E. Anscombe and P. Geach, *Descartes: Philosophical Writings,*
          London, 1964.
K   A. Kenny, *Descartes' Philosophical Letters,* London, 1970.

    1. This subtitle appears first in the second Latin edition, 1642; HR I,
144; AT VII, xxi.
    2. AG 117. See also note 30.
    3. January 1642, AT III, 491; K 127–28.
    4. For Hobbes' view, HR II, 61; for Gassendi's, HR II, 142. Descartes'
replies: HR II, 63 and 211.
    5. AG 69.
    6. HR II, 25.
    7. HR II, 83.
    8. K 123; AT III, 474.
    9. K 144.
    10. The phrase is part of the title of the Second Meditation.
    11. See *Études sur le rôle de la pensée médiévale dans la formation
du système Cartesien,* esp. 2ᵉᵐᵉ pt., 1.
    12. *Discours*, III, AT VI, 30; P. Olscamp, *Discourse* etc., Indian-
apolis, 1965, 25.
    13. July 22, 1641, K 109; AT III, 420.
    14. May 21, 1643, K 139; AT III, 667.
    15. "Postquam autem ulterius perrexi," AT VIII, 440; HR II, 253.
This suggests a temporal order in Descartes' thinking that cannot be taken
literally.
    16. HR II, 253–54.
    17. April 26, 1643, K 135–36; AT III, 648–49.
    18. Compare *Principles*, pt. 2, art. 37: "The first law of nature: that
each thing as far as in it lies, continues always in the same state; and that
which is once moved always continues so to move." Art. 39 asserts that "all
motion is of itself in a straight line." HR I, 267. For an illuminating account
of Descartes' concept of inertia and its influence on Newton see A. Koyre,
"Newton and Descartes," in his *Newtonian Studies*, Cambridge, 1965, 69–76.
    19. *Metaphysics*, Z, 8, 1033ᵃ–4ᵃ. But compare L, 4, 1070ᵃ. This pas-
sage seems to allow a possible exception in the separate existence of the
forms of natural beings and, in particular, of the rational soul of man. The
same kind of suggestion is made at H, 2, 1043ᵇ, "Whether the substance
of destructible things can exist apart is not yet at all clear; except that ob-

viously this is impossible in some cases; e.g., a house or a utensil. Perhaps indeed, neither of these things themselves, nor any of the other things which are not formed by nature, are substances at all; for one might say that the nature in natural objects is the only substance to be found in destructible things," W. D. Ross, Oxford, 1908. It must be noted that Aristotle speaks here of forms by themselves as "substances." On this confusing alternative usage he does not apply the term to composites of form and matter, although this is commonly his practice elsewhere. At 1070^b–1^a Aristotle states flatly, "Some things can exist apart and some cannot, and it is the former that are substances." These passages very much conform to the conception of soul-like separable constituents, capable of causing motions in things of which they are forms, that is, the very conception that Descartes ascribes to the scholastics and then rejects.

20. *Metaphysics,* H, 3, 1043^{a-b}.

21. *Metaphysics,* H, 6, 1045^{a-b}.

22. *Physics,* I, A, 1, 193^a.

23. *On the Heavens,* Bk. 1, 1, 7–8, 276^{a-b}; and Bk. 3, 2, 300^a.

24. *On the Heavens,* Bk. 1, 1, 8.

25. *On the Heavens,* Bk. 3, 7, 314^b–6^b, and *On Generation and Corruption,* Bk. 2, 4, 331^a–2^a.

26. Holders of the sort of view to which Descartes refers are not limited to Aristotle and the Schoolmen of the thirteenth century and later who were so deeply affected by the rediscovery of Aristotle's works. Even Saint Augustine voices both the idea that heavy things are directed to goal-like natural places by their weight, and the idea that this activity of heavy bodies resembles human desire-guided behavior. Augustine says, "Our body with its lumpishness [Augustine has merely 'corpus pondere'] strives towards its own place. Weight makes not downward only, but to his own place also. All things pressed by their own weight go towards their proper places. . . . Things a little out of their places become unquiet. Put them in their order again and they are quieted. My weight is my love. By that I am carried wheresoever I be carried." *Confessions,* Bk. 13, ch. 9; trans. W. Watts, London, 1912, 391.

27. *Physics,* Bk. 2, 3 and 7.

28. *Physics,* Bk. 2, 1, 412^{a-b}; and Aquinas, *Summa Theologica,* I, q 76, a 4.

29. *De Anima,* Bk. 2, 1, 412^{a-b}; trans. J. A. Smith.

30. *De Anima,* 413^a. I take this to be the precedent for Descartes' pilot-ship analogy in the Sixth Meditation.

31. Gilson shows that these doctrines are prominent in the manuals from which Descartes was taught as a boy at La Flèche. See *Études,* 155 and 161 n. For a full survey of the Aristotelian concept of form and substantial

form in patristic, scholastic, and Renaissance thought see "Form and Materie," in *Historisches Wörterbuch der Philosophie*, ed. J. Ritter, Basel, 1971, vol. 2, 978–1015.

32. Aquinas, *Summa Theologica*, I, q 76, a 4, Dominican trans.

33. *Le Monde*, AT XI, 7. See also Gilson's discussion of this passage, *Études*, 152–53.

34. AG 94.

35. *Descartes' Conversation with Burman*, J. Cottingham, London, 1976, 19.

36. HR II, 254. The view that self-preservation is the biological function of our confused experience of pleasure and pain is also presented in the Sixth Meditation, without reference to the inadequate theories that Descartes thinks this confusion tends to promote. HR I, 197.

37. HR II, 255.

38. HR II, 255.

39. HR II, 255.

40. See Crombie, A. C., *Medieval and Early Modern Science*, New York, 1959, vol. 1, 128, and vol. 2, 46 and 68ff. Crombie also reports medieval theories involving natural place influenced by Plato's *Timaeus* and incorporating the un-Aristotelian notion of multiple worlds (no one center) such as that of Nicolas of Cusa. Such accounts are part of the historical background of Descartes' vortex theory of planetary motion. Insofar as these alternative medieval cosmologies accepted some version of the idea of natural motion, they are simply further illustrations of what Descartes took to be a universal error.

41. Art. 17, Latta, R., *The Monadology* etc., Oxford, 1898, 228. Latta also quotes Leibniz's "Commentatio de Anima Brutorum," (1710): "Whence it follows that, if it is inconceivable that perception arises in any coarse 'machine' whether it be made of fluids or solids, it is equally inconceivable how perception can arise in a finer 'machine'," Gerhardt, ed., *Phil. Schriften*, vol. 7, 328.

42. AT XI, 223–24.

43. AT XI, 224.

44. AT XI, 225.

45. AT XI, 226.

46. For a survey of Descartes' discussions of automata and an interpretive investigation see F. Alquié, *La découverte métaphysique de l'homme chez Descartes*, Paris, 1950, 52–54.

47. See *Discourse*, HR I, 116; and *Principles*, IV, art. 203–4; HR I, 299–300.

48. AT XI, 31.

49. AT XI, 120.

50. That is, the *sensus communis*, a hypothetical organ or faculty which integrates the input of the several senses according to Thomas and other scholastics.

51. AT XI, 201–2.

52. *Passions*, art. 32, HR I. 346.

53. This is Gilbert Ryle's penetrating epithet, from *The Concept of Mind*, London, 1949, 19.

54. See my "Could Our Beliefs Be Representations in Our Brains?" *Journal of Philosophy*, 76, 1979, 225–44.

55. *Dioptrique*, I, AT VI, 84.

56. AG 73.

57. *Cogitationes Privatae*, AT X, 213. See also H. Gouhier, *Premières pensées de Descartes*, Paris, 1958, 67.

58. For example, Aquinas, *Summa Theologica*, I, q 4, a 2.

59. See note 54.

60. Cottingham, 19.

61. Cottingham, 19.

III

The Metaphysical Elements of Spinoza's Philosophy of Mind

1. The Objectives of This Study

One of the attractions of Spinoza's philosophy for readers today is that it rejects the metaphysics of mind-body dualism, and as a consequence, it appears to avoid the mystery of ethereal mind-stuff and the hopeless problems of mind-body interaction. At the same time Spinoza does not endorse the classical materialism enshrined in Lucretius and rehabilitated by Spinoza's contemporaries Hobbes and Gassendi. In spite of the difficulty of Spinoza's doctrines, and in spite of the obscurity enhanced by his exposition *ordine geometrico*, and perhaps also, partly, because of this difficulty and obscurity, Spinoza's philosophy seems subtle and modern. It has become standard to find in his thinking anticipations of Freud as well as anticipations of the latest mind-brain identity theory or functionalist identity theory of the mind. The overall aim of the present study is to present a clear enough analysis of some of Spinoza's main ideas to make it possible to evaluate these current assessments. His system is an intersection of a large number of intellectual forces. As such I think it extremely interesting and worth much study. Furthermore, Spinoza's objectives are admirable, and I share them. But most of the connections between his and contemporary thought are, I believe, more enthusiastic than reasonable. On the whole there are in Spinoza more retrogressive elements looking back to medieval and Greek thought than there are progressive elements consonant with the scientific outlook of his contemporaries, much less elements prefiguring later scientific developments. Spinoza is secular, tolerant, antiauthoritarian, rational, learned, and humane. His supremely rational "religion" may be regarded as the crowning achievement of Renaissance secularism. In contrast, Descartes is still an apologist in the tradition of Augustine and Thomas Aquinas. But in his philosophical views themselves Spinoza is unappreciative of the radical achievement of Descartes and out of touch with the ideas and style of thought that were to become science.

It is said that there are two strands of thinking in Spinoza. One is rational and scientific. The second component frequently discerned is mystical. Perhaps his accomplishment in this dimension is not accessible to an explicit sympathetic and imaginative examination of his assertions and the arguments that defend them. If there is such a mystical side of Spinoza, the present discussion will not capture its virtues. We will confine ourselves entirely to the rational, the discursive, and the coolly logical perspective to which Spinoza himself expresses commitment in all of his writings. This is the side of Spinoza that leads Stuart Hampshire to feel that "in the philosophy of mind [Spinoza] is nearer to the truth at certain points than any other philosopher has ever been." I sympathize with this judgment only to the extent that every effort to think around and beyond dualism deserves our attention and general praise. In very broad terms Spinoza's philosophy of mind is not in very close touch with our thinking at all because he presents, not a mind-brain identity hypothesis, and not a mind-body identity hypothesis, but a mind-matter identity hypothesis. Contemporary antidualist philosophy of mind has the Cartesian emphasis on consciousness for its chief historical antecedent. This is one of the important sides of Descartes' thought to which Spinoza is least responsive. Spinoza's thinking about mind has little to do with those centers of episodic conscious thought that we think of as minds and that some philosophers hope to identify with neural things and activities.

The philosophy of mind is presently the scene of energetic investigations from many sides. There is little that is stable or satisfactory in it. But I would certainly include Stuart Hampshire among philosophers who have got closer to the truth in the philosophy of mind than Spinoza ever was.

2. The Concept of Substance

Spinoza's great thesis identifying God or nature as the sole independent existent being, which is both a thinking and an extended being, rests on his analysis of the concept of substance. Pressing the notion of independence to the limit, Spinoza reserves the concept of substance for being that is free from every conceivable taint of conditionality or contingency. Part one of the *Ethics* amounts to an exploration of this concept of substance and an elaboration, in the most abstract metaphysical terms, of the implications of the contrast between independent and dependent existence for the understanding of reality.

The broad lines of this analysis are simple. Nothing has an independent existence if it is caused. For to say of something that it is caused is just to say that it depends on whatever it is that causes it. Of course, we have to ask what "causality" means to Spinoza, but we can be sure that some version of this kind of dependence will be part of whatever causality is. The whole of the natural world is a realm of causes and effects, and all the causes of things that we encounter in the world are themselves effects of more remote causes. Nothing independent can be found among the particular things we know. Furthermore, for the entire Judeo-Christian intellectual tradition all of this world of particular causes and effects is understood to depend upon God for its existence. God's creation is a kind of causality. This alone makes the theological vocabulary of Spinoza's metaphysics natural. In Spinoza's hands this theme becomes the foundation of a very secular religion, but he never considers abandoning it altogether. God is the unique uncreated being, the necessary being, the *causa sui*. The very idea of creation brings with it the idea that everything other than God owes its existence to him. Given that independent existence is a required feature of substance, it follows that God is the only substance.

The difficulty of part one is not the uniqueness of substance nor the identification of substance with God. These are virtually self-evident consequences of Spinoza's concept of independence developed in the framework of a conception of God as creator. The difficult thesis is the claim that everything else exists *in substance* and that, as a consequence, nature and all the particulars it contains are incorporated in God. In Spinoza's system the effect is contained in the cause. Divine causality *is* the created world. God *is* the nature that he creates. Dependence is never separate existence, but always something like the dependence of the part on the whole, and even this idea really gives the dependent individual too much independ-

ence, since we so easily think of parts as conceivable and possibly existent outside the whole in which they are parts in fact. Independent
substance necessarily exists, and all components of it only exist and
necessarily exist within the whole. Dependence is a question of perspective. Dependent things exist only relative to a view which does
not take in the whole. It seems as though things other than substance, things merely contingent on what *is* necessarily, truly dependent beings, creatures in the ordinary sense, do not really exist at all.
Independent necessary existence of a seamless whole is the only existence. Finitude, contingency, and individual existence is something
like an illusion.

Earlier philosophical conceptions of substance afford some help
in trying to understand this radical and difficult side of Spinoza's
metaphysics. Traditional treatments of substance offer a bewildering
variety of ideas, but the notion of independence is so prominent
among them, either explicitly or implicitly, that it serves as a thread
by which the diversity is connected and unified. One familiar and ancient line of analysis distinguishes the bearers of attributes or properties as substances, because accidents and properties could not exist at
all without their bearers, as a smile cannot exist without a face, while
a face can exist smiling or unsmiling. From the point of view of
discourse the same distinction is made when the ultimate subjects of
predication are identified as substances, while the referents of predicates are properties and features to which substantial status is denied.

This sense of "substance" is present in the definition Spinoza
framed for his early *Principles of Descartes' Philosophy:* "Every object
to which belongs, as to a subject, some property or quality or attribute . . . is called substance."[1] On this understanding, which goes
back to Aristotle, concrete individuals such as a piece of wax or the
man Peter are substances. There is an obvious sense in which Spinoza
later rejects this idea of substance, for he does not admit any plurality
of substances, much less allow concrete individuals under the heading "substance." But the idea of ultimate subjecthood and the idea
of the ultimate bearer of properties are retained in Spinoza's conclusions about substance in the *Ethics.* The version of this idea that refers to subjects of predication brings out the connection here. Truths
are sentences in which something is properly predicated of a subject,
and that means that the object named by the subject term has the
property referred to by the predicate. Since there is, for Spinoza, only

one true substance, there will only be one ultimate bearer of all attributes and one subject of all predication and all truth. The language that we ordinarily speak does not reflect these metaphysical
constraints, but that is merely a manifestation of the inadequacy of
our ordinary thought and speech.

Adverting to another line of thinking that overlaps the
understanding of substance just considered, we find that *form* and
matter, and *thought* and *extension*, are also called substances in prominent philosophical usage well known to Spinoza. Again, such
things are called substances in view of their fundamental or irreducible role in reality relative to things which are contingent and dependent. For the hylomorphism of the scholastic-Aristotelian tradition
every existing thing has to have a form and has to be composed of
some matter, but form and matter do not themselves have to be
formed or composed of something more elementary. At the same
time it is usually said that neither the form nor the matter can exist
in separation from the individual things which have form and are
composed of matter.

For Descartes extension and thought are substances, though
they are created by God, because of their relative independence.
They cannot be generated or suffer dissolution. They are not reducible to one another or to any more fundamental constituent of things.
As they are producible only by God's creation, so they are indestructi-
ble save through annihilation by God. In Spinoza's system thought
and extension are attributes of the one substance he recognizes. In
large measure he models extension on the Aristotelian conception of
matter, and he models thought on the Aristotelian form.[2] For Aristotle the form makes an individual the particular thing it is. Form constitutes the intrinsic intelligibility of things that gives a footing in
them to understanding and science. Furthermore, Aristotle's conception of the mind is assimilated to his doctrine of form. Aristotle describes the rational soul of man as the highest of a hierarchy of forms
of the human body and speculates on the possible separate existence
of this particular kind of form. Under the influence of the Aristotelian
tradition Spinoza welds form and matter into a single substance in
virtue of the fact that neither one can exist without the other, which
means that they are not independent existences. At the same time he
identifies these now united elements with Descartes' substances:
thought and extension. After rejection of the idea of externally cre-

ated substances, these become attributes of the unique substance which is God.

Finally, a tradition that identifies *space* as a single substance, or an irreducible and indivisible entity, influences Spinoza. This idea is present in Descartes' concept of space identified with matter, an identification which Spinoza accepts. It is clearer in the thinking of those who, like Henry More, rejected the equation of space and matter, while retaining the concept of space as a unique all-embracing substance. In Spinoza's usage spatial containment is a general metaphor for dependence. Individual things like physical objects, and particular events like the stimulation of a nervous system on an occasion, are called finite modes of substance.[3] Their dependent status is brought out by the fact that they exist and are conceived of as existing, not *in* themselves, but *in* something else. Color exists *in* a red cube of wax, so the cube is substantial relative to the color. But the cube of wax can only exist *in* space. It is, thus, like all other bodies, merely a mode of extended substance. Again in this context individual existence tends to be absorbed in Spinoza's metaphysics into the independent existent or substance. The unique substance is an infinite extended thing, and finite things can only exist *within* this indivisible whole.

3. Appearance and Reality

Other prominent rationalists like Descartes, Malebranche, and Leibniz share with Spinoza the view that sense perception is inevitably a source of confusion, error, and prejudice. When reason leads us to a conception of reality that is far from compatible with the world of things that we seem to encounter and talk about in our ordinary experience, the rationalists are willing to ascribe the incompatibility to the intrinsic unreliability of conceptions of things derived from the senses and the imagination. Spinoza's rational exploration of the concept of substance generates a gap between the way things seem to be and the way things are that is wider and more permanent than that envisioned by any philosopher since Parmenides.

Plainly all the discrete particular things that figure in our ordinary experience are finite things whose existence is not guaranteed by some self-contained essence or cause. The contingency of all the physical objects and persons that we encounter in ordinary life is made prominent at once by the fact that these things all exist *for a time*. None of them are eternal things. Anything that qualifies as a substance will be such that it is contingent on nothing. Its essence will involve its existence. Hence the necessity of the existence of substance. Temporally bound things, or things with what Spinoza calls "duration," are not necessary. More than the essence of the thing is required for the existence of things with duration. They do not have to exist, for at times they do not exist.

Our thought about finite individuals including ourselves falls very low on the scale of intellectual processes as these are ordered by Spinoza. Things with duration only figure in thinking based on what Spinoza calls "perceiving things after the common order of nature." Not only the particular beliefs that we form about such things but the entire conceptual scheme within which we frame such beliefs comes in for drastic qualification. The beliefs thus formed about individuals are intrinsically inadequate. The inadequacy is traceable to the presumed finitude and contingency of the things we have beliefs about. We think of things as truly discriminable entities that exist for a while in mutual interaction with other things of the same sort. The inadequacy of such thoughts is an inevitable aspect of the individuality and separateness from the whole of the things we consider.

This theme emerges most decisively in connection with the idea of duration. Propositions II:xxx and II:xxxi tell us that following the common order of nature, we have only "very inadequate knowledge of the duration of the body" and "a very inadequate knowledge of the duration of particular things external to ourselves." This phrasing suggests that we might attain a more adequate knowledge of ourselves and of external things from some other epistemic quarter. In part, Spinoza does mean to cover in this observation the idea that mere acquaintance with things does not suffice for determining how long they will last. For this we need a complete understanding of the causal setting of individual existence. But this kind of explication does not do justice to the radical intent of Spinoza's condemnation of our ordinary thought of finite individuals with duration. Greater adequacy involves progressive elimination of the particular. In a true understanding of reality, an ideally adequate understanding, both particularity and duration will be deleted.

In *On the Improvement of the Understanding* Spinoza contrasts imagination with intellectual grasp afforded by the understanding. When we attain understanding, we do not have a better or perfected appreciation of the same individuals that we grasp weakly and confusedly when relying on sense-based imagination. When thinking about things is freed of reliance on the imagination, "it does not consider either their number or duration," whereas in imagining them "it perceives them in a determinate number, duration and quantity."[4]

Spinoza defines "an adequate idea" as one which "considered in itself, without relation to the object, has all the properties or intrinsic marks of a true idea."[5] Spinoza's ordering of things here, like Descartes', asserts that we recognize the existence and character of objects of ideas insofar as the ideas themselves pass an epistemological test. Spinoza's "adequacy" is the analog of Descartes' "clarity and distinctness." In other words, we do not rule that ideas are inadequate because they fail to correspond to their objects. Indeed, we are in no position to make any such comparison. We rule, on the contrary, that a suitable object corresponds to our idea because we recognize the adequacy of the idea. Applied to the context of ideas of things generated in perception in "the common order of nature," to say that these are inadequate ideas means that nothing really corresponds to them.

Leibniz presents a similar view. The order of physical objects apprehended in perception constitutes the realm of *phenomena bene fundata*. This system of ideas is an imperfect intellectual product which manages to represent reality, although there are no referents, metaphysically speaking, for the referring terms of the phenomenal vocabulary. The only real referents are monads, which are substances, and which are represented only in a crude and aggregated fashion in phenomenal thought and discourse. We may think of discourse about individuals with duration in Spinoza's system as *phenomena* in a similar sense, but with the important difference that Spinoza adds no clause equivalent to "*bene fundata*" in his conception. Leibniz thought of *phenomena* as offering the terms in which scientific descriptions and explanations must be framed, since we are not in a position to attain a monad-by-monad representation. But Spinoza's conception of science involves the abandonment of the phenomenal in favor of "common notions," by which he means an abstract mathematical representation in which the inadequate vocabulary suitable for phenomenal individuals disappears. In part, Spinoza asserts here the idea, retained in recent philosophy of science, that proper scientific

laws do not make reference to the individual. But we cannot legitimately equate Spinoza's claim with this plausible methodological
principle because his view is inextricably wrapped up with the opinion that reference to the individual drops out of scientific discourse
because there really are no individuals.

In confirmation of this reading we find Spinoza saying in the
Short Treatise, "Part and whole are not true or real beings but only
beings of thought, and consequently, in nature, there are neither
wholes nor parts."[6] He goes on to explain that parts would be things
that could exist though the whole in which they figure should disappear. Nature cannot be constituted of such parts any more than space
could be constituted of particular figures ontologically independent
of one another. The same metaphysically unreal fragmentation per-
vades all our thinking about individuals with duration. The knowledge that God has that corresponds to my knowledge of individuals
includes the completed web of relationships of which but a fragment
appears in my thought. "These ideas of modifications [finite modes
or individuals] in so far as they are referred to the human mind
alone, are as consequences without premises, in other words, confused ideas."[7]

In a letter to Ludwig Meyer, Spinoza resolves problems of the
infinity and indivisibility of extended substance in terms of the contrast between imagination and understanding. "Imagination" is pejorative, as is standard for the rationalist philosophers.

> . . . [Q]uantity is conceived by us in two ways, namely, by abstraction
> or superficially, as we imagine it by the aid of the senses, or as sub-
> stance which can only be accomplished through the understanding. So
> that, if we regard quantity as it exists in the imagination (and this is
> the more frequent and easy method), it will be found to be divisible,
> finite, composed of parts and manifold. But if we regard it as it is in
> the understanding, and the thing be conceived as it is in itself (which
> is very difficult), it will then, as I have sufficiently shown you before,
> be found to be infinite, indivisible and single.[8]

Spinoza goes on to identify time, measure, and number as the instruments of abstract thinking and imagination which introduce duration and other forms of separation into our thinking about substance. Time, measure, and number are then said to be "mere aids
to imagination."[9] Understanding does not impose these divisions on

substance. The thought of the separate individual, the existent that endures for a time, the contingent being, belong only to the unsatisfactory conceptual scheme that imagination generates.

The fragmentary and inadequate conception that we have of reality framed in terms of finite contingent individuals is improved when we understand the relationship of these individuals to others. Spinoza construes this widening horizon of understanding as a progressive ontological shift in favor of more and more comprehensive units of being which incorporate what are taken to be independent things at earlier and even less adequate levels of thought. The ultimate end of this procedure is the thinking of God, where all interdependence is fully represented, and the final comprehensive individual is the totality of everything which is God himself. Everything short of this is inadequate and involves presumptions of independence which are based on ignorance and have no metaphysical standing at all. The conception we have of our own free will is an illusion based on just this ignorance of causes that supports the idea of independence. Ideally adequate thought would be subject to no such illusions. Spinoza's thinking tries to occupy the precarious ground of one who, as a finite human mind, can only think in the framework of an illusion of individuals, including himself, which he is able to recognize as an illusion. He therefore denies the credentials of the only discourse that is available to him.

In the proof of the second corollary to II:xliv Spinoza says that reason adopts the perspective of eternity:

> We may add that the bases of reason are the notions which answer to things common to all, [that is, mathematical notions that fit extension in general], and which do not answer to the essence of any particular thing; which therefore must be conceived without any relation to time, under a certain form of eternity.

Here again Spinoza prefigures later understandings in the methodology of science which permit no reference to time in equations expressing laws of nature, except in derivatives representing, for example, velocity and acceleration. But here, too, Spinoza's thinking is not separable from the conviction that time itself belongs to the set of illusions engendered by the finite and falsifying perspective of human thought. The all-embracing individual reached by the progressive incorporation of effects in their causes, in an ever-more comprehensive being, does not have a duration at all. All the temporal boundaries will be somehow erased when the provisional part-whole style of thought gives way to apprehension of the unitary and simple being of substance. In the *Cogitata Metaphysica* we find that "time is not an affection of things but rather a mode of thought or, as we have said, a logical being."[10] The inadequacy of our knowledge of finite things that occupy parts of time is, in the end, a consequence of the fact that time, and duration, and finite things fall short of true being. As Hegel said of this side of Spinoza's understanding of things:

> The mode is the individual, the finite as such which enters into external connection with what is "other." In this Spinoza only descends to a lower stage, the mode is only the foregoing [that is, the higher stage of substance] warped and stunted. Spinoza . . . takes mode, alone, as a false individuality. . . . and thus determinateness continually vanishes from his thought.[11]

Spinoza presses himself to this doctrine merely through rigorous observance of the demands of the concept of independence. Clarity, reason, and understanding yield this characterization of reality in relation to which our familiar conception of a world of individual things has to be branded confused, inadequate, illusory, and false. Ironically, this doctrine, supported only by what Spinoza takes to be the demands of undiluted reason, is the foundation of the common opinion that Spinoza is a sort of mystic. Perhaps it is reasonable to agree that only a philosopher with a strong mystical bent could allow a cool logic to press him as far as the acceptance of Spinoza's picture of ultimate reality that saves so very little of the phenomena.

4. Causality and Intelligibility

We have said that Spinoza's analysis of being tends toward the elimination of individual existence. The intellectual mechanism that reveals this pattern most clearly is Spinoza's thinking about causality. Causes ultimately incorporate and do not merely explain or condition their effects.

Starting from a broadly shared understanding, we can say with Spinoza that causality involves dependence. A caused entity has but a conditioned existence. The mere conception of it does not suffice for its existence, since we can conceive of a caused thing but not know whether there is such a thing because we do not know whether the needed cause itself exists. Where we do know that the cause exists, we can assert the existence of the effect. Causal analysis allows us to deduce the real occurrence of the effect from that of the cause.

This line has a misleadingly familiar rhythm. Contemporary analyses of causal explanation assert the deducibility of what is causally explicable from premises that assert the occurrence of causal factors and other premises that formulate natural laws. Then Spinoza's deductive conception of causality and his intuition of the thoroughgoing interconnectedness of things can appear to be a version of up-to-date thinking about explanation and the unity of science. Little of this, however, survives a closer look at what Spinoza means by a causal relation. The notion of a law assisting in the deduction of the effect from the cause is entirely alien to Spinoza's thought. The idea that observed regularities or statements asserting regular conjunctions might have a role in our causal understandings is even more remote from Spinoza's notion of causality. An adequate conception of the cause, by itself and without any supplementary general premise, suffices for the deduction of the effect within the setting of Spinoza's conception of a cause. Appeal to regularities would amount, in Spinoza's view, to the admission that the effort to reach the true intelligibility of a causal connection had failed.

Where we do know that a cause exists, we can assert the existence of the effect. The effect is never a substance, as is demonstrated by the very fact of causal conditioning. That means that the essence of an effect never suffices for its existence. Spinoza thinks that where A is the cause of B, the essence of B is contained in the essence of A, and this relation underwrites the validity of the deduction of B from A. If A is itself caused, the known causal relationship between the essences of A and B does not yield any existential conclusion. The existence of B will only follow from the essence of A together with the existence of a further cause, the cause of A. The world of contingent existences contains such causal chains. Spinoza regards them as nested essences. The question of existence is always deferred in such chains or nestings, since the containing essence or cause is itself causally conditioned. If we were able to pursue this kind of chain back to an unconditioned existent, the essence of that ultimate cause would need no cause in order to exist. It would be a *causa sui*. An ontological argument would prove the existence of this cause and with it the existence of all the conditioned members of the chain of effects. The very fact that the cause suffices for the logical deduction of the effect shows that the effect has to be wholly contained in the cause, not merely universally connected with it.

Spinoza's metaphysical thinking makes a leap to the conception of the ultimate cause which is an essence in which the essence and existence of everything is contained. But he does not envision a scientific passage from the conditioned to the unconditioned. The existence and character of the perceived world is better understood, scientifically, insofar as we succeed in tracing causal connections through a wider network. From the finite human perspective all of the causes that we ever discover are conditioned by further causes as yet unknown. Therefore, we cannot deduce the existence of finite things from known causes, although we can deduce the essences of effects from the essences of causes. The causes of finite things are finite, so that the knowledge of the cause of a finite thing never suffices for deducing the existence of anything.

Proposition I:xxviii makes it clear that a chain of finite causes never reaches back to an uncaused cause.

> Every individual thing, or everything which is finite and has a conditioned existence, cannot exist or be conditioned to act, unless it be conditioned for existence and action by a cause other than itself, which also is finite and has a conditioned existence; and likewise this cause cannot in its turn exist, or be conditioned to act, unless it be conditioned for existence and action by another cause, which also is finite, and has a conditional existence, and so on to infinity.

The totality of this web of causally interconnected finite existences is identical to being, nature, and God. But no element of this web, nor any stretch no matter how comprehensive, is intelligible within itself. Exploring this web, we remain in the realm of contingency in that no individual or system that we can survey is an unconditioned thing, and the unconditioned whole is not accessible from within. Logic assures us that everything is necessary, and this is the burden of the very next proposition, I:xxix: "Nothing in the universe is contingent." But investigation is always limited to a relative necessity. From a metaphysical point of view that which is only relatively necessary and only relatively intelligible is also only relatively real.

From the perspective of Cartesian subjectivism we are entitled to two orders of thinking about existence and essence. Our rational logical investigations do engender only logical relations of essences like the angle-sum theorem, which, as Descartes notes, does not assure us of the existence of triangles. In the same spirit Leibniz once said that necessary truths are all conditional, and assertions that entail existential claims are always contingent. This is much in accord with Spinoza, but the Cartesian subjectivity also permits the entrance of existence into our understanding in the guise of the existence of the thinking subject. Here our thinking runs from effect to cause. This is embodied, in the first instance, in Descartes' argument for the existence of God as the needed cause for the existence of the idea of God that I find in my self-conscious mind, the existence of which, together with its contents, is secured by the *cogito*. The pattern of this theological exercise is repeated in other domains with appealing results. Descartes' argument is what has come to be called a transcendental argument. The facts of my own existence and thought entail whatever can be understood to be necessary conditions of that existence and thought. The empiricist tradition has repeatedly followed this Cartesian precedent in arguments that defend claims about the external world as required conditions for the existence of mental data of perception which are certainly known to exist because they figure in immediate subjective experience. Kant's transcendental arguments flesh out the same project refined by his critique of idealism.

There is no representation of this pattern of thinking in Spinoza. Although his exposition of Descartes' philosophy is admirably lucid, the Cartesian egocentric subjectivism is either wholly overlooked or wholly unattractive to Spinoza. To quote Hegel's judgment again, there is in Spinoza's

> . . . system an utter blotting out of the principle of subjectivity, individuality, personality, the moment of self-consciousness in Being. Thought has only the signification of the universal, not self-consciousness.[12]

As a consequence, the inference from the existence of the effect immediately apprehended in subjective consciousness to mediately known causes is not encountered in Spinoza. All of the ideas encountered in our conscious experience have to be subjected to logical tests before any existential claim is based on them. Mere presence in consciousness is not a credential of any standing from the rigorous metaphysical point of view to which Spinoza adheres. This is part of the message of II:xxviii and xxix where Spinoza asserts that ideas of the body which make up the human mind do not give us an adequate or unconfused idea of that mind. Our conscious experience is not a source of indefeasible premises for Spinoza.

It is only logical, and not scientific or factual analysis, that leads us to the conception of infinite substance, that is, to the essence that suffices for its own existence. And when we have attained this conception, it proves to be impossible to connect it with the finite world and the web of causal connections of finite things. From the infinite as such only infinite, necessarily existing attributes and infinite, necessarily existing modes are deducible. In the proof of I:xxi the idea that finite things might follow from the absolute nature of the infinite is shown to be incoherent. Thus, the web of finite interconnections is not reached from the infinite, just as the infinite is not reached from the web of finite conditions, even when this web is extended infinitely, as in I:xxviii. Here is the gap between what reason bids us to accept and the only order of existence that we can perceive and investigate. It separates the adequate ideas of unity, simplicity, indivisibility, and eternity, and the substance that these ideas characterize, from the inadequate concoction of sense and imagination which is the world of parts and duration and contingency. This is the gap between the infinite and the finite. Leibniz called it "the labyrinth of the continuum." Faced with the failure of connection here, Spinoza always leans toward the logical and demotes the web of the finite to the level of ignorance and confusion.

There is an atmosphere of classical Greek thinking in this Spinozan program that contrasts the realm of complete being so starkly with the world in which we seem to live. Spinoza's substantial world even suggests the Aristotelian heavens where the absence of "violent motions" insures that nothing can really happen. No generation and corruption spoils the tranquil permanence and perfection of this domain. The world closer to hand is all imperfection. It is the scene of unnatural motions that counteract one another and produce a trackless wilderness of events. The elements mix and transmute. Individuals are created and destroyed. Like the other constituents of this order, we endure but for a time. This is the world of competition, striving, and of failure. It is the world of corruption both physical and moral. Akin to the substantial world of Spinoza, Aristotle's astronomical heaven is all completeness, eternity, and perfection. Furthermore, Spinoza's contrasting domains of necessity and contingency are reminiscent of themes in Plato's division between the perceived flux of unstable material concatenations and the permanent, logically accessible but unperceivable, reality of the forms. No apprehension of the world available in perception deserves to be called knowledge, and the objects of perceptual beliefs do not attain the status of true being. These are Spinozan motifs too.

The reason for Spinoza's evident bias in favor of the logical, the necessary, and the infinite lies in part in the connection between his ideas of substance and of cause. We must remember that Spinoza has not abandoned the thought that a substance is a true subject of predication. When our discourse contains terms that purport to refer but that do not pick out substances, the possibility of literal truth is immediately foreclosed. We cannot correctly ascribe a property to something if our conception of that something fails to pick out anything that really exists. When Spinoza construes causality as involving a conditionality destructive of the claim to substancehood, it follows that discourse that ascribes features to effects will have to be reorganized so that the ascriptions are all allocated to the unconditioned cause, which really does exist and which *contains* the essence of the effect. At the level of practice, success in trading inadequate for adequate referring terms is always relative, since the causes we discover are themselves conditioned by further causes. Substancehood retreats up the chain of causal connections, and with it the prospect for entirely successful reference. Only the ultimate cause-of-itself is a substance, and that will, a fortiori, absorb all predication in the final divine reorganization of true statements. There is just nothing else about which one might speak truly. To that extent ascriptions of properties to other subjects are all more or less false.

There is in this an anticipation of the outlook of the idealist philosophers, like those G. E. Moore sought to refute, that is, the philosophers who believed that there is, in the end, only one fact, and that every assertion of commonsense and of science is false. Like Spinoza these idealists incline to think that time is unreal, that the subject of thought and the object of thought are metaphysically identical, and that all relations between things are internal or essential. Like the idealist versions, Spinoza's theory of internal relations undermines the reality of the items that are to be internally related.

5. The Rejection of Dualism

The development of part one of the *Ethics* can be understood as the reorganization and correction of Descartes' fundamental metaphysical scheme. In a straightforward sense Spinoza actually takes over Descartes' theory of substance. Descartes emphasizes independence and unconditional existence as defining features of substance,[13] and, just like Spinoza, he finds that there is only one truly independent entity, namely, God. Descartes' dualism of mental and material substances, or thought and extension, employs the concept of substance in a diluted and compromised sense. Thought and extension are "created substances," and they are, for that reason, not truly independent and unconditional existences at all. They are dependent upon God, and their existence is conditioned by his existence. The two pillars of this doctrine are the idea that there could be more than one substance and the idea that God, being a substance, might have created the other substances. The Spinozan theory is reached when these two ideas are set aside. The notion of the production of one substance by another is expressly eliminated in I:vi,[14] while the impossibility of more than one substance appears as early as the explanatory note to I:viii and is reasserted of the substance, God, in I:xiv.[15]

We have described in general terms Spinoza's rejection of substantial status for the finite individual. In the context of dualism Spinoza begins by rebutting the idea that there could be many substances with the same attribute,[16] such as a plurality of substantial bodies or a plurality of minds regarded as independent substances.

There are medieval precedents for part of Spinoza's understanding of matters here. Aristotle identifies the mind as a form of the body, and this view itself prefigures and influences Spinoza's doctrine that the mind is the idea of the body. In the Aristotelian account the bodily component provides what came to be known as the principle of individuation. It is only the matter constituting the bodies of Peter and Paul which makes it possible for us to distinguish them and count them. And this is merely the application to the case of human individuals of the more general Aristotelian doctrine that exemplification in some matter is required for the existence of an individual having any form whatever. Furthermore, Aristotle ascribes a kind of intelligence and/or intelligibility to all being in his concept of a universal *nous* of which the individual human mind is a manifestation.

Here, too, Aristotle's doctrine reappears in another guise in Spinoza's conception of the attribute of thought in which everything participates. The Aristotelian theory of individuation via matter or the body, especially as applied to the distinctness of human beings, became a focus of theoretical and theological discussion in the scholastic traditions. The Averroists held, following Aristotle's principles, that the individual mind or soul cannot survive the dissolution of the body and must be supposed to be reabsorbed into a single human soul in general. The Averroists rejected individuation in the absence of a material constitution. It is as though Spinoza accepts this much and goes on to argue that even with a material constitution individuation fails. The failure to secure substantial individuals via the body is a consequence of the identification of space with matter that Spinoza takes over from Descartes. In Descartes' understanding the idea of different bodily objects is wrapped up with our discriminations of sensuous qualities such as color and warmth in different regions of space. Since Descartes holds that all of these discriminations are only subjective, there is nothing left of our concept of an outer objective realm beyond that of an entity that conforms to our pure geometrical ideas. That entity is space itself. Upon this identification matter ceases to be a stuff of which individual things are constituted and becomes, for Spinoza and to some extent for Descartes, a single comprehensive entity in which extended things inhere and are mutually locatable.

Spinoza retains the Averroist-Aristotelian conception of the special role of the body in his doctrine that the individual human mind is the idea of that human individual's body. But this retained sense of individuation via the body does not distinguish *substances*, either mental or material. Separate parts of space (even if moveable and divisible as Descartes makes them) are not independently existing things and could not exist without space as an infinite whole. As we have seen, Spinoza thinks that ideas of individual minds and bodies are confused ideas. The defects of thinking about individuals are only repaired by rising to thought in terms of notions common to all things, where the resources for discourse about individual things are left behind.

The collapse of the three Cartesian substances—God, extension, and thought—can be appreciated through the problem of mind-body interaction that Descartes' ordering of things immediately produced. In the development of Cartesianism immediately following Descartes, his grotesque theory of interaction in the pineal gland was discarded in favor of a resigned acceptance of the rational impenetrability of the relation between the mental and material orders of things. The "occasionalism" that replaces Descartes' blatantly paramechanical theory relocated the source of the fit between mind and body in God's direct control of things. This theory was developed by contemporaries of Spinoza. Whether or not such thinking actually influenced him, the very idea of occasionalism sheds light on Spinoza's monism. The occasionalist simply abandons the hope of rational understanding of reality. The fit and parallelism of mind and body is just a brute consequence of God's will and involves no intellectually trackable process at all. Nothing is less congenial to Spinoza than this sort of resignation and final appeal to the nonrational and brute. The separateness of thought and extension as created substances makes their interaction unintelligible. Spinoza saw this as the occasionalists did. Their solution is an essentially miraculous parallelism of the two substances through the arbitrary will of a third. This is doubly unacceptable to Spinoza. The relationship of mind and body is incomprehensible and so is the relationship of both to an external creator. The only intelligible foundation for the thoroughgoing correspondence of the material and the mental is the fact that they are not two realities at all. Hence the view that they are attributes of the same substance, two expressions of one and the same being. The idea of creation by an external substance merely compounds the incomprehensibility to which occasionalism is committed. Spinoza can accept neither the miracle of creation nor the miracle of interaction. The two Cartesian substances are really attributes, and the external creator is really an indwelling causality.

The relaxation of the rationalist demand for intelligibility manifested in the occasionalist philosophy has its roots in Descartes' own thought. Descartes recognizes a wholly nonrational foundation when he argues that God *might* have placed ideas of an external order in our minds even though there is no such external order, no realm of extension. He could have done this either by directly creating in our minds the ideas that we have of bodily things, or by creating some intermediary cause for those ideas which suffices for generating them in us but which is itself not an order of extended things. In the Sixth Meditation it is ultimately the goodness of God, and no rational principle, that assures us that there really is an external world and that that world actually possesses at least the geometrically describable constitution that our ideas impute to extension. Within the occasionalist rearrangement of these matters it seems that God *does* directly cause our ideas of extended things. They cannot be causally traced to their objects because of the general failure of the Cartesian theory of interaction. Then God also causes directly the detailed extended things and material events that correspond to our mental experiences. This second use of God's creative resources seems to be wasteful, since all our thinking will be just as it is whether or not God bothers with a realm of extended things. The more economical philosophy of Berkeley results when this creative excess is eliminated from our conception of God's activities.

It is also worth noting that prominent aspects of occasionalist theory fit in very well with Spinoza's views. In Malebranche's opinion our human thinking is a kind of participation in the all-embracing mind of God. All the ideas we have exist in God and are perceived in God. God is the "place of minds just as space is the place of bodies." These sentiments agree with Spinoza's assertion that our ideas are themselves constituents of the divine mind but incompletely apprehended.[17]

Occasionalism is representative of a tendency away from the claim of rational intelligibility in the history of thinking about causality. There is a strong echo of occasionalism in Hume's epistemological atomism. The Humean assertion of the logical independence of every particular matter of fact, and the logical independence of effects and their causes, is the diametrical opposite of Spinoza's conception of things. It is as though Hume and Spinoza share a deep conviction that only a logical bond can yield an intelligible relationship. Constant conjunctions offer no footing to reason. If any aftermath from a given cause is as reasonable as any other, then there is nothing to understand in the sequence of things. That is why there is no rationally defensible extrapolation from patterns in observed sequences. Hume advances from the shared premise that relations must be logical to be intelligible to the conclusion that there is, indeed, nothing to understand in causal connections, while Spinoza insists that nothing is understood as long as we grasp merely de facto connections. For Hume the fact that we develop expectations based on exposure to constant conjunctions, and the fact that we have the notion of necessary connection from subjective "impressions of reflection," does not give us a rational ground for those expectations. In occasionalist style Hume actually ascribes the salutory consequences of acting on these expectations to a fortunate "pre-established harmony."[18] This Humean option is anticipated with repugnance by Spinoza when he berates "those who are ignorant of true causes" and therefore "think that trees might talk just as well as men—that men might be formed from stones as well as from seed; and imagine that any form might be changed into any other."[19] Spinoza's use of the word "form" (*forma*) tells us a lot here. The form is the indwelling principle which makes the development and behavior of the thing intelligible. On the Humean understanding anything could develop from anything; any individual might behave like any other. Spinoza is the great champion of resistance to the modern abdication of the claims of reason.

6. The Apparatus of Substance and Attributes

The actual proofs of Propositions I:v (there cannot be two substances with the same attribute) and I:vi (one substance cannot produce another) are not stated in terms of extension and thought. The anti-Cartesian objectives of the argument are pursued in the opaque terminology of substances, attributes, and modes, seldom relieved by the least indication of the philosophical discourse to which the proved propositions might be relevant. The early propositions establish that if two substances are to be individuated at all, it must be by appeal to either a difference of attributes or a difference of modes. Spinoza uses "modes" to cover both individual things conceived under an attribute (such as individual bodies) and general determinations rooted in the essential nature of an attribute. In keeping with the latter clause Spinoza calls not only finite bodies but also motion and rest "modes of extension." Similarly, not only Paul's belief that Peter is present, but also believing, desiring, and willing generally are called modes of the attribute of thought. This is an alarming latitude in the concept of a mode. In any case Spinoza's proof proceeds briskly.

Distinct substances must differ either in attributes or in modes. "If only by the difference in their attributes it will be granted that there cannot be more than one with an identical attribute." That is, if the distinction between the substance A and the substance B rests only in the fact that A has attribute a and B has attribute b, they will not be an instance of two substances with the same attribute, and the case will not threaten the thesis of I:v.

Spinoza turns immediately to the job of ruling out the thought that there might be two different substances with the same attribute but different modes of the same attribute. Perhaps this would be illustrated by the Aristotelian-Averroist individuation of person-substances in virtue of their participation in the same attribute, extension, where each person's extended aspect is a different finite part, or mode, of extension. Or Spinoza may mean to cover the possibility of two infinite substances which are alike in being extended but differ in that one contains only, say, triangular individuals, while the other has only rectangular individuals. These supposed possibilities can be excluded, Spinoza says, because "substance is prior to modification," so that if A and B are distinct substances, we have to be able to recognize their distinctness prior to consideration of modes.

Distinctions limited to modifications cannot be part of the essences of substances. If A and B are infinite extended substances, and A in fact contains triangular modes while B does not, it could have been the other way around. Since both are extended, both offer scope for the existence of finite modes such as triangles. But then it will also be possible that A should have just the same constituent modes as B: they could both have triangular modes, the difference in their finite modes being inessential. Therefore, if A and B could differ only because they are differently modified, they could also differ as substances if they happened to have the same modifications. But that is contrary to the previously proved assertion that they must differ in either modes or attributes. Similarly, A and B could not be thought of as distinct substance-persons in virtue of their identification with different extended things viewed as finite modes of extension. The priority of substance means that were they substances, A and B would have to be distinguishable even in the absence of the existence, inessential to them, of the finite units of matter that make up the bodies of A and B.

Readers following Spinoza into the detail of this argument will wonder why he does not try to rule out the possibility that two substances might have one attribute in common but differ nonetheless, not in virtue of the shared attribute, but in virtue of two other attributes, one possessed exclusively by one of the substances and the other possessed exclusively by the other substance. The possibility that substance A might have the attributes a and c, while the substance B has the attributes b and c, has not been expressly ruled out. Is it not even a possibility worth considering in Spinoza's understanding? If it is not a possibility, why not?

Leibniz raises just this question in a discussion of Spinoza's proof of I:v.[20] In an analysis of the issue, including Leibniz's objection, Martial Gueroult vindicates Spinoza's proof as it stands. Gueroult believes that Spinoza means to restrict his investigation to the case of substance with a single attribute and that this restriction covers the first eight propositions of part one. He thinks of this restriction as characteristic of Spinoza's orderly geometrical procedure that builds up gradually to the complex substance with infinite attributes that is God after first developing a theory for a hypothetical substance with a single attribute. Perhaps Gueroult's understanding has plausibility in terms of its broad conformity with Spinoza's habits of thought. It appears, however, to rest on extremely slender textual evidence, to wit, the phrase, "substantia unius attributi" in the demonstration of I:viii.[21] Apart from the fact that this one appropriate phrase appears only in the proof of the last of the propositions that Gueroult takes to be governed by the restriction to substances of a single attribute, even that one appearance requires a meaning incompatible with Gueroult's interpretation. Spinoza has to be saying at I:viii that there can only be one substance with *any one given* attribute: "Substantia unius attribute non, nisi unica, existit (per Prop. v.)." On Gueroult's construction that would mean that there can only be one substance consisting of a single attribute. But Proposition v, adduced by Spinoza, makes no such claim but rather asserts that there cannot be two substances having the same attribute. Further, Gueroult's rendering would serve no purpose in the argument Spinoza is constructing since it would be a claim compatible with the existence of several substances of many attributes, one of which could be the same as that of the "substance of a single attribute." And this possibility, unruled out by Gueroult's reading, would be compatible with the finitude of the one-attribute substance, while the assertion that Spinoza seeks to prove is that every substance is infinite. Gueroult's interpretation vitiates the proof.[22]

An ambiguity in the statement of Spinoza's definition of "attribute" seems to explain why it is that he did not think it necessary to canvass the possibility of substances sharing one attribute while differing in another. The definition runs: "By an *attribute* I mean that which the intellect perceives as constituting the essence of substance."[23] In the Latin as well as in the English translation this definition can put the ontological burden of attributes either on the substances whose essences are grasped by the intellect, or on the mental grasp, that is, in the representations of the substances that the intellect forms, according to the definition. For example, we can mathematically represent geometry so that "line," "point," and "intersection" are the fundamental terms for grasping the subject matter. We can also represent the very same mathematical domain using triplets of numbers, sets of such triplets, and set-membership as the fundamental ideas. The difference does not lie at all in the formal structure we are representing, now in one way, now in another. Sometimes Spinoza's use of "attribute" suggests that differences in attributes can be merely differences in representation, as in this example. On the other hand, we can think of different attributes as different features of a thing which it has and which are different whether we represent the thing or not. Then we understand different attributes as offering a systematic foundation for different representations. For photographic representation various kinds of radiation such as visible light, infrared light, and X-rays can all be the basis for production of contrasting representations of things. The capacities to radiate or reflect different forms of radiation are different features of the thing represented, and they give rise to different kinds of pictures because the attribute of the thing that generates the picture is different in each case.

Does Spinoza illicitly exploit both of the interpretations to which his ambiguous definition is open? The interpretation of "attribute" that places all the weight on the representation is the one that would answer Leibniz's objection to the proof of I:v. In the context we readily accept that two representations of necessarily existing infinite extension are just two representations of the same reality. Perhaps Spinoza simply extends this style of thought to cover all attributes. They are all intended as different conceptions of the essence of being, not conceptions of the essence of different beings. Then differences in attributes are automatically simply different characterizations of the same thing, and Spinoza, not thinking otherwise, does not mention the possibility of substances that differ in attributes.

This understanding is reinforced by the proof that God is the unique substance at I:xiv. Spinoza says that another substance would have to share some attribute with God and that I:v has already demonstrated the impossibility of two substances with the same attribute. This appeal to the proof of I:v requires that the impossibility of two substances with the same attribute be intended by Spinoza so as to exclude Leibniz's case by itself. I:v must read so as to exclude the possibility of two substances sharing one attribute, *no matter what other attributes they have*. No other meaning makes sense of Spinoza's text:

> . . . if any substance besides God were granted, it would have to be explained by some Attribute of God [since God will have all the attributes], and thus two substances with the same attribute would exist, which (by Prop. v) is absurd.[24]

In contrast, both the definition of God and Proposition I:ix appear to demand the interpretation of "attribute" that puts the ontological burden of multiple attributes in the thing and not in the representation. The definition of God says that he is "a being absolutely infinite — that is, a substance consisting in infinite attributes" (*hoc est, substantiam constantem infinitis attributis*).[25] And I:ix says that "the more reality or being a thing has the greater the number of its attributes."[26] This proposition is proved by the merest reference to the definition of "attribute" with no discussion at all. These contexts are not really intelligible if we restrict the idea of different attributes to the difference in representations. Although they are consistent with the claim that all attributes are, in fact, attributes of the same thing, these assertions of Spinoza's make it hard to understand why he does not feel the obligation to consider the kind of case that Leibniz raises.

The view of these matters that Spinoza ultimately purports to establish colors his fundamental conceptions of substance and attribute and makes understandable just the ambiguity that we have been examining. In the long run the two options in virtue of which the definition is ambiguous are not separable in Spinoza's thinking. Different attributes are different graspings by the intellect, and to that extent they are just mental things which we are tempted to think of as requiring no corresponding distinction in the thing represented. But Spinoza thinks of forms of intelligibility not only, and not primarily, as the content of investigative activities exterior to what is

grasped. The intelligibility that we commonly think of as incorporated in representations such as pictures or descriptions is, for Spinoza,
simply the reality of what is represented when considered under the
attribute of thought. So the possibility that attributes are patterns of
intelligibility by which things are representable does not contrast
with the idea that attributes are intrinsic features of substance. The
very terms in which the ambiguity of "attribute" can be explained are
undercut by the monism that Spinoza embraces. Although I do think
that the eventual coalescence of thought and thing expressed in II:vii
is responsible for the contours of Spinoza's thinking in the definition
of "attribute," I do not mean to say that the resulting metaphysical
unity of being and thought, representation and represented, leaves
us with a clear view of things.

7. The Infinity of Attributes

The claim that substance has infinite attributes of which we
know only extension and thought has been the subject of unsettled
controversy since Tschirnhausen's sharp questioning addressed to
Spinoza himself.[27] Discussions have brought forth suppositions as
radical as the claim that by "infinite" Spinoza really means "all that
there are," which in this case may be *two*.[28] The equation "Infinity
= two" is surely a desperate expedient in the face of the obscurity
of Spinoza's doctrine. It is not at all in the spirit of his definition of
God as consisting in (*constantem*) infinite attributes. Could Spinoza
say that the more reality a thing has the more attributes it has [29] if
this were compatible with the possibility that the all-embracing reality has a total of two attributes? Why would Spinoza speak of "infinite attributes" again and again if he meant "all the attributes there
are," when "all the attributes there are" is an expression that was
surely accessible to him? Might Spinoza have said with equal plausibility that there are infinite substances, meaning "all the substances
there are" and thus *One*?

The infinity of the attributes of God was a standard doctrine in
scholastic metaphysical theology.[30] The medieval theologians never
listed more than a relatively small number of these infinite attributes,
but they do speak explicitly of more than two, and they unmistakably
imply that the attributes of God are uncountably numerous, and

under no circumstance would a few attributes be compatible with the ascription of infinite attributes to God. The actually stated part of traditional lists often say that God is one, complete, perfect, eternal, powerful, wise, good, and so on. We cannot simply suppose that Spinoza directly takes over this kind of list. He plainly thinks that while all these things are rightly predicated of God, they are only *properties* of God, while extension and thought are the only known attributes.[31] Nonetheless, Spinoza's idea that God has infinite attributes is surely related to the precedent of these medieval versions of the very same idea.

The most striking difference between Spinoza's conception of the attributes of God and the thinking of his medieval predecessors is the fact that extension is one of the attributes on Spinoza's list. Extension becomes an attribute of God with Spinoza's rejection of the Cartesian theory of created substance. As a consequence, Spinoza's concept of attributes of God has two very different sources: the medieval theory of infinite attributes and the corrected Cartesian theory of extension and thought as created substances. A passage from the *Short Treatise* makes these two sources of the doctrine quite clear, and the passage employs two different conceptions of what is predicated of God, one compatible with the traditional scholastic style of thought about God and the other reflecting Spinoza's redescription of Descartes' dualism. The passage is in the dialogue between Love, Understanding, Desire, and Reason. Desire has distinguished thought and extension as infinite substances and has claimed that no third substance can be conceived to have produced itself and also these two. Elements of this reasoning which rejects the Cartesian theory of created substances represent Spinoza's true opinion. But the characterization of thought and extension as two different substances with nothing in common is rebutted in the following lines given to Reason in the dialogue:

> Thus, O Desire, when you say that you note several substances, I tell you that is false, for I clearly see that there is only one which exists through itself and is the subject of all other attributes. Since you want to call the bodily and intellectual "substances" relative to the modes that depend on them, so they must also be called "modes" relative to the substance on which they depend, because you do not conceive of them as existing through themselves. You conceive of willing, feeling,

conceiving, loving and so on, as several modes of what you call thinking substance, in which you bring them all together and make a unity
of them—so I conclude following your own example, that infinite extension and infinite thought together with the other infinite attributes—
or according to your way of speaking other substances—are nothing
but modes of the one, eternal, infinite, self-constituting being. The
single being or unity composed of all these attributes, outside of which
no thing can be imagined, we take to be established.[32]

Here Spinoza sees Descartes' substances as attributes and includes
the speculation that there may be other such attributes. He thus opposes the claim Desire has made that thought and extension must ex-
haust reality. But all of these known and unknown attributes are as
modes relative to the unique substance to which Spinoza ascribes the
features one, eternal, infinite, and self-causing. This list does not include thought and extension at all, but it is quite reminiscent of the
traditional lists of the infinite attributes of God.

Spinoza's exchange of letters with Tschirnhausen also bears on
the meaning of the doctrine of infinite attributes. Tschirnhausen
takes up Spinoza's notion of a multiplicity of attributes in addition
to extension and thought with which we have no acquaintance and
of which we can form no idea. He develops questions for Spinoza by
projecting the idea of further unknown attributes into roles that seem
to make them parallel to the attributes we do know. Our bodies are
our constitution under the attribute of extension; our minds, under
the attribute of thought. It seems that *we* are not constituted under
any of the other attributes, for if we were, our minds would contain
ideas of the modes of those further attributes, as our minds do in fact
contain ideas of our extended nature. Tschirnhausen speculates on
the existence of other creatures who might partake in an unknown attribute X and have minds composed of ideas of their own X-hood,
as we have minds composed of ideas of our bodies. A realm of X-ness
ought to be an infinite self-contained system, somehow parallel to extension, and it ought to be accompanied by a system of all the ideas
of all the X-things and their modes, just as extension is expressed in
a system of ideas of all of the modes of extension. A creature "based
in" a different attribute would be unable to imagine extension as we
are unable to imagine X-ness. This is a free expansion of the line of
thinking Tschirnhausen adopts.

On the basis of such reflections Tschirnhausen asks Spinoza if

such creatures would not amount to populations of "other worlds."
In his brief responses to Tschirnhausen, Spinoza seems little concerned with the danger that his theory of attributes will generate other
worlds and other minds with which we are permanently out of contact. His first reply[33] concentrates on the view that a human mind
consists of ideas of a human body and that, in consequence, the attributes of extension and thought, and no other, are known to us and
can figure in our accounts of reality. What we do not know we do not
know, so Spinoza seems to be simply unwilling to enter into the
speculation that Tschirnhausen proposes. He recommends study of
the notes to II:vii and I:ix. The moral to be drawn from this study
is, presumably, that a multiplicity of attributes is not a multiplicity
of substances or existing things, so that participation of existing things
in other attributes should not count as the existence of other worlds
which would require a population of different entities and not merely
expression of the same entities in different ways. This is the relevant
import of the note to I:ix, while the note to II:vii emphasizes the idea
that we must confine our concerns to thought and extension, and our
explanatory ambitions must remain within the attribute systems with
which we are acquainted:

> . . . so long as we consider things as modes of thinking, we must ex-
> plain the order of the whole of nature, or the whole chain of causes,
> through the attribute of thought only. And in so far as we consider
> things as modes of extension, we must explain the order of the whole
> of nature through the attribute of extension only; and so on, in the
> case of the other attributes.[34]

Spinoza seems to mean that other attributes could not engender the
possibility of other worlds. They would offer only further expressive
means with which we could also "explain the order of the whole of
nature" as we can explain it in terms of thought and in terms of extension. But the discussion at II:vii in fact concedes a certain obscurity, ending with the sentence "I cannot for the present explain my
meaning more clearly."

In his second explanatory reply Spinoza makes things much
more uncertain. Here Spinoza allows the ascription of infinite attributes to God to involve him in the extreme view that each individual, such as an individual constituted in extension by a human
body, has infinite minds, each in separation from all the others.

> But in answer to your objection I say, that although each particular
> thing be expressed in infinite ways in the infinite understanding of
> God, yet those infinite ideas, whereby it is expressed, cannot con-
> stitute one and the same mind of a particular thing, but infinite
> minds, seeing that each of these infinite ideas has no connection with
> the rest.[35]

Spinoza means that ideas of extension float a complete account of the
order of nature, that is, of "the whole chain of causes," which is complete and independent of any other ideas, so ideas of another attribute of being would float an independent account of the whole.
In spite of the metaphysical identity of what is accounted for, the account of an individual in ideas of one attribute will make a different
mind from that constituted by ideas of the same individual in
another attribute.

This development under the pressure of Tschirnhausen's questions is a major calamity for Spinoza's metaphysical picture. Each of
the infinite minds of one individual will have the same foundation
in the only substance that there is. So these minds will only differ
from one another as different expressions of the same reality differ.
But this cannot be right since, as minds, all these different expressions are expressions under the same attribute, namely, thought. We
lack any means for distinguishing between them, since the distinction between expressions of the same substantial reality is supposed
to be provided by the concept of different attributes. Without notic-
ing what has happened, Spinoza has destroyed the parallelism of the
attributes and made of thought a super attribute in which the expressions of reality of all of the other attributes is reexpressed.

Apart from the deep problems created by this startling idea of
infinite minds for individuals, Spinoza's response does not seem to
be an adequate way of disposing of the question. Since all these
minds are unconnected with one another, Spinoza's scheme seems to
deserve to be called a system of multiple worlds. Do not all the extended things and the minds that are ideas of them seem to make
a world in themselves? Do they not make up "our world"? For all his
parsimony of substances, Spinoza's deformed conception of attributes has created a system of epistemologically independent worlds
anchored in one substance.

In the exchange of letters Spinoza is led into this maze of speculations to no advantage to his metaphysical system. Any option in

this morass seems equally unattractive. The idea of infinite attributes has led Spinoza into an uncharted region of imaginative exercise that he is unprepared for conceptually. Perhaps much of this is not really intended by Spinoza at all.

Let us look at the issue again from the perspective of the traditional lists of attributes of God that ascribed to him power, wisdom, goodness, and so on. It is reasonable to think that when Spinoza says that God has infinite attributes, he is encouraged by the thought that this harmonizes with the traditional ascription of power, and wisdom, and goodness to God. Descartes himself regularly ascribes such "attributes" to God. With things like these in mind there would be no problem of other worlds populated by beings constituted under the attribute of, say, goodness or power. There are no finite modes of wisdom and power as there are finite modes of extension and thought, or if there are, in some sense, then at least there are not finite modes of wisdom and power *in addition* to finite modes of extension and thought. Wisdom, power, goodness, unity, simplicity, and so on do not offer any purchase to speculations like those in which Tschirnhausen embroils Spinoza.

How are the traditional lists of infinite attributes of God that do include things like wisdom and power related to the Spinozan list that does not include these and that starts with thought and extension and then ends abruptly with our inability to name even one more of the infinite attributes? We should stress the fact that "thought" is no more conspicuous on the traditional lists than is "extension." On reflection, this is entirely natural. A list of attributes that does not assign a bodily nature to God, as Spinoza does, will also not assign to him the contrasting constitution as thought. A list that does not include one of the attributes constructed out of Descartes' substances will not include the other. A spiritual rather than a bodily nature is presupposed by all the attributes on traditional lists. All the attributes of God on those lists are nonmaterial attributes. In a sense the expanded Spinozan list can be understood to include the whole traditional list with the addition of the single attribute extension. All the others belong to the realm of the nonextended, the immaterial, the spiritual, and they are, therefore, included in the attribute "thought." In fact, only the one new Spinozan attribute, extension, offers something under which we can plausibly think that creatures might be constituted, as we can think of a human being constituted under extension together with ideas of and generated by that extended thing. The job of Cartesian extension and Aristotelian matter is precisely the constituting or embodying of things. Hence the special role of the body in individuation. Spinoza never gives any reason at all for thinking that there are other attributes relevantly like extension, and Tschirnhausen's speculations are unsupported by anything definite to which Spinoza is committed. If this is the right way to understand Spinoza, there is a sense in which Spinoza's infinity of attributes does boil down to two, not because Spinoza means only "all the attributes that there are" and there are but two, but because the attribute "thought" will cover all the infinite attributes which do not have to *embody* things. Spinoza's thinking about attributes arises out of the traditional idea of infinite nonembodying attributes and the amended Cartesian idea of attributes of body and mind.

We have said that the exchange with Tschirnhausen brings to light an unresolved tension in Spinoza's conception of the parallelism of thought and extension. Spinoza falls naturally and unguardedly into the supposition that attributes in addition to extension would be attended by representations in the attribute of thought, just as the body is attended by ideas of this mode of extension, namely, the mind. Thought will take in and represent all of the other attributes, while none of them will be so related to the others or to thought.[36] The foundation for this unmanageable idea resides in Spinoza's conception of attributes and does not depend on the theory of additional unknown attributes. The parallelism Spinoza wants to assert is destroyed by the very idea that thought represents the world of extension, and, in particular, that the mind is the idea *of the body*. In up-to-date terms, ideas are intentionally related to the things of which they are ideas, and for Spinoza these are extended things. This relationship is at the heart of Spinoza's concept of ideas. It is of the essence of ideas to represent the physical things of which they are ideas. Is there a parallel relationship in which extended things have ideas as their *objects*, or in which extended things represent ideas? Extended things are not "of" anything in the way in which ideas are essentially ideas of something. Bodies are not intentional entities having ideas for objects. The representational relation works in only one direction in spite of Spinoza's willingness to speak of extension itself as an "expression" of the being of substance.

The lack of true parallelism between extension and thought is an instability that runs through the whole of Spinoza's system. His monism appears to be an advance from Descartes' dualism of mind and body insofar as we can think of extension and thought as two aspects of a more ultimate being. This is the program in which thought expresses, not extension, but the more ultimate being which is also expressed in the system of extended things. The trouble is that Spinoza cannot avoid making extended things, and not the reality that they too express, the system of objects for ideas. This is obvious, for example, in the critique of ordinary everyday thinking that Spinoza invites us to accept. Conceptions of reality based on perception are inadequate and confused, but this is not because everyday thought envisions a reality of extended things. The deficiency is a matter of representing extended things *badly*. Insofar as everyday thinking and imagination project extended objects they are sound. Error consists in imputing divisibility and duration and secondary qualities like warmth and cold to the objects of our ideas of extension. When ideally corrected, they will still be ideas of extension.

As a consequence, Spinoza's monism of nonparallel attributes threatens to collapse into a more familiar and, perhaps, less attractive materialist or idealist monism. Ideas are conceptions of extended things and of whatever other systems of objects for ideas there may happen to be. Spinoza's scheme of things veers toward idealism whenever he reflects, in Cartesian fashion, that ideas can never be compared with their objects, since having ideas of them is as close as we can get to objects. We have to recall that Spinoza insists that considering things as modes of thinking, "we must explain the order of the whole of nature . . . through the attribute of thought only."[37] As Pollock puts this point, "The perception of things as extended is not a relation between the extended thing and the perceiving mind, for they are incommensurable."[38] This is so, although Spinoza seems to assert a correspondence theory of truth which suggests comparison of an idea with its related extended object. So Axiom vi of part one says, "A true idea must correspond with its ideate or object." Since we cannot observe any such correspondence, our recognition of truth must actually be based on "reflective knowledge" of the ideas themselves. The adequacy of our ideas is offered as a self-contained mark of truth and, therefore, an indication of the correspondence the quoted axiom calls for. The definition of "an adequate idea" in part two asserts of such an idea that "in so far as it is considered in itself, without relation to the object, it has all the properties or *intrinsic* marks of a true idea."[39] This view of truth conforms with *On the Improvement of the Understanding* where Spinoza says:

> . . . the reality (forma) of a true thought must exist in the thought itself, without reference to other thoughts; it does not acknowledge the object as its cause, but must depend on the actual power and nature of the understanding.[40]

Spinoza's most striking discussion of truth, committing him to a radically idealist position, is in the chapter "On the True and the False" of the *Short Treatise*. Although true ideas agree with things and false ideas do not agree, they are both only "modes of thought," and "it is only in thought, and not actually, that their agreement and disagreement with things can be distinguished." The puzzling situation is supposed to be resolved when we reflect that truth and falsehood must be self-revealing in our true and false ideas.[41] Spinoza's idealist stance is more radical than Descartes', because Descartes works with the doctrine that his ideas have extramental causes, while Spinoza rejects this doctrine.

The corresponding tendency to materialism is simply the fact that the ultimate reality is that of the extended things with respect to which the realm of thought has a parasitic existence as a system of representations. Without extended things there would be nothing to represent, while bodies could exist even if there were no representations or ideas of them at all. No doubt it is just this possibility that Spinoza hopes to rule out by saying that the intrinsic intelligibility of bodies is their existence in the attribute of thought. We are not free to conceive of extended things as they are but denuded of their intelligibility. For this intelligible side is as much an essential part of them as their space-filling nature. Much stands in the way of simply accepting this saving advice.

Spinoza's thinking on the parallelism of the attributes is riddled with difficulties. The tensions here are never resolved and never really appreciated by Spinoza. Taken together, these tensions are not resolvable. Spinoza's definition of an attribute as the expression of the essence of substance is fundamental. If we adhere to this definition, then we cannot think of our ideas as representations of extended things in the attribute of thought. For that would be to regard ideas as representations in one attribute of reality as already represented in another attribute. The definition and the claim of parallelism give us no license for this ordering of things. Ideas are expressions of reality in the attribute of thought, and extended things are expressions of the same reality in the attribute of extension. There is no footing here for the notion that ideas are *of* extended things any more than there is footing for the notion that extended things are *of* ideas.

In the passage just cited, Spinoza introduces the "idea of a circle" as an illustration. How are we to construe the phrase "of a circle"? "Of a circle" can denote either the object of the idea or the content of the idea. Insofar as we confine our discussion to the content of ideas the idea of a circle is a certain kind of idea and not a relation between an idea and an extended thing. Spinoza elides these two interpretations of "of a circle." His theory of attributes and their parallelism only gives scope to the content-specifying sense of "of" in "idea of a circle." His effort to present a plausible account of the relationship between ideas and the material world leads him to slip into an object-specifying sense of "of" to which his definitions and principle assertions do not entitle him.

If Spinoza were consistent in restricting ideas to expressions of reality and did not confusedly also think of them as expressions of reality as already expressed in another attribute, then his system would be a form of idealism. Since it is just ideas and their content that we have to deal with as thinkers, we would "express the whole of nature in the attribute of thought only," for this is what the system of ideas does according to Spinoza. The existence of another attribute which also expresses the whole of nature would be hypothetical. On the other hand, if Spinoza were explicitly to make room for the view that in having ideas we are acquainted with extended things and not merely with the contents of our own ideas, then the parallelism of the attributes and the definition of "attribute" would be overthrown.

8. Aristotle and Spinoza

The effort to follow Spinoza's identification of the intrinsic intelligibility of things with their participation in the attribute of thought brings us again to his conception of causality. From one point of view that idea that thought is rooted in things and not in

an external survey of things is the direct outcome, in Spinoza's
system, of his appreciation of the impossibility of mind-body interaction. The occasionalist solution to this problem is no solution not
merely because it invokes the idea of created substances which have
to be kept in harmonious relationship by their maker but also
because it makes the fact of correspondence between ideas and *ideata*
arbitrary and, in the end, superfluous, as in Berkeley's philosophy.

The involvement of thought in the very essence of its own objects is responsible for the peculiar epistemological cast of the basic
metaphysical definitions and axioms of part one. The legitimacy of
defining substance and attribute and mode in terms that make explicit reference to how this or that is conceived and can be conceived
rests on the idea that the intelligibility of reality is not a matter of
inspection by an external intelligence but is constitutive of the things
that are intelligible in themselves. This very difficult and elusive
idea, although it is the very core of Spinoza's rationalism, does not
truly represent an advance relative to the thinking of Descartes. It is,
rather, a regression. Some commentators see in this view the influence of Neoplatonic mysticism and the Cabala.[42] It is quite possible that Aristotle's influence outweighs that of esoteric sources in this
connection. The indwelling intelligibility of things captures much of
the force of Aristotle's notion of *form*. The "formal cause" in Aristotle's theory of the four *aitia* is quite close in spirit to the rational intelligibility of substance that Spinoza envisions.[43] Spinoza's version of
the Cartesian dualism of thought and extension, unlike Descartes'
original, conveys much of Aristotle's ubiquitous contrast of form and
matter.[44] Descartes blamed the scholastic metaphysicians for projecting "little souls" into physical things, even inanimate physical things.
These were precisely the Aristotelian substantial forms in light of
which the development and behavior of individual things were supposed to be accessible to understanding. On the whole, Spinoza, like
Leibniz, wants to put these mental constituents back into the realm
of things from which Descartes took pains to exclude them.

Spinoza himself connects the claimed identity of thought and
the object of thought to a thesis "dimly recognized by those Jews who
maintained that God, God's intellect, and the things understood by
God are identical."[45] Commenting on this statement, Harry Wolfson
sees Aristotle behind Maimonides and the other Jews alluded to.
Wolfson quotes the *Metaphysics:*

> As the intellect (νοῦσ) thinks (νοεῖ) itself because it shares the object
> of thought (νοητοῦ); for it becomes an object of thought in coming
> in contact with and thinking its object, so that thought and object are
> the same.[46]

Aristotle held that "the mind is in a sense potentially whatever is
thinkable." Spinoza expressly repudiates the distinction between
potential and actual employed here, but he retains the Aristotelian
identification of thought and object.[47] The supposed actual mental
side *of things* for Aristotle is their intelligibility. We have no available way of expressing this view without using the dispositional notion of intelligibility rather than some categorical description. It is
this dispositionality that Spinoza rejects in rejecting the idea of a
"potential intellect." To grasp Spinoza's intent we have to try to think
their intelligibility as a nondispositional character of things.

Many of Spinoza's particular views can be found in Aristotle.
For example, Spinoza's claim that adequate ideas depend on notions
common to all things that we can understand corresponds to Aristotle's assertion that thinkability of diverse things may require that
"mind contains some element common to it with all other realities
which makes them all thinkable."[48] The idea Spinoza shares with Descartes that simple ideas cannot be false is also found in *De Anima*.[49]
Finally, the rather mysterious doctrine of the intellect in *De Anima*,
III, 5, is remarkably suggestive of Spinoza's overall view.

> Actual knowledge is identical with its object: in the individual poten-
> tial knowledge is prior to actual knowledge, but in the universe as a
> whole it is not prior even in time. When mind is set free from its pre-
> sent conditions it appears as just what it is and nothing more: this
> alone is immortal and eternal (we do not however remember its former
> activity because, while mind is in this sense impassible, mind as pas-
> sive is destructible) and without it nothing thinks.[50]

Aristotle's idea of mind "in its present condition" may be something
akin to Spinoza's conception of the essentially inadequate mental
processes that characterize the finite human perspective in contrast
with the infinite intellect to which our thought must be referred.
Even Spinoza's culminating recommendation of "intellectual love of
God" as the activity befitting the wise echos the theological con-
templative posture Aristotle envisions as the crowning achievement
of wisdom.

The many relations between Spinoza's system and Aristotle's philosophy justify us in thinking of Spinoza's secular rationalism as a backward-looking reassertion of the impersonal theology-metaphysics of Aristotle and not as a post-Cartesian secularism anticipating the modern wholly independent scientific point of view. Although Spinoza follows Descartes in the denunciation of Aristotelian teleology, in the appendix to part one, he confines his understanding of teleology to the doctrine of final causes, and he actually readmits the psychologistic point of view in physics that Descartes took great trouble to eliminate. The theory that makes thought an inhering essence in all things is out of touch with, or contrary to, developing patterns of scientific understanding in the seventeenth century.

9. The Order of Ideas

In the philosophy of mind Spinoza's monism finds general expression in Proposition II:vii, which we have already had much occasion to discuss: "The order and connection of things is the same as the order and connection of ideas." The terminology "of things" (*rerum*) and "of ideas" (*idearum*) suggests an ontological distinction between the mental and the real which is promptly excluded in the corollary and the scholium, where it is made clear that "things" is intended to cover realities under the attribute of extension, while "ideas" are the same realities under the attribute of thought.

The proof of II:vii is as obscure as it is short. Spinoza says that it follows directly from part one, Axiom iv: "The knowledge of an effect depends on and involves the knowledge of a cause." This defends the proposition at hand, "For the idea of everything that is caused depends on a knowledge of the cause, whereof it is an effect." Here again we find that peculiar Spinozan blending of the epistemological and the metaphysical. In one sense the axiom means to assert that we do not really understand something until we can appreciate its existence and character in light of the broader matrix of realities that have made it what it is and how it is. This theme is connected with the downgrading of perceptual acquaintance which involves only a confused, superficial, and subjective representation, devoid of any true understanding. The axiom and the proof of II:vii seem to make a reasonable claim if we suppose that they speak of *our ideas* and assert the contrast between *human* scientific knowledge and inadequate perceptual acquaintance. On closer inspection, however, it turns out that Spinoza is not really talking about human mental activities and the different merits of different human representations at all.

Once again a comparison with Descartes' outlook can be helpful. The idea of a survey of "the order of ideas," meaning the ideas that human thinkers find in their conscious mental lives, is familiar in Descartes' investigation and classification of his ideas in the Third Meditation. Descartes is engaged, as Spinoza *seems to be*, in assessing the parallelism of his system of mental representations and the system of things that he takes them to represent. When in the corollary to II:vii Spinoza associates reality *formaliter* with extended things and the correlative reality *objective* with ideas of those extended things, the echo of Descartes' use of the same scholastic terminology in his discussion in the Third Meditation becomes very strong. The reality *objective* of an idea is, so to speak, its representational pretension. Having an idea A, we know what a thing would have to be like in order to qualify as the thing of which A is an idea. The features of an idea that set these desiderata for an object of that idea constitute the reality *objective* of the idea. The system of features of the existing thing, that is, the features in the object satisfying those desiderata (assuming that there is such an object) make up the corresponding reality *formaliter*. The corollary asserts the thoroughgoing parallelism of reality *objective* and *formaliter*:

> . . . whatsoever follows from the infinite nature of God in the world of extension (*formaliter*) follows without exception in the same order and connection from the idea of God in the world of thought (*objective*).[51]

But the corollary also makes it clear that Spinoza is not really engaged in an enterprise similar to Descartes' at all.

Descartes hopes to draw conclusions about "things" from premises confined to the ideas he encounters. For this project he relies on causality, and this, too, suggests affinity with Spinoza's proceedings at II:vii which makes dependence "on the knowledge of the cause" so prominent. Descartes says that the ideas that he finds present to his mind must themselves have causes. He argues that the causes of ideas must contain, either *formaliter* or *eminenter*, as much reality as exists *objective* in the ideas themselves. To see what this means we need to understand one further bit of scholastic apparatus: the object will contain the required features *formaliter* only if the features exist in the object just as they do in the idea. For example, our idea of space is of a three-dimensional domain. Since space is three-dimensional, it has the reality *formaliter* that the idea has *objective*. The causes of an idea will contain the required reality *eminenter* but not *formaliter* if they fail to correspond to or resemble our ideas of them but, nonetheless, contain sufficient reality to produce those ideas in some other or higher form. Thus, *"eminenter"* can be translated "sufficient but in a different form." Ironically, *"objective"* means, more or less, "subjectively"; and *"formaliter,"* more or less, objectively. The argument from ideas as effects to extramental realities as causes is employed by Descartes to establish the existence of God in the Third Meditation and the existence of an external material world in the Sixth Meditation.

Although Spinoza's discussion has all the same conceptual ingredients—ideas and things, causality, reality *formaliter* and *objective*—the pattern of his argument diverges utterly from that of Descartes. Ideas are not regarded as givens from which the existence of extramental causes might be inferred. On the contrary, the main burden of the proof is an inference *to the existence of ideas*, "For the idea of everything that is caused depends on a knowledge of the cause, whereof it is an effect." Spinoza means that we can be sure that there are ideas to go with the whole "order of things" because the epistemological relation between knowledge of a thing and knowledge of its cause will mirror the ontological relationship between caused things and their causes. But what sort of epistemology is this? It is as if the entire system of causal relations of extended things were given, and we are to infer the existence of a correspondingly complete system of mental representations. It is certain that *I* do not have ideas "of everything that is caused," which would supposedly entail the existence of ideas of the causes. It cannot be *my* ideas of causes that I am inferring from *my* ideas of effects here. Of course, from the egocentric Cartesian perspective there is no question of inferring the existence of my ideas at all. If I have them, I know it, and if I do not know I have them, I do not have them. This is the heart of Cartesian epistemology. But in the corollary to II:vii it is clear that it is God's ideas and God's knowledge that are being discussed.

Spinoza makes no appeal to the existence of an extramental cause for any idea. Indeed, any such appeal involves the theory of mind-body interaction that Spinoza certainly rejects. Spinoza is not saying that ideas for all the details of the material world exist in either God or man because those material things cause the ideas to exist. No idea is caused by an extended thing in Spinoza's philosophy. Causality connects the order of extension into a single unified whole. In the proof of II:vii Spinoza merely *asserts* that the causal system is completely mirrored by a system of ideas. Perhaps Spinoza is encouraged by the view that we know something about this mirroring in our own intellectual life. That is, we do, in fact, attain a better understanding of things the more we grasp the existence and character of things in a matrix of causal relations with other things. Our own experience, however, gives us at most some illustrations of this principle. The proposition asserting a complete parallelism of the orders of thought and extension is certainly not to be read as an inductive inference from those few cases wherein we have appreciated the causes of things.

Spinoza makes no use at all of the first-person perspective which Descartes exploits to such effect. As a matter of fact, the ideas that we actually have of things always fall far short of the true causal understanding to which II:vii appeals. The most comprehensive network of causes within which we actually understand anything is always insignificant in contrast to the infinite network of all causes. It is simply Spinoza's conception of ideas and causes that guarantees Proposition II:vii. Causal relations, as we said, are intrinsically relations of intelligibility. This is the rationalism that contrasts with Humean and occasionalist conjunctive relationships, impenetrable to the understanding. This rational intelligibility of causes is what the axiom to which Spinoza appeals here really asserts. So the unified network of causes is a network of intelligibility and, *eo ipso*, a network of ideas. The shift to the ideas of God and knowledge of God includes the elimination of the episodic external conception of thought altogether in favor of the elusive theme of thought as an inhering aspect of the reality of things.

10. Mind and Physiology

In the scholium to II:vii Spinoza reminds us that the difference of attributes does not imply a multiplicity of subject matters: "sub-

stance thinking and substance extended are one and the same substance comprehended now through one attribute, now through the
other." He goes on to apply this global doctrine to matters of detail,
saying, "a mode of extension [under which individual bodies are in-
cluded] and the idea of that mode are one and the same thing expressed in two ways." The thesis that the mind of an individual
human being is the idea of the body of that individual (Proposition
II:xiii) is an instance of the general claim about modes and ideas of
them. The person, we may suppose, is identical with both this finite
mental system and this finite material system, for they express "one
and the same thing." Although the scholium warns against mixing
the explanatory idioms suitable for the two attribute systems, the
underlying reality is identical, so that Spinoza does not ascribe a composite nature to a person. At a level of even greater detail Spinoza
says that particular mental states or activities are the expression in the
attribute of thought of the very same reality that is constituted of particular states and activities of the body.

In other words, a man's mind is the idea of his body, and the
mental particulars—the thoughts, perceptions, beliefs, emotions,
and so on—that collectively make up the individual mind are ideas
of bodily particulars. The subjective conscious mental life, to which
Descartes gives such prominence, comprises a subset of such mental
particulars. For Spinoza these Cartesian mental particulars are identical with a subset of bodily particulars which they merely express in
the attribute of thought. A conscious mind is a set of mind-body particulars. In this doctrine Spinoza suggests something like twentieth-
century mind-brain identity theories.

That Spinoza's intended meaning lies in this direction is much
confirmed in the sections of part two that follow the first thirteen
proved propositions. The course of the reasoning is interrupted after
II:xiii by the introduction of new axioms, lemmas, and postulates.
The objectives to be secured by the new material are clear. They introduce elements of a science of bodily things chosen to prepare for
the development of a physiological foundation for Spinoza's fundamental assertions in epistemology and the philosophy of mind.
The six postulates and Propositions xiv through xix present this scientific conception in extremely general terms, but the account includes
the basis for a physiology of perception and a physiology of memory.
It is worth emphasizing that II:xiii has not only made the striking

claim that the mind is the idea of the body, but it also bespeaks the confinement to the body of the objects of the several ideas constituting the mind of an individual.

> The object of the idea constituting the human mind is the body, in other words a certain mode of extension which actually exists, *and nothing else.*[52]

II:xiv explains that perception of external things is underwritten by the physical sensitivity of the body which receives impressions from the environment. II:xix states:

> The human mind has no knowledge of the body and does not know it to exist, save through the ideas of the modifications whereby the body is affected.

In other words, all our knowledge of extended things, including our knowledge of our own bodies, depends in the first instance on the ideas that we have of states and activities of our bodies. Our thoughts of things external to the body depend, in addition, on physical relations between our bodies and the external things we get to know. Although Spinoza's characterization of these relations is very abstract, it is clear that the discussion is meant to cover the causal processes that are involved in sense perception and that engender changes in the body, especially in the organs of perception and the nervous system. The mental side of these modifications of our own bodies is the foundation of all our thinking about external things. Such thinking about external things reduces to having ideas about extended things, but these are only ideas of *internal* extended things, that is, modifications internal to the body. Thus, when I perceive an object such as the body of another person a characteristic modification of the "soft parts" of my body occurs. The aspect of this bodily impression in the attribute of thought amounts to the fact that I "will regard the said external body as actually existing and as present to [myself]."[53]

Recognition, memory, and all the mental states that we would call intentional states where the intentional object is not present or does not exist are explained by the fact that habitual exposure reinforces physical modifications giving them an endurance that outlasts the presence of the physical cause.[54] As a consequence, the corollary to II:xvii tells us that "the mind is able to regard as present external bodies, by which the human body has once been affected, even though they are no longer in existence or present." Thus, perception and the physiological aftermath of it make it possible for me to have ideas of external things, and to think about them when not perceiving them, and to make perceptual errors and form mistaken beliefs about external things. It is important to stress that all of these mental contents are expressions in the attribute of thought of modifications of my own body. My mind and all of its constituents are ideas of my body "and nothing else."[55] The notion that these modifications or our ideas of them are *representations* of the things outside the body that figure in the causal history of the modifications is, so far, unexplained. Put in contemporary terms, Spinoza is saying that mental entities are neural entities, and man's awareness of his own mental life is actually an awareness of neural goings-on.

That this is, indeed, Spinoza's opinion seems to be indisputable in light of the explanatory discussion that follows the corollary to II:xvii:

> . . . we clearly understand what is the difference between the idea, say, of Peter, which constitutes the essence of Peter's mind, and the idea of the said Peter which is in another man, say, Paul. The former directly answers to the essence of Peter's own body, and only implies existence as long as Peter exists; the latter indicates rather the disposition of Paul's body than the nature of Peter, and, therefore, while this disposition of Paul's body lasts, Paul's mind will regard Peter as present to itself, even though he no longer exists.[56]

In terms of the ontology of thought and extension, then, the thoughts constituting my total mental being are ideas of my body, and, in their detail, they correspond to detailed modifications of my body and not to extended things which might, as Spinoza says, not exist without changing anything at all in my mental life. The mode of extension that is identical with Paul's idea of Peter is a modification of Paul and not Peter. Paul's idea of Peter is, properly speaking, an idea of this modification or "disposition" of Paul, as Spinoza also calls it.[57] "Disposition" is presumably a reference to the account of recollection that we have summarized from the proof of II:xvii. It is also suggestive of dispositional analyses of psychological concepts familiar in twentieth-century philosophy. We would say that the reinforced physical trace is the foundation of the disposition to say that Peter is present, to act as though he were, and so on, rather than calling the trace the disposition itself. But Spinoza's thinking is running along the same lines as contemporary dispositional analysis.

There is something in this general understanding that is suggestive of empiricist and idealist developments of Cartesian thinking. According to these developments the immediate data on which all our claims to know anything about the world must be rested are constituted of our inner perceptual experiences. The very existence of corresponding things making up an external world is the subject matter of relatively tenuous hypotheses. Then, for dogmatic idealists, as Kant called philosophers like Berkeley, the existence of things corresponding to ideas is just an error promoted by extravagant interpretations of the speech of the vulgar. The idea that an external world corresponding to my ideas is a matter of hypothesis is the solipsist perspective, and Spinoza shares in it insofar as he limits objects of ideas to inner realities or modifications of my own body. The idealistic motif is enhanced at II:xix when Spinoza says that we only know anything at all, even of our own body and its existence, through the ideas we have of modifications of it. This could be read as the view that we confirm hypotheses, in which the existence of our own body and of outer things is asserted, in terms of evidence consisting wholly in ideas. In view of the identity of mind and body asserted in II:xiii, such an interpretation should not be correct, although it seems to be supported by the propositions that follow in which Spinoza seems to place our knowledge of external reality at an even further remove from the external things themselves. Proposition II:xxii says that the human mind perceives not only modifications of the body but also it perceives its own ideas of those modifications, and II:xxiii seems to complete the picture of an inner sphere of ideas to which conscious acquaintance is limited, asserting:

> The mind does not know itself except in so far as it perceives the ideas of the modifications of the body.

In Spinoza's theory of the mind the introduction of ideas of ideas of modifications of the body covers the notion of consciousness of one's own mental activities. Consciousness of ideas is especially relevant to Spinoza's enterprise in two ways. First, the epistemological attitude of the *Ethics* and of *On the Improvement of the Understanding*, as well as the attitude of all of Descartes' philosophical writings, gives a special prominence to consciousness of one's own thinking. This is true not only because consciousness itself becomes a special domain of ultimate evidence in Descartes' philosophy. As I have said, this subjective epistemological emphasis is completely ignored by Spinoza. Consciousness of our own ideas is prominent in all these works in a more direct and simpler way. As philosophers joining in projects like these, we are assessing our own ideas, testing our thoughts and beliefs, trying to discard the defective elements in our thinking and to find a foundation for the rest. In order to do this we focus conscious attention on our own thinking. The critical epistemological undertaking is a critique of representations, not of things.

In the second place, special provision for consciousness of ideas is needed just because Spinoza has asserted that the order of ideas perfectly mirrors that of extension. Our own mental histories have to be construed as illustrations of the parallelism. A particular experience is the reality in the attribute of thought of what is, as an extended thing, a modification of the body. This kind of illustration and the affinity suggested with contemporary mind-brain theories threaten to undermine the general parallelism. Mind-brain materialists today do not claim that there are mental states and events for everything that goes on in the brain, much less in the whole body. We certainly do not have any experiences to go with most of our bodily modifications. But if II:vii can be believed, they must all have their representation in thought, and these representations must be constituents of the mind. The notion of ideas of ideas resolves the problem of the absence from our mental life, as we experience it, of ideas to correspond with most of the things that occur in our bodies. The Cartesian mental life that we can report with such authority is limited to those ideas of modifications of which we have second-order ideas.

If this is correct, then Spinoza does mean to assert that we have in our minds ideas of everything bodily that goes on within us. We have no ideas of most of these ideas of modifications, so that most of our ideas are unconscious. This passage of thought is similar to Leibniz's contrast of mental processes in general and conscious *apperception*, in which the vast detail of unconscious perception is lost.

When Spinoza says that our knowledge of our own bodies and external things depends upon the second-order ideas we have of our own ideas of modifications of the body, he is uncharacteristically taking up a Cartesian viewpoint. He is speaking of the conscious knowledge we have, the knowledge we are able to state. We reach a conscious knowledge of our body only because we recognize that the objects of our second-order ideas are ideas of modifications of our bodies. And we reach a knowledge of external things only because we recognize that the modifications, of the ideas of which we have second-order ideas, are modifications caused by external things. Since, for the most part, Spinoza pays no attention to Cartesian consciousness and Cartesian epistemological problems, the concept of second-order ideas of ideas has little role to play. He makes no comparable distinction about the ideas of God. The thought of God is not conscious thought.

11. The Problem of Objects for Ideas

Although Spinoza does not involve himself in the Cartesian subjective epistemological project, elements of this idealist epistemology find their way into his scheme of things. In the Cartesian tradition the immediate objects of thought are all internal mental objects. They are all ideas. If Spinoza's immediate objects of thought include extended things as well as ideas, they are all, in any case, internal objects like those of the Cartesians. Spinoza discusses no problem of the existence of the material world because the idea and the modification in extension are one and the same thing (although Spinoza does not worry about explaining how we might know this). Since they are but aspects of the same reality, it is not possible that ideas should exist in the absence of extended things. The ideas constituting my mind are not premises from which the existence of bodily things can be inferred. We do not need argument here if these ideas and their objects are just two expressions of the same reality.

Beyond the general difficulty of this central Spinozan doctrine, a particular tension emerges when we recall that Spinoza says that we may have ideas of some object although that object is not present, and even if it does not exist. How can I have an idea of something that does not exist if the idea and the thing of which it is an idea are but the same thing expressed "now in one way, now in another"? Spinoza tries to handle this problem by identifying the real object of the idea, not with that outer thing which may not exist at all, but with the inner modification that, in the ordinary case, is produced by causal processes originating from the outer thing.

Things are not really going well for the theory here. If the inner state is the thing of which my idea is an idea, in what sense can I have ideas of outer things at all? The idea of Peter that has Peter for its object is always going to be Peter's idea of Peter. Of course, we do allow that the inner state is, ordinarily, caused by the outer object, and, therefore, we might speak *loosely* of the outer cause as the object of the idea. But no idea that is part of my mind can *strictly* be an idea of an outer thing simply because it must always be the expression in the attribute of thought *of part of me*. Expressions of outer things in the attribute of thought may be ideas of those outer things, and, as such, they may go into the constitution of minds, but they cannot be part of the constitution of *my* mind, for the outer thing cannot be, as it were, detached from the idea which is *its* expression in the attribute of thought. So we are left with no way of understanding how we can be said to gain knowledge of outer things or have any ideas of them as a consequence of the modifications they induce in us.

Spinoza is traversing a familiar philosophical course here. In the usual Cartesian idealist version I reflect that my conscious thoughts are as they are and that I am perfectly secure about that, however disappointing external realities may prove to be. When I suffer an hallucination like Macbeth's, I certainly do pick out *something* that is dagger-shaped and oriented with handle toward my hand. Since this experience can be just as it is without a real dagger, we must provide an inner surrogate object of perceptual experience. The indisputable existence of the object of my consciousness leads philosophers to postulate a fail-safe phenomenal object. In just this way Spinoza is attracted by the thought that Peter cannot possibly be the object of my perceptual idea of him because my idea of him would be just as it is even if he did not exist, as long as the state of my body is just as it is. We all understand this reflection. Suppose someone could simply install in my brain just the neural realities that ordinarily exist only if I have a normal visual experience of Peter. They would be able to produce that experience in me. So the aspect of my experience in virtue of which we think of it as an experience *of Peter* must be reconsidered. I experience something, but not really Peter. It is the fail-safe object, an inner object for my idea. This is the very step habitually taken by the idealist Cartesian, but the difficulties that are always created by taking the step are more legible in Spinoza's version.

The idealist internalization of the object of a perceptual idea derives plausibility from the thought that the internal object is something like the external thing that one might naively suppose to be apprehended directly in perception. If we decide to say, with the idealist, that I really apprehend a mental image of Peter, the newly supplied inner object has a lot in common with the outer object as naively conceived. The mental image of Peter looks like Peter, to put this common ground bluntly. The plausibility that comes from the available resemblance of mental images and outer things is wholly unavailable to the Spinozan version of the required fail-safe inner object. It is plain that the internal bodily modification, the neural state, say, induced in perception of Peter, is not something that looks like Peter. When we move from the naive outer object — namely, Peter — to this inner object — namely, a neural state — we move to something that does not resemble the outer object at all. But according to Spinoza, such an inner modification is the object of Paul's idea of Peter. This modification is what Paul's idea expresses in the attribute of thought. If the idea is the intrinsic intelligibility of the thing, then Paul's idea when he sees Peter is the intrinsic intelligibility of Paul's neural state, not the intrinsic intelligibility of Peter. The concept of the adequacy or inadequacy of an idea generated in perception is a matter of its success or failure in representing, not the external object, but some complex internal state, presumably, of the brain.

It would be putting the thing mildly to say that my perceptual idea when I see Peter is an inadequate representation of my own neural state. If my ideas are ideas of neural states, they utterly fail as vehicles of information about their objects. Even more strangely, the valuable information that my perceptual ideas do seem to have, information about external objects, has to be discarded as worthless. Following the internalization of the idea, the idea counts as an idea of Peter only in the loose and extended sense, which really means only that the proper object of the idea has been caused by Peter. The loose and extended sense cannot be allowed to import the suggestion that the proper object of the idea is something like Peter, which, indeed, it certainly is not, since it is a neural state. My idea of the bodily modification cannot reflect the causal history of the modification back to its cause and, in some sense, include that cause. It is precisely because the modification will engender the idea whether or not there is the usual cause that we introduced an inner object in the first place.

Spinoza is sensitive to the need for a mental bridge to the outer that will correspond to the causal bridge. He tries to close the gap in Proposition II:xvi.

> The idea of every mode, in which the human body is affected by external bodies, must involve the nature of the human body, and also the nature of the external body.[58]

The proof appeals to causality and, again, to the idea that knowledge is through causes. The first corollary to this proposition makes the desired connection: "the human mind perceives the nature of a variety of bodies together with the nature of its own."[59] The second corollary, however, tends in quite the opposite direction.

> . . . the ideas which we have of external bodies indicate rather the constitution of our own body than the nature of external bodies.[60]

Then Spinoza adds that this conclusion has been illustrated in the appendix to part one, where he has in fact suggested a version of the theory of secondary qualities. He includes warmth and cold in a list of evaluative and everyday moral terms that are to be discounted as merely subjective.[61] There are so many strands here that Spinoza's actual passage of thought is virtually untrackable. The broad lines of a self-defeating vacillation stand out clearly enough. The causal origins of modifications are reflected in those modifications. Properly understood, the idea of a modification will, therefore, include the idea of the cause. Thus, the human mind "perceives the nature of a variety of bodies," namely, the causes of the modifications. But the idea in a human thought can only express in thought the modification itself and not the cause. In recognition of this constraint the second corollary takes back that which the first asserts. Ideas said to be "of external things" only really convey information about our own bodies. They "indicate the nature" only of the caused modifications and not of the causes. Hence the appeal to the idea that warmth and cold are misunderstood when they are taken to describe the outer and objective. Therefore, having a perceptual idea does not deserve to be described as perception of "the nature" of an outer thing.

The difficulties are compounded if we try to take seriously the allusion to the subjectivity of the qualities of things encountered in perception. Are we to think of the warmth we naturally ascribe to outer things as, in reality, a feature of something in our own body? That is quite possible. The warmth we feel is really the warmth of our own hand. But the extension of this to perceptual ideas generally runs against the unsuitableness of the inner modification that we have commented on already. The sounds and colors of things cannot be features of the inner object if that inner object is construed, not as a mental image, but as a physical modification such as a neural state. Spinoza has detached the sensuous features of things from the outer world in the manner of the Cartesian idealist. But in his amended account the internal object cannot receive those features, and they are left in a metaphysical limbo without any owners at all.

12. Representation and Knowledge of the External

There is a commonsense level of thinking about perception which is rejected by Spinoza and, at the same time, tacitly exploited. In perception I get to know what outer things are like insofar as they have features accessible to my senses. Seeing Peter, I come to know what color Peter's hair is, for example. When I see something, the object of my perceptual consciousness is what I see. Spinoza, like all philosophers, draws on this preliminary understanding. It is the sole and sufficient foundation for saying Paul has an idea of Peter in the first place. Of course, no one will deny that there are all sorts of physical and physiological activities that go on in vision and that Paul would not be able to see anything if they did not go on in him. But, from a prephilosophical perspective, visual perception gives Paul no acquaintance with any of these physiological processes when he sees Peter.

Only scientists know much about these processes that go on in the body in perception. Let us suppose that, in the course of these inner processes, there are phases which, when we understand them scientifically, we will naturally think of as distinct bodily modifications that *correspond* to the thing that we see. The existence and the correspondence of these bodily modifications will be understandable in light of complex causal relations with the seen object. As far as I know, this is just unsupported speculation about what might be found by neurophysiologists in the future. In any case, let us suppose that just such detailed and corresponding modifications are discovered. From the preanalytic point of view we still have no temptation at all to think that we gain some information about these discrete modifications of our nervous systems in the course of perceiving things visually. It will be understandable if these inner items are called "representations" in virtue of their correspondence to the outer object. We may, for instance, further speculate that neurologists will be able to tell what it is that a man sees from information about the neural representations in his brain. Such brain scientists would be reading modifications of the nervous system as if they were encoded descriptions of the outer object seen. But, in the absence of theory and, for that matter, in spite of philosophical encouragement to the contrary, it is quite absurd to suggest that we gain any information at all about these inner sensations when we see the things we do.

It is even more absurd to suppose that we, or our brains, like these imagined future scientists, in some way do already "read" such encoded descriptions. It is just incomprehensible to suggest that it is such physiological reading of things in the brain that somehow enables us to tell what it is that we are perceiving, just as reading modifications might indeed enable a scientist to tell what someone else is perceiving. The incoherence of this kind of suggestion is clear when we note that a scientific brain reader will only have any idea of what the object that causes the neural modifications is like because he can perceive such an object himself. He can know, for example, that a certain pattern in the nervous system is only produced when the seen thing is red, but he will only know what it is like for something to be red because he can see red things himself. If his information were limited to "indications of the nature of the modification" of someone's body, he would not be able to form any idea whatsoever of the external cause of that modification. If we try to reduce our own concepts of outer things and their perceivable features to our own apprehension of, or response to, these inner modifications, the significance of thinking of the modifications as descriptions or representations will be eliminated. The neural states do not have the features that outer things have, and if they were what we really encounter in perception, then we would encounter nothing that has any such features, and descriptions of things in terms of such features would be unintelligible. But this idea of apprehension of the inner is Spinoza's concept of perceptual consciousness.

Spinoza's theory holds that Paul's own inner bodily modification is the object of Paul's idea when Paul sees Peter. Because, according to Proposition II:xvi, the modification in Paul is a causal consequence of a process starting from Peter, Paul gets knowledge of both the nature of Peter and of the nature of the modification. But, as we noted, the second corollary cancels this. We find that Paul's so-called "knowledge of the nature of Peter" is really only an indication to Paul of the nature of the modification of Paul. Just this prepares for the detailed restatement of the vast difference between Paul's and Peter's ideas of Peter at the end of the scholium to II:xvii, which we have already quoted.

The characteristic Cartesian epistemological and speculative physiological lines of thought do operate here in the formation of Spinoza's account. We see these themes in Spinoza's preoccupation with the case wherein Paul "sees" Peter but Peter does not exist, and in Spinoza's repeated account of perception of the outer in terms of the generation of inner modifications on which, he asserts, our knowledge of the outer is wholly based, as in Proposition II:xxvi. But Spinoza's thinking involves a third element which is not present in the customary dualistic or idealistic inner-object theory of perceptual consciousness. Spinoza's ambitions are not limited to an epistemological account of our knowledge of external things. In fact, we have stressed that he is not interested in the traditional epistemological problems at all, although he follows the traditional path for a long way. Spinoza is interested in a metaphysical account of the mind and in the relationship between the mind and the body. We said that his rejection of interaction and dualism involves Spinoza in a theory that is quite like Aristotle's account of knowledge and perception. A mind-like component is out there in all things. The realm of thought cannot be understood at all if it is made into an external, ultimately supernatural survey of bodily things, which are considered merely concatenations of intrinsically mindless inert stuff. Thought has to be rooted in the things that are objects of thought. Thought *is* the intrinsic intelligibility of things, and the human mind has to be understood as an instance of this intrinsic intelligibility. There is no option here, once the mental is identified as substance expressed under one of the attributes. The inevitable ubiquity of mind is expressed by II:vii. The usual picture that we have of the mind as offering an all-embracing personal perspective from which the world is surveyed has to be adjusted to this fundamental conception of mind as coextensive with being. Causality is the mechanism for this adjustment in Spinoza's thought.

Paul's mind is the expression under the attribute of thought of the same reality that Paul's body amounts to under the attribute of extension. Since thought is indwelling, one might say that Spinoza holds that everything thinks itself. Human minds are not different from the mental aspect of other things on this account. They seem different because of the extreme complexity of the human body and its complex causal relations with other things. The causal registration in the body of so much from its environment is traced to the cohesion and lasting integrity of the body through growth and nutritional interchange of parts that Spinoza sketches in the seven lemmas that follow his two special axioms of motion in part two.[62] The body contains, from a causal point of view, information about its environment on a scale immeasurably beyond that contained in a stone. The insensitivity of a stone amounts to the fact that it does not enter into subtle causal relations with the extended things around it. Nothing happens in a stone comparable to the modifications of my body occasioned by light, reflected from surrounding things, falling on the complex structures of the eye. Therefore, when my body thinks itself, there is a lot more to it in the realm of ideas than when a marble statue thinks itself, as, in a sense, it surely does. The principle of the mental is the same in the two cases. A human mind is just a much fancier bit of being expressed in the attribute of thought than the mind of a marble statue.

This way of connecting Spinoza's conception of thought as an attribute of substance with prephilosophical thinking about human mentality leaves two grand problems. We all think of human minds as individual centers of consciousness and personality. Some philosophers raise consciousness to the level of the essence of the mental. Descartes seems to do this. While Spinoza is not obligated to confer an exalted Cartesian status on consciousness, we do have to understand what individual conscious mentality is according to his theory. Second, although the complexity of the body can make it understandable that the human mind, which is its idea, will be correspondingly complex, this in itself does not give us any understanding of the fact that human minds can attain knowledge of the world outside the human body. Simple or complex, Spinoza's equation of mind and intelligibility gives no hint as to how anything other than the body can be known to the mind. As we have seen, the causal account of the inner modification tends to shrink the representational scope of the ideas in it so that they fail to reach beyond the body at all. The mind is only a representation of the very complex thing that is a human body and of the complex changes and states that arise in it when it is affected by other things.

We have already touched on both of these problems. We said that Spinoza's theory of second-order ideas is his account of conscious mind, and the contrary messages of the corollaries of II:xvi represent Spinoza's struggles with the problem of the knowledge we attain of the outer. The investigation of the interconnection of these two themes will be the end of our study of Spinoza's effort to construct a non-dualistic philosophy of mind. The Spinozan solution to the problem of consciousness will lead us to the conclusion that the problem of the external is insoluble. Spinoza's monism ultimately collapses to a speculative metaphysical hypothesis that he fails to connect with human intellectual concerns in any matter of detail.

We said above that consciousness seems to come into his picture of the mind with Spinoza's provision of second-order ideas of modifications of the body. We have ideas of ideas of modifications, and these are our conscious ideas. Is this account of second-order ideas compatible with the universal parallelism of the orders of thought and extension? The idea of the inner modification is the expression in the attribute of the thought of that modification itself. To what extended reality does the idea of the idea of that modification correspond? As far as I know, Spinoza does not give an answer to this, but it is not really an embarrassing question for his theory of ideas. We have to suppose, and we do suppose, that the complexity of the body involves sensitivity not only to modifications engendered through the sense organs but also to complex inner relations in which lower-level modifications are causally related, via neural mechanisms of synthesis and integration, to higher level modifications. Spinoza's ideas of ideas will be expressions in the mental order of these higher neural states and activities. This is so much in the spirit of Spinoza that we can take it to be the Spinozan theory, although he does not speak of the physiological underpinning for ideas of ideas.

On the surface it looks as though this account of consciousness of ideas will reproduce the problem of knowledge of the external wholly within the realm of physiological functioning. To be sure, one modification of the brain may represent, as an effect, another modification, and we may rightly think of these as higher- and lower-level modifications because only the lower modifications engender the higher, as outer things engender the lower. But this does not explain why it is that the idea which is the expression in the attribute of thought of the higher-level modification should count as an idea *of* the lower-level modification and its idea. The lower level will be, so to speak, "external" to the higher-level modification. We can allow that the higher-level modification will correspond to an element in the order of thought. This element will be the idea of that higher-level modification "and nothing else" as Spinoza says. But we introduced these levels in order to explain how one idea can be the object of another idea. Just as we found in the case of the perceptually produced modification, here again we find that Spinoza does not give us a foundation for the view that an idea can be anything other than the expression in thought of one particular extended reality. Both within and without the body he needs a way of seeing an idea as an expression of two extended realities, one the effect and the other the cause.[63]

When this problem is posed for Spinoza in the context of ideas of ideas, or the context of self-consciousness, it gives rise to a Spinozan solution which is so plausible and so thoroughly in the spirit of the *Ethics* that it can hardly be refused acceptance. The solution is very simple. The point is that we can count ideas of higher-level modifications as ideas of ideas because the causal relationships that engender higher-level brain states from perceptual input are part of our physiology. These causal processes are speculative, but whatever they are, they will take place entirely within our bodies. Here both the causes and the effects will be parts of the extended thing that is the body of an individual. The idea that expresses that human body in thought is entitled to express the higher level as the effect of the lower level because the whole causal relationship is part of the extended mode which that mind expresses. We said that for Spinoza everything thinks itself. If we consider just that neural event which is a higher-order modification, by itself, then the expression in thought of just that event cannot incorporate its own causal history and cannot count as knowledge of the lower-level modification which figures in its genesis. In just the same way we said that the neural state cannot be described as knowledge of the outer thing because the idea of it, however complicated it may be, just expresses *it* and not its cause. We illustrated this saying that Peter cannot properly be part of what Paul's idea expresses in thought because Peter is outside Paul's body, while Paul's mind, with all his ideas, is just the idea of Paul's body. When we rehearse the same steps for the relations of modifications and ideas in the brain, we are allowed to include the reality of the cause with the effect in the extended thing in which the entire causal relationship exists and which the mind of the individual expresses. The acceptability of the account of consciousness of ideas rests upon the thought that both the causes and the effects are within the body.

Knowledge extends to the cause, and the cause can really be thought of as the object of an idea, only if the cause is part of the same extended reality as the effect, so that an idea can be regarded as the expression of this connection. This principle of the literal *incorporation* of the cause with the effect in one whole is satisfied in the case of internal neural relationships, but it is not satisfied, and not satisfiable, when it comes to external things which cause inner modifications.

When Spinoza thinks of the understanding that God has of things, he develops the notion that all the extended things together make one integrated causal network, which is all within the infinite extended thing that is God. Therefore, when Spinoza tells us that the ideas that we have in inadequate fragmented form are adequate in the context of the thought of God, this superiority amounts to the fact that all the causes and effects are internal to God, while only a few effects are internal to us.[64] The whole system of causes and effects has the whole system of intelligibility for its expression in thought, while a part of the system of extension is expressed by a part of the system of intelligibility. And that means that a part is only partly intelligible. The intellectual representation of the part is inevitably inadequate.

The trouble with this is that it makes nonsense of the idea that we might improve our knowledge by extending the scope of causal interconnections included in our representations of the world. Spinoza tries to connect the idea of a better representation with the concept of complex causal interaction, in the course of which details of the outer world are differentially registered in the body. In this spirit II:xiv recommends an empiricist attitude. It seems if we want to have a better understanding of things, we have to interact with as many things as we can, generating a maximum of discriminations in the effects of interactions with the outer world to correspond with distinctions in the outer causes themselves. This coheres with the Spinozan thought that scientific understanding grows insofar as we achieve successively a more comprehensive picture of the causal matrix of things and are not left confronted with effects that cannot be understood as necessary. But it turns out that we are not really capable of representing outer reality at all. In consequence one representation is not better than another. All our knowledge is confined to inner effects. We could only get to know something about the cause of a modification of the body, and we could only rightly think of our idea as an idea *of that cause*, if we could make that cause part of us, as it is a part of God. Insofar as Spinoza allows the causal concept of the inner modification to obliterate the representational conception, only absorption of causes will make possible knowledge of causes. A more comprehensive being will have more comprehensive knowledge. A being that is merely more sensitive, without being more comprehensive, remains confined to representation of its own more detailed being. The representation of outer things drops out of the mental for finite minds, however sensitive. It also drops out for the infinite mind. God, too, represents nothing external to him, but then nothing is external to God.

We saw in the first parts of this study that the difficulty he encounters in connecting the infinite and the finite incline Spinoza to downgrade the reality of the individual, the contingent, and the temporal in favor of the truer being of the simple eternity of substance. His treatment of causality and representation involves him in a second major denigration of the individual. Since the causal relation is ultimately destructive of the pretensions of representations, a superior understanding will only be conceded to a superior being, and that will mean a larger being that takes in more of the causal web.

There is in this an ironic revision of Aristotle's theory that the mind *becomes* what it knows and perceives. For Aristotle this meant that the intelligible *form* of the known is somehow transferred or taken in, without the matter of the external thing, so that the representation in the mind comes to have the same form as the external item. In the Spinozan reincarnation of this Aristotelian theory of the intelligibility of things the mind becomes what it knows in a more drastic and literal sense. The mind could only really know an external cause of a modification by actually engulfing that cause, so that the cause of the modification and the modification caused are both within the extended reality that the mind is in a position to express. In just this way God engulfs the world, and he expresses all of it in thought.

The Spinozan moral perspective is not unaffected by this incorporative epistemology. Spinoza proposes that the narrow, vain desires and pursuits of men can be set aside if we attain an understanding that makes the necessity and appropriateness of all existence intellectually accessible. This tolerance takes on a different color when we reflect that the expanded point of view really comes from the identification of the mind with a larger and larger unit of being. The desires of the individual are set aside not because of their vanity or foolishness as desires *for that individual*. They are set aside because they are not the desires of a being that would consist of a larger chunk of the total of reality. Spinoza recommends that we adopt the appetitive outlook of the largest or most comprehensive creature. Again, it appears that Spinoza discredits the individual perspective because it is that of an individual. He does not really show that the desires and disappointments of individuals are inappropriate as desires for individuals, or are not disappointing to individuals if they are wise. Of course, many desires, activities, and disappointments of individual men are vain and foolish. But Spinoza only shows that those human traits would not be shared by an all-embracing being. He does not establish which desires are foolish for individuals nor that everything that ever happens ought to be greeted with the same satisfaction and equanimity by human beings. The tranquil acquiescence on the part of nature as a whole in the face of everything that happens offers no solace to individuals faced with personal catastrophe, and it is odd that admirers of Spinoza's moral outlook should think otherwise. But his view in this particular does cohere with the fact that Spinoza does not rate individuals very high on the scale of being.

NOTES

Abbreviations used in these notes are:

Elwes I-II R. H. M. Elwes, *Works of Spinoza*, New York, 1955.
Geb. I-IV   Carl Gebhardt, ed., Spinoza *Opera*, Heidelberg, 1924.

1. This definition is directly based on that given by Descartes himself in the "synthetic" presentation of his views at the end of his replies to the second set of Objections to the *Meditations;* HR II, 53.

2. For this relation see the discussion in Wolfson, H. A., *The Philosophy of Spinoza*, Cambridge, Mass., 1934, I, 232-35.

3. Spinoza's definition is extremely broad: pt. I, def. v, "By *mode*, I mean . . . that which exists in, and is conceived through something else."

4. Elwes I, 40.

5. Elwes I, 82.

6. See *Spinoza's kurzgefasste Abhandlung von Gott, dem Menschen und dessen Gluck*, Schaarschmidt, C., trans., Leipzig, 1907, 14-15.

7. From the proof of II:xxviii, Elwes I, 105-6.

8. Elwes I, 319.

9. Elwes I, 320.

10. *Spinoza: Earlier Philosophical Writings*, Hayes, F.A., trans., Indianapolis, 1963, 120.

11. *The History of Philosophy*, Haldane, E.S., and Simson, F.H., trans., London, 1895, Vol. III, 260-61.

12. Haldane and Simson, Vol. III, 287.

13. See definitions v, vii, and x, HR II, 43; and Descartes' reasoning from the concept of substance in *Meditations* II and III.

14. The proposition states, "One substance cannot be produced by another substance."

15. The first occurrence of the claim of uniqueness occurs in these lines: "Jam quoniam ad naturam substantiae . . . pertinet existere, debet ejus definitio necessariam existentiam involvere, et consequenter ex solâ ejus definitione debet ipsius existentia concludi. At ex ipsius definitione . . . non potest sequi plurium substantiarum existentia." Geb. II, 51.

16. I:v: "There cannot exist in the universe two or more substances having the same nature or attribute."

17. Malebranche says,"il est absolument nécessaire que Dieu ait en lui-même les idées de tous les êtres qu'il a créés,. . . .Il faut de plus sçavoir que Dieu est tres étroitement uni a nos ames par sa présence, de sorte qu'on peut dire qu'il est le lieu des esprits, de même que les espaces sont en un sens le lieu des corps." *De la recherche de la verité*, III, 2, vi.

18. *An Inquiry Concerning Human Understanding*, V,2.

19. Elwes I, 48-49.

20. Gerhardt, *Phil. Schriften*, I, 142. See Gueroult, M., *Spinoza*, Paris, 1968, I, 120, for a discussion of Leibniz's remarks.

21. The view is presented in the chapter "La substance constituée d'un seul attribut," of Gueroult's exhaustive study. For the textual citation see *Spinoza*, I, 109.

22. Proposition I:viii: "Omnis substantia est necessariò infinita. Demonstratio: Substantia unius attributi non, nisi unica, existit (per Prop.v), & ad ipsius naturam pertinet existere (per. Prop. vii). Erit ergo de ipsius naturâ, vel finita, vel infinita existere. At non finita. Nam (per Defin. ii) deberet terminari ab alia ejusdem naturae, quae etiam necessariò existere (per Prop. vii); adeóque darentur duae substantia ejusdem attributi, quod est absurdum (per Prop. v). Existit ergo infinita. Q.E.D." Elwes' translation "There can only be one substance with an identical attribute" seems to me to be in the right direction, although somewhat obscure. Shirley, S., trans., *Baruch Spinoza: The Ethics and Selected Letters*, Indianapolis, 1982, says "There cannot be more than one substance having the same attribute," and this is what is required by the argument and supported by I:v.

23. "Per attributum intelligo id, quod intellectus de substantiâ percipit, tanquam ejusdem essentiam constituens." Geb. II, 45.

24. Elwes I, 55.

25. Geb. II, 45.

26. Elwes I, 50; Geb. II, 51.

27. Letters 63 through 66 (Elwes' numbering) mediated by G.H. Schaller; Elwes I, 396-401.

28. For this view see Wolf, A., "Spinoza's Conception of the Attributes of Substance," in Kashap, S.P., ed., *Studies in Spinoza*, Berkeley, 1972, 26; and Bennett, J., *A Study of Spinoza's Ethics*, Indianapolis, 1984, 76.

29. Proposition I:ix.

30. Wolfson, *The Philosophy of Spinoza*, I, 225ff.

31. See Wolfson, I, 227.

32. The original Latin of the *Short Treatise* is lost. I have translated this passage from the German version of Schaarschmidt, Leipzig, 1907, 19-20.

33. Elwes I, 399.

34. Elwes I, 87.

35. Elwes I, 401.

36. For a good discussion of this issue see Pollock, F., *Spinoza: His Life and Philosophy*, London, 1880, 173-75.

37. Elwes I, 87.

38. Pollock, *Spinoza*, 175.

39. Elwes I, 82.

40. Elwes I, 26.

41. Schaarschmidt, 73.

42. For a discussion of this connection see Pollock, *Spinoza*, 99ff.

43. See Randall, J.H., *The Career of Philosophy*, New York, 1965, I, 349.

44. See Wolfson, *The Philosophy of Spinoza*, I, 233-34.

45. Elwes I, 86.

46. *Metaphysics*, L, 7, 1072^b 19-21; quoted and translated by Wolfson, *The Philosophy of Spinoza*, II, 24.

47. For Spinoza's views on this Aristotelian contrast see Propositions I: xxx and I:xxxi, and especially the scholium to xxxi.

48. *De Anima*, 429^b.

49. *De Anima*, 429-30.

50. *De Anima*, 429. Smith, J.A., translator.

51. Elwes II, 86.

52. II:xiii: "Objectum ideae, humanam mentis constituentis, est Corpus, sive certus extensionis modus actu existens, & nihil aliud." Geb. II, 96.

53. Proposition II:xvii.

54. II:xvii and II:xviii.

55. "et nihil aliud"; see note 52.

56. Elwes I, 99.

57. For example, "disponitur" and "dispositum" in the proof of II:xviii, and for the assertion in general, II:xxvi.

58. "Idea cujuscunque modi, quo Corpus humanum à corporibus externis afficitur, involvere debet naturam Corporis humani, & simul naturam corporis externi." Geb. II, 103.

59. "Hinc sequitur primo Mentem humanum plurimorum corporum naturam unà cum sui corporis natura percipere." Geb. II, 104.

60. "Sequitur secundò, quod ideae, quas corporum externorum habemus, magis nostri corporis constitutionem, quam corporum externorum naturam indicant; quod in Appendice partis primae multis exemplis explicui." Geb. II, 104.

61. Elwes I, 79.

62. Elwes II, 93-97.

63. This is the need expressed in II:xvi.

64. For example, "God has the idea of the human body, in so far as he is affected by very many other ideas, and not in so far as he constitutes the nature of the human mind." From the proof of II:xix, Elwes I, 102.

IV

The Unity of Leibniz's Thought on Contingency, Possibility, and Freedom

1. The Defects of Cartesian Physics

That it fails to accommodate force is Leibniz's fundamental criticism of Descartes' physics. Descartes tried to reduce physics to geometry. A conceptual scheme restricted to geometrical concepts lacks resources adequate for the representation of physical forces. In the context that is best known and most often discussed by Leibniz, he attacks Descartes' conception of the conservation of the "quantity of motion," and he substitutes the idea of the conservation of *vis viva*, or active power, which is what we would call the conservation of energy.[1]

When we try to state the issues here in up-to-date terms, at least in the terms of modern classical physics, it can appear that Leibniz is insisting on the conservation of the product of mass and velocity-squared, while Descartes calls for the conservation of the product of mass and velocity. Since mv^2 (kinetic energy) and mv (momentum) are both conserved, some commentators say that Descartes and Leibniz are both right and that debate is out of place.[2]

This conciliation is not satisfactory. Nothing like the modern concept of mass is actually employed by Descartes. Were we to try to introduce "mass" where he speaks of "quantity of matter," we would have to make amendments in his thinking along the very lines which Leibniz requires. Mass eludes any merely geometrical description, and the shortfall is only made up by appeal, in one way or another, to something like force. Furthermore, Descartes actually thinks in terms of what we might call "speed," that is, motion along any path, straight or curved, while the conservation laws only hold for rec-

tilinear speed. This distinction becomes significant in Descartes'
metaphysics when he tries to reconcile mind-body interaction with the
thoroughgoing mechanical determinism that he supposes to rule the
material world. Descartes' idea of conservation and his laws of impact
express this determinism. The problematic mind-body interaction
takes place, Descartes hopes, when purely mental influences manage
to "deflect" the subtlest material particles of the animal spirits in the
pineal gland. Such deflection is supposed to change the direction but
not the quantity of motion of particles affected.[3] In the parlance of
classical physics, this solution fails because it violates the principle of
the conservation of energy. The deflection of a particle would constitute a change of velocity (though not necessarily of speed) and,
therefore, a change of energy. This addition or subtraction of energy
would not be charged to any account in the material world. Leibniz
makes this point.[4]

These faults in Descartes' ideas are not just details on which he
remains at an unsatisfactory and preliminary level relative to later
science. On the contrary, the difficulties spring from views which are
among Descartes' most important and best insights. The claim "My
physics is nothing but geometry"[5] is widely recognized as the expression of his deepest inspiration in science, but this view is also, as
Leibniz thought, responsible for the most obvious defects in
Descartes' physics. Why are we supposed to agree that physics is just
geometry? In part this is supposed to follow from the fact that nothing sensuous is allowed to characterize "outer," spatial, material reality by Descartes' epistemological analysis. All sensuous characteristics
like color, sound, and heat, that is, all the so-called secondary qualities,[6] are not really *out there*. They exist only in the play of mental
states and perceptions in our minds. Contact with outer things is
causally responsible for the generation of *ideas* with sensuous features,
but material things do not have such features themselves.[7] On reflection it appears that nothing is left with which we can rightly describe
the nonmental space-filling world except nonsensuous concepts like
figure, magnitude, and motion.

When sensuous distinctions are no longer thought to distinguish different regions of space, we are reduced to a defoliated universe of moving particles having geometrical features only. To Descartes this seems a great intellectual advantage and a trustworthy sign
of the correctness of his epistemology. In fact, it would be better to

say that his epistemology is motivated in major part by his scientific objectives. He intends to filter away the sensuous so that a mathematically suitable subject matter will be left for scientific theory. His epistemology provides just the interpretation of reality needed by Descartes and others who were convinced that scientific understanding becomes possible only when we manage to delete the unmanageable, subjective, sensuous aspect of things and to characterize the subject matter of science exclusively in the vocabulary of abstract mathematics. In the argument of Descartes' *Meditations* and in the *Principles of Philosophy* the proof for the existence of an external world of material things is simply a proof that the abstract mathematical and geometrical truths, which we are able to appreciate in pure thought, do have a subject matter outside of our thought which they fit and describe. This subject matter is *res extensa*, that is, space, as an existing manifold or entity.

Descartes does not confine his purification of our conception of the material world to the purge of sensuous characteristics. The prevailing scholastic-Aristotelian tradition was dominated by biological and psychological paradigms for the explanation of change. Within this tradition, as Descartes read it, the understanding of physical phenomena involved projecting into the physical realm various soul-like agencies and, in particular, the substantial forms of the scholastics. Descartes' reduction of physics to geometry means the elimination of this psychologism and teleological thinking from the scientific explanation of the motions of bodies. The material universe which survives the elimination of both the sensuous surface and the inner determinants of motion is Descartes' plenum of indefinitely subdivisible particles, all of whose motions are determined by collisions that conserve an initial sum of motion given to the system at the beginning of things by God.[8] Matter itself contains no principle of action nor disposition to move or not to move. All concepts of determinants of motions residing in material things are eliminated in Descartes' rejection of the animism of the scholastic-Aristotelian tradition.[9]

At a level near common sense we can represent the shortcomings of the Cartesian identification of space and matter and the resulting purely geometrical physics as follows. A theory in physical science has to provide concepts with the help of which we are able to see what happens as the instantiation of clear regularities. Motions observed in ordinary experience are usually too complicated for analysis, but at

least for the scientific explanation of motion, rules should be formulable that cover very simple artificial or imaginary ideal cases.
Descartes himself thinks of the obligation of scientific theory in this
way, and he formulates seven laws of which ideal cases of impacts of
particles are supposed to be the instances.[10] If such laws are satisfactory, they will enable us to predict what will happen when situations
fitting the conditions specified (here the specification of simple collisions) are realized. This elementary reflection is usually summed up
by saying that a scientific theory generates predictions when initial
conditions are satisfied. Now Leibniz's critique of Descartes' physics
can be stated as the thought that no such predictive validity is accessible to a physics framed with Descartes' attenuated concepts. Using
a priori arguments, Leibniz is able to show that the specific laws
Descartes presents are incoherent and could not possibly be empirically adequate.[11] But the larger point is that no laws based on Descartes' concepts can succeed. Leibniz sees this permanent inadequacy
in the fact that Descartes has no conceptual means for distinguishing
between instantaneous motion and instantaneous rest.[12]

Suppose we are going to predict the future position of bodies
in the solar system. In order to do this we need rules expressing the
patterns of motion which they instantiate, and we need initial conditions in the form of specifications of the positions, velocities, and ac-
celerations of the various heavenly bodies at some particular time.
But geometrical concepts only yield determinations of position at a
particular time, that is, at an instant. Descartes' purification of the
concept of matter has left him nothing with which to express the difference between a moving body and a stationary body at one moment, and he has no reason for thinking that there is any *intrinsic*
difference. The obstacle to predictive success within Descartes' conceptual scheme can now be put very simply. Initial conditions that
characterize material things at one moment of time accessible to
Cartesian physics will give the positions of particles only. But the future development of a system of bodies depends upon velocity and
acceleration, and not merely on position. So the Cartesian scientist
will inevitably find different developments arising out of what he sees
as identical conditions. If the conditions are identical, however, the
very idea of scientific regularity requires identical predictions. So
predictive success cannot be forthcoming. Ad hoc efforts to generate
predictions conformable to experience must result in laws which are

arbitrary and incoherent, as Leibniz finds that the Cartesian laws of impact are in fact.

The characterizations that successfully distinguish motion and rest at an instant are just those that are accessible to the infinite mathematical methods of the calculus which Leibniz himself developed. Leibniz thinks of Descartes' "matter" as *incomplete*. It is a mistake to think that merely space-filling stuff could constitute a substance.[13] In this there is the influence of Aristotelian conceptions of matter and form which Leibniz does not repudiate. Neither matter nor form, by itself, can constitute an existing thing. But Leibniz's view is also determined by his understanding of the irreducible status of force in physics. In his thinking, momentary material existence is an abstraction from the reality of temporally extended things. Substances are not constituted of densely laminated temporal slices which are their constituent realities as the cards are the constituents of the deck. Substances, rather, correspond to functions with values extended in time. Thus, the monad contains all its temporal states as the values of a function are contained in the law *which is* the function itself. The fundamental metaphysical description of the world must be in terms of such functions. Such a description can never be reached by aggregating consecutive momentary distributions of merely space-filling stuff. In contrast, time does not enter into Descartes' characterization of *res extensa* at all.[14] So in Cartesian physics moving bodies have to be constructed out of momentary stationary bodies.

Descartes did attempt to present a theory of motion in his laws of impact. Furthermore, his scientific writings present an enormous number of explanations of various phenomena most of which are now merely picturesque relics. Some of his explanations are reasonable and correct. On the whole, however, it seems to me that Descartes was never entirely clear about the appropriate expectations for scientific explanation, once the field had been cleared by his elimination of both sensuous qualities and occult inner determinants of change.

No one emphasized the role of mathematics in science more than Descartes. Yet he seems to have had very little confidence in the possibility of really detailed mathematical explanations of real events, and he did not foresee anything like the kind of success mathematical physics was to attain, so soon after his lifetime, in the work of Newton. Sometimes Descartes writes as though the chief intellectual job of science is *completed* when substantial forms and teleological explanations have been dropped, so that the material world can be understood to be a matter of moving and colliding particles.

The explanations that Descartes actually gives of particular phenomena are usually very much like ad hoc scholastic explanations in their ambitions and their explanatory horizons, however unlike scholastic explanations they are in content. Like the scholastics, Descartes offers imaginative stories that are plainly without predictive force or intent. They are broad ways of *seeing* the phenomenon in question within the framework of a geometrical particle universe.

In a remarkable passage Descartes says that since he came to appreciate the real character of physical reality, that is, that it is a spatial manifold of particles, and since he came to appreciate the nature of physical events, that is, that they are collisions of particles, he has found that he can solve any problem of science that is proposed or that occurs to him in a very short time.[15] This is not so much an outrageous boast as it is an illuminating indication of what Descartes expects from explanation in physics. The solutions to problems which he can produce so promptly are obviously merely broad hypotheses providing, with the help of humble empirical analogies, a way of seeing this or that event as a particular form of particle motion. So the phenomenon of planetary motion is *explained* when we see that an ocean of particles might carry suns and planets in vortices, as a whirling eddy of water carries a leaf in a closed path. Magnetic phenomena are *explained* by the imaginative hypothesis, again based on the observable world of everyday objects, that there are screw-shaped pores in bodies, which impede but do not prevent the passage of screw-shaped particles, just as the threaded nut impedes but does not prevent the passage of the threaded bolt. Combustion is explained to the same limited degree as the progressive destabilization of the structure of a burning object by a storm of fast-moving particles. And the refraction of light is supposed to be intelligible on the model of tennis balls deflected from their path when they encounter the light resistance of a thin veil. In sum, explanation does not go beyond the provision of a hypothesis that makes it reasonable that the phenomenon in question is observed even though the world is just a plenum of moving particles. Particular explanations rely on a rough empirical analogy to show how such particle collisions could constitute the phenomenon in question. It is only such hypotheses, dependent upon empirical analogy, that Descartes was able to think of in a short time, and that is what he means by "solving" the problems that come to his attention. Given this conception of explanation, it is quite understandable that Cartesian physics should tolerate divergent developments from initial conditions that are identical when described in the terms that Cartesian science permits.

Near the end of the *Principles of Philosophy* Descartes quite explicitly expresses his conception of the irreducibly conjectural character of theoretical explanations. He recognizes that accounts in terms of particle motions involve positing events (the particular particle motions and collisions) which are not accessible to the senses. Then in Principle CCIV of part four Descartes tells us:

> That touching the things which our senses do not perceive, it is sufficient to explain what the possibilities are about the nature of their existence, though perhaps they are not what we describe them to be (and this is all that Aristotle has tried to do).[16]

In the following passages Descartes says that we would not find his individual explanations compelling if we considered them independently of one another. The real support for his system is that so many explanations are generated from so few ideas (namely, those that go into the scheme of a plenum of particles), yielding a simple coherent picture of the world.[17]

If we look at Leibniz's critique in the context of Descartes' repudiation of teleology and his reduction of nature to a wholly mechanical system of particles in motion, we find that Leibniz urges the rehabilitation of teleology and is prepared to reinstate the Aristotelian biological paradigm for all substances complete with the *entelechies* and substantial forms that were so deliberately expunged from the physical world in Descartes' thought. This must appear to us as a considerable step backward. A number of Leibniz's prominent excesses such as his panpsychism, his denial of the reality of death, his theoretical assimilation of all causes of change to a more-or-less mental "appetition," and his ubiquitous teleology are all of them regressions in comparison with the conceptual restraint achieved by Descartes. Leibniz only manages to preserve any plausible and recognizably scientific perspective at all by segregating teleological and mechanical explanations and holding that everything that happens in the physical world can be explained mechanically, without invoking the agency of any entelechy or deploying any teleological pattern of

explanation.[18] Teleological thinking is conveniently allocated to a
higher metaphysical level. Teleological understanding, in the form,
for example, of least action principles, guides our discovery of mechanical laws without introducing a teleological aspect into those laws
themselves. Leibniz says, for example, that the thought that light
always takes the shortest path operates essentially in the understanding that led to the discovery of Snell's law.[19]

I do not want to give the impression that Leibniz's defense of
teleology is entirely inappropriate. Leibniz did not simply slump
back into already discredited styles of thought. On the contrary, his
insistence that reason-giving explanation must be reconciled with a
mechanical universe and his idea that the two patterns of explanation
operate at different levels embody important truths.

2. Nature Itself

Attempting to delete spurious psychologism and teleology, Descartes eliminates all activity from the material world and paves the
way for an Occasionalist philosophy in which God is directly responsible for each thing that happens. The ultimate passivity of material
substance is expressed in Descartes' thought that matter does not
even contain any principle sufficient for its own continued existence
into the next instant of time. All temporal continuity of existence
depends on God's continual recreation of things.[20] How could a particle, unable to struggle through a second of continued existence
without help from God, have any continued and independent effect
on things other than itself? Furthermore, the Cartesian exclusion of
every means for distinguishing one region of space (which is matter)
from another undercuts the very idea of occurrences in the material
world. At each moment every region of space or matter exactly resembles every other region. It follows that at every moment the structure of the whole of space or matter is exactly what it is at every other
moment. The universe is at every moment a plenum of indefinitely
divisible particles. Then anything that happens will leave things exactly as they were: a plenum of indefinitely divisible particles.[21] If,
somehow, we could attach meaning to motion in this universe, we
would still be unable to make sense of Descartes' idea that God has
caused an initial motion of particles and ordained the subsequent

conservation of that motion. For Descartes' conceptual parsimony leaves us no way to grasp how it is that motion might continue without the continued action of God.

At first impression we are apt to think that Descartes can reasonably propose that God has created an essentially inert, wholly passive, and motionless universe, which he then sets in motion at the beginning of time. We will have in mind analogies like the initial winding of a motionless clock which creates a motion that endures in the clock without our continual intervention. Leibniz sees that this understanding of motion in nature cannot survive close inspection if we are thinking in terms of Descartes' physical concepts. Clocks can be wound so that they will run continuously precisely because of the nongeometrical features of bodily existence on which Leibniz insists. The compression of the mainspring of the clock represents a force, an inner determinant of future motion. This intrinsic potential cannot be represented as a particular arrangement of particles. Within Descartes' framework of ideas the compression of the spring would bode nothing for future motion. A mere arrangement of space-filling particles will not induce any further changes. A further rearrangement will need an external cause. Ultimately, God will have to move the hands of the clock himself. This is the prospect for "the new philosophy which maintains the inertness and deadness of things."[22]

Leibniz mounts such criticisms in his 1698 essay "On Nature Itself."[23] If we are to imagine that God has arranged things to conserve the initial motion that he has caused in matter, we must suppose that he has imparted to material a foundation for continued motion that is intrinsic to that reality.

> For since this command [calling for conservation of motion after the initial motion was imparted] . . . no longer exists at present, it can accomplish nothing unless it has left some subsistent effect behind which has lasted and operated until now, and whoever thinks otherwise renounces any distinct explanation of things, if I am any judge, for if that which is remote in time and space can operate here and now without any intermediary, anything can be said to follow from anything else with equal right.[24]

and

> . . . if things have been so formed by the command that they are made capable of fulfilling the will of him who commanded them,

> then it must be granted that there is certain efficacy residing in things, a form or force such as we usually designate by the name of nature, from which the series of phenomena follows according to the prescription of the first command.[25]

In other words, no matter what role we assign to God, we must impute active powers to nature if we are to formulate intelligible explanations.

"On Nature Itself" is Leibniz's contribution to a German debate occasioned by Robert Boyle's contention that appeals to "Nature" should be deleted from science.[26] For Boyle the repudiation of Nature meant the rejection of scholasticism and scholastic forms. In this Boyle is following Descartes. For the specious concept "Nature" Boyle wants to substitute "mechanism" as the foundation of all explanations in the material world. The German Cartesian point of view supported Boyle's claim and reasserted the essential passivity of material substance.[27]

Leibniz does not argue against Boyle's mechanism, nor does he claim *here* that mechanical explanations ought to be supplemented by teleological explanations, though this is certainly his view. In this context it is the Cartesian concept of mechanical explanation that Leibniz finds defective as a consequence of the limitations of Descartes' concept of material substance.[28] Descartes tries to exclude ad hoc psychologism and teleology.[29] But the resulting conceptual platform is so feeble that no explanations at all can be mounted on it. Then God's ad hoc intervention is required at every point. If that is so, then it turns out that the only explanatory pattern that finds any application in Descartes' material world will be the teleological pattern of intended purposeful behavior. God causes each and every thing that happens for his good reasons. Then all explanations are psychologistic, the very thing Descartes sought to eliminate completely. Although Leibniz is rightly known as the defender of teleology, his insistence here that activity be ascribed to *nature itself* is founded on the claim that, failing an active nature, each and every mechanical event in the universe would have to be understood as an intended action on the part of God.

Perhaps the most interesting idea of "On Nature Itself" is Leibniz's thought that we should bring under a single philosophical perspective both the mechanical events studied and explained by

physicists and the free actions of men. Leibniz sees that the independence of the human will and the independence of mechanical
forces from God's actions are parallel requirements if we are to
understand human responsibility and the motions of bodies respectively. The passivity of created substance finds expression in the
Cartesian doctrine "that things do not act but that God acts in the
presence of things and according to the fitness of things." Natural application of this to the mental realm of thinking and willing would
mean reassignment of the cause of the sequence of our thoughts and
desires and resolutions from us to God. The Occasionalists such as
Malebranche who seem to espouse such a view have not really
established it and do not appreciate its destructive implications. We
must believe in our own spontaneity.

> To doubt this would be to deny human freedom and to thrust the
> cause of evil back into God, but also to contradict the testimony of
> our internal experience and consciousness by which we feel that what
> these opponents have transferred to God without even the appearance
> of reason belongs to ourselves.[30]

Furthermore, the very idea of an *independent substance* is wrapped
up with action so that were actions all assigned to God,

> God would be the nature and substance of all things—a doctrine of
> most evil repute, which a writer who was subtle indeed but irreligious,
> in recent years imposed upon the world, or at least revived.[31]

Equally appropriate to mechanical causality and free action,
these ideas show us what is best in Leibniz's thought about teleology
without the encumbering metaphysics and theology with which his
insights are ordinarily accompanied.

What is at stake in the dispute over active powers as far as
mechanical explanation is concerned? Consider a simple example.
The wind blows dead leaves from the branches of trees in the
autumn. Leibniz's intuition is that our science must offer a mechanical understanding that really succeeds in attributing the detachment
of the leaves to the force of the wind. Of course, Leibniz thinks that
God has arranged the laws of nature and that these laws are as contingent as the particular events that obey them.[32] But to say that is
not to say that God really removes each leaf, that God twirls it in the
air for a while, and that God then deposits it on the ground. On the

contrary, things are so ordered that the wind removes the leaves, and no action of God's is present or required. To assume that God knows just how each leaf will move is to assert the infinity of his understanding but not the ubiquity of his will. To think otherwise is to destroy the idea of "laws of nature" and to replace them with mere generalizations the truth of which is only a consequence of the consistency of God's actions. Therefore, our mechanical conceptions must be rich enough to capture causal action in relationships that obtain between natural events. Descartes has produced a physics that is too weak for this job.

Turning to voluntary human behavior, Leibniz finds the same pattern in a setting of very different philosophical issues. When we raise the question which preoccupied Leibniz throughout his career, that is, the question of God's responsibility for the failings and evils of human conduct, we are asking whether or not human beings are truly active in the world. Of course, Leibniz thinks that men are created by God and that in his creation God fully appreciates the powers, limitations, and liabilities of his creatures. Moreover, being omniscient, he knows exactly what circumstances they will face and how they will act. This much is parallel to the fact that God makes the things of the material world and the laws of nature, and he knows in advance just what will happen. But to say that men have any powers at all implies that when those powers are exercised, it is men who act and not God. When I vote, it is not God who casts a ballot, any more than it is God that tears the leaf from the wind-whipped branch. No doubt we would not hold a man responsible for his actions if he were a mechanism like a clock or if his "acts" were caused by the wind. So there is more to responsibility and free agency than independence of God. In "On Nature Itself," however, Leibniz sees the common ground of mechanism and volition. In understanding action we have to make fundamental explanatory appeal to the human agent. In understanding mechanical events we must make fundamental appeal to physical determinants of change. The creativity of God no more constrains physical forces than it does human actions.

This line of thought also clarifies Leibniz's often-expressed view that there is a mechanical explanation for everything that happens in the world while, at the same time, teleological explanations have their own validity within the same world of events.[33] The physical world is not a continuous sequence of miracles, as it would be if active

powers were excluded from nature. The physical world is ordered by
the intentions and creativity of God. But to say that is to say that he
has created a mechanically functioning system wherein what happens
is explained by physical causes for motions and not by the will of
God.

The wisdom of this conception is partially concealed from us by
the theological trappings of Leibniz's customary discussions. It becomes correspondingly clearer when we translate the conceptual relationships envisioned by Leibniz back to the level of human purposeful action in a mechanical world. What is required for the simplest
self-consciously purposive action by a human agent? Suppose, for example, a man drives a nail into a wall in order to hang a picture. The
format that Leibniz proposes urges us not to confuse the aptness of
the teleological explanation, "He put the nail into the wall in order
to hang the picture," with a mechanical explanation of the motion
of the nail: "The force imparted by collisions with the hammerhead
caused the relatively rigid nail to penetrate the relatively fixed wall."
We should not think that the mechanical explanation competes with
or rules out accounts that cite purposes and reasons. Thus, Leibniz
says that there is a mechanical explanation for all motions. The mechanical explanation is not merely *compatible* with a reason-giving
explanation. Leibniz is asserting that a mechanical explanation is *required* if the reason-giving explanation is to be intelligible. We could
not act as we do, when we want pictures hung, were it not for the
fact that nails are *mechanically caused* to move by collisions with
hammerheads. Leibniz appeals to a notion of levels of explanation,
saying that there are mechanical explanations for everything which
are not teleological, and that there are also teleological explanations,
applicable to the same reality, which are correct explanations.

Leibniz thus stands against all reductive programs that would
try to convert teleological explanations into mechanical explanations.
Such a reduction is the common aspiration of Hobbes's conception
of the material embodiment of deliberation and will, of Descartes'
theory of deflections of particles in the pineal gland, and of contemporary mind-brain materialism applied to action and motivation.[34] In
Leibniz's view mechanical causes are organized as they are as a consequence of God's intentions. But it is physical forces that explain what
happens mechanically, and God's intentions are not physical forces.
The same pattern of relationships holds for human purpose-fulfilling

actions. Human intentions have a secure explanatory role. But this
never removes the need for a mechanical explanation for the motions
of things. Human intentions are not mechanical causes any more
than divine intentions are mechanical causes.

In his theological presentations we can all understand with Leibniz, although perhaps few of us will agree with him, the thought that
the laws of nature are instituted by God in the course of bringing into
existence the kind of world he wants. But in understanding just this
much Leibniz shows that we must be envisioning two kinds of explanation which are correlative and not in conflict with one another.
We are supposing that God sets up the world and its laws with a purpose and to fulfill his plans and intentions. This is a reason-giving explanation belonging to the general teleological pattern. But this idea
would not be intelligible at all, and explanations would collapse into
the assertion of sequences of miracles, if we did not *also* suppose that
the arrangements God makes give scope to another very different
kind of explanation, namely, the mechanical explanations of the motions of things that appeal to physical powers and forces in nature
rather than God. In the absence of an explanatory role for natural
forces, appeals to God's ordinances reduce to the Occasionalist's at-
tribution of each and every event to the direct intervention of God's
will. Following the same pattern, while deleting the theological context, we can understand a purpose-oriented explanation of human
behavior, but we would not be able to understand it, for it would
mean nothing if it were supposed to rule out or to compete with
mechanical explanation of what happens. If it were supposed to rule
out a mechanical account, a reason-giving explanation would have to
assert that the will moves objects directly. But we neither understand
nor have any use for this efficacy of the will. We do understand that
someone has arranged matters to realize his objective just insofar as
we also understand that there are mechanical causal relations which
he has foreseen and wittingly exploited in his action. If we thought
that teleology eliminates mechanism, we would convert every purposeful act into a man-made miracle.

The idea of purposive action in a mechanical world has seemed
to many philosophers to require a gap in the mechanical order of
things through which the will can find expression in what happens.
Leibniz's insight here shows us that the envisioned gap could serve no

useful purpose. A motion that is not mechanically explicable would not be graspable as a purposeful act, but, instead, this uncaused motion would belong to the realm of the miraculous, as though our every action involved a kind of levitation.

We tend to credit the question "How can my reasons have anything to do with what happens if there are mechanical causes for all motions?" This natural-sounding complaint implies that my reasons could be relevant if only some events were not determined by any mechanical cause. Then those things at least might be determined by "my reasons." But this line of thought is hopeless. If my reasons could produce some motion in things, this will be either an unintelligible miracle and, thus, no explanation, or "my reasons" will just be an expression for some further mechanical cause, as both seventeenth-century and twentieth-century reductions will have it. But if appeal to reasons is actually only appeal to mechanical causes, then purposes, objectives, that is, true reasons, drop out altogether, and explanation operates merely by appeal to sufficient prior determinants of motion.

Without the cloud of dust that philosophical reflection about causality and freedom inevitably raises, I do not think we would find an apparent inconsistency or any other problem in the fact that the force of hammer blows moves a nail, and that I, at the same time, claim to have a reason for its being in the wall. Only a philosopher would ever think that the correctness of the reason-giving account implies that I must have moved something "with my will," so that either my will is also a physical cause or the mind can mysteriously intervene in the physical order and violate conservation laws in the process. In Leibniz's thinking the choice between these unpromising options is not forced upon us. Teleology is not mechanism, and it does not presuppose a gap in the mechanical order. Quite the reverse is the case. Leibniz shows that if the relevant motions are not explicable mechanically, the teleological explanations will not get any explaining done. This is the most profound message of the understanding of activity and explanation presented in "On Nature Itself."

Our thinking about action is often beset by another speculative temptation. We are willing to allow that the mechanical force of hammer blows surely accounts for the motion of the nail head. But then we simply want to look further back in the physical and physiological chain of events for the point at which appeal to reasons and purposes finds its real footing. Of course, I did not simply will the hammer to move any more than I simply willed the nail into the wall. I picked up the hammer, and that means, *inter alia*, that forces applied to the hammer by my hand explain its motion. Could it be that the will only produces its own nonmechanical effects when applied to parts of my own body? This would enable me to orchestrate the mechanical relationships of things in the world beyond my body so as to achieve desired objectives. This attractive thought comes to a dead end with the appreciation that the motions of bodily parts are not in any relevant way different from the motions of external objects. Conservation laws alone mean that there must be mechanical explanations for motions of protoplasm as well as for motions of rocks. There are known physiological-mechanical (speaking loosely) explanations for the motions of my hand, of my muscles, and, no doubt, there are as yet undiscovered explanations for all the subtle electrochemical goings-on within the muscles, the nerves, and the brain. Should we not suppose that my control of my body, to the extent that I have such control, presupposes and exploits just these mechanical relationships? To think otherwise will be merely to project the miracle of *willed motions* into some physiological recess where our scientific understanding is presently incomplete and does not as yet, therefore, make such willing as unintelligible as the idea of willing a hammer to move. Willing things to change and move is really a concept with no more application within the body than without. And voluntarily moving things that we can move does not imply that no mechanical account of their motion is correct.[35] Leibniz's view that purpose explanations do not replace or conflict with mechanical explanations appears to be the only defensible understanding.

This conclusion does not mean that Leibniz provides any philosophical analysis that removes the feeling of incompatibility that surrounds the issue of freedom and causality. The understanding of teleological explanation and its relation to efficient causality or mechanism remains to be achieved.[36] Leibniz's view of the distinctness and the interdependence of these explanatory patterns is both subtler and more promising than many approaches that are still defended. This Leibnizian view, as I have tried to show, is independent of theological commitments and of Leibniz's too-bold opinion that there is a teleological explanation for everything that happens.

3. Analyticity

All the events and actions that are explained either mechanically or teleologically are contingent according to Leibniz. True propositions asserting such occurrences are contingent truths. By a contingent truth Leibniz means a truth of which the denial expresses something *possible* and is not inconceivable or contradictory. I want to emphasize Leibniz's assertion of the contingency of all of these subject matters, because there is an interpretation of his thought, and it is the dominant interpretation now, according to which he does not really think that any of these matters are contingent. On this, the dominant understanding of Leibniz, he takes all truths to be *analytic* truths, and, as everyone agrees, no analytic truth can be contingent. It is an obvious and essential feature of analytic truths that their denials are contradictory. So in saying that Leibniz thinks that all truths are analytic, supporters of this interpretation assert that he cannot really distinguish between the class of truths whose denials are contradictions and any other class of truths whatsoever. So his real opinion is supposed to be that there are no contingent truths at all and that everything true is necessarily true.

In considering this contention we have, first, to note that *there is a sense* in which all these contingent truths are also necessary. They are "hypothetically necessary" in Leibniz's customary terminology.[37] By this he means that there is a coercive reason why this event or action occurs rather than some alternative to it. Thus, given the laws of nature and the relevant circumstances preceding a mechanically caused event, that event must follow. This is entailed by the presumed universality of natural laws. Leibniz recognizes that the conditional statement that expresses hypothetical necessity is itself logically necessary, or, as he expresses it, *metaphysically* necessary and *absolutely* necessary. It is a feature of any absolutely or logically necessary truth that its denial is a contradictory statement. Therefore, in saying that an event is hypothetically necessary Leibniz is associating that event with a conditional statement that is absolutely necessary.

This is not an extreme view of Leibniz's, nor one that we should think of as expressing a characteristically rationalist perspective. An ideally simple schema can bring out the points in a way that makes them noncontroversial, or nearly so. Suppose that the only law relevant to the occurrence of the event E is the simple conditional: "If circumstance C obtains, then event E follows." E is shown to be hypothetically necessary by adverting to this law together with the fact that the circumstance C did obtain in the actual context of the occurrence of E. This can be summed up in the logically necessary conditional:

> If it is the case that the law "if circumstance C, then event E" holds; and if circumstance C does obtain, then event E follows.

All those philosophers of science who envision a deductive relationship between scientific laws, initial conditions, and statements asserting the occurrence of explained events are committed to this Leibnizean viewpoint. Most empiricists adopt this view. That the relationship of the *explanans* to the *explanandum* is deductive is just another way of saying that propositions with the above form, and those with much more complicated laws and instantiating conditions, are logically true. Leibniz once asserted, "As for eternal truths, we must observe that at bottom they are all conditional, and say, in fact, such a thing posited, such another thing is."[38]

The necessity of conditional statements connecting laws and conditions with explained events is all that Leibniz means by "hypothetical necessity" in the sphere of mechanical explanation. Such hypothetical necessity leaves open the possibility that some other event might have occurred, rather than the actual event, had the laws and initial conditions been different. For factual circumstances, and the laws of nature, are themselves contingent according to Leibniz.[39] Thus, the denial of the occurrence of a hypothetically necessary event is not contradictory.

Parallel points are to be made in understanding Leibniz's conception of the contingency of free actions. Leibniz consistently rejects what he calls "the freedom of indifference." By this he means to exclude choices which are entirely arbitrary and motivated by nothing but the disposition to choose. Freedom, for Leibniz, never eliminates the need for a reason for what is done which distinguishes it in some intelligible way from all alternative actions and makes clear why it was chosen over alternatives. To suppose that a man could actually make a random or arbitrary choice between alternatives would be to allow an element of unintelligibility into our idea of reality. A single inexplicable node in the causal network of things would infect the whole scheme of an explicable world.

The vulnerability of this conception is revealed in exchanges with Samuel Clarke, who points out, among other things, that Leibniz must rule against the very possibility that God, or a man, could ever be faced with equally desirable means to some desired end.[40] In the manner of the problem of Buridan's ass, the value-equivalence of the means would prevent selecting either of them, on Leibniz's principles, no matter how urgently desired the end.

In spite of such penetrating criticisms, we should bear in mind that the idea that everything that happens is explicable is not merely a rationalist dogma. It seems to be a presumption of all investigations of things, one that is extremely difficult to set aside.

For better or worse, Leibniz's view is that an agent must always have a definite reason for choosing the action he does perform from the alternative courses available to him. The reason is coercive in the sense that once an agent determines what course he prefers, which Leibniz expresses as "what course appears best to him," he will inevitably adopt that course. He likes to compare deliberation with weighing things in a balance. The very idea that a man could act in the absence of a determining reason is, for Leibniz, like the idea that a balance might incline to one side although there is no greater weight in that side than in the other.[41]

The principle "men always choose the course that appears best to them," is the analog of a scientific law, and the particular assessment preceding an action will be the analog of prior circumstances. Again, conditionals of the following type can be formed:

> If a man is choosing for the best, and if A appears better than any other option that he recognizes, then he will do A.

This pattern fits the actions of God as well as of finite agents, with the difference that God's infinite power enforces his choice and to God's infinite wisdom what appears best is best.[42] In both the divine and the human case the absolute necessity of conditional statements of this form never means that other actions could not possibly have been performed. On the contrary, it is an ineliminable part of the idea of action that all of the alternative actions could be performed by the agent. This is the minimum meaning of calling them alternative courses of action. The question of choice only arises on the irreducible assumption that an agent could do more than one thing. Only then does the question of preference, the best, the apparent best, and assessment become relevant. Therefore, actions themselves, although hypothetically necessary, are never absolutely necessary. Other preferences and principles of action might have issued in other actions. The denial that a particular action was done is never a contradiction.

The contingency of mechanically explicable motions and the contingency of motivated actions is essential to Leibniz's thinking about these matters. If it were absolutely impossible for a particular motion not to occur, if its nonoccurrence were inconceivable and contradictory, and the assertion of its occurrence, thus, metaphysically necessary, then talk about mechanical causes would be as inappropriate in physics as it is in geometry. If a man's behavior were absolutely necessary, the desirability of an action would be as irrelevant as the desirability of a theorem in pure mathematics. Then, as Leibniz says, it would be as easy to be a prophet as to be a geometer.[43] Like geometrical proofs, scientific explanations and explanations of actions can be expressed in deductive arguments. The crucial difference is that the premises of mathematical deductions are themselves necessary truths, while the premises from which actions and events can be deduced are contingent.

Apart from God, the existence of all material things and all human agents is contingent. Thus all statements that describe finite existences and say what happens to them and what they do are contingent truths if they are true statements.[44] Plainly all statements about mechanically caused events involving bodies and all statements about the free actions of human agents will fall into the class of contingent statements.

The popular idea that Leibniz makes all truths analytic[45] is certainly wrong. It flies in the face of his frequent and careful statements on these issues. It makes nonsense of his most important views and of his philosophy as a whole. It imputes logical inconsistencies to a great logician that are so obvious that no beginning student could miss them. There is just no question of testing this proposed understanding of Leibniz against his writings in order to see whether it may be an adequate or an unavoidable expression of his real opinion. The only interesting question is how it can have happened that this reading has managed to gain, not merely currency, but ascendancy in the views of so many who study Leibniz's philosophy.

First, we need a rough review of the concept of analytic truth that is used in this bad interpretation of Leibniz. The roughness of our treatment here intentionally avoids twentieth-century controver-

sies over analyticity[46] and avoids all of the niceties concerning logical
form that would require attention in a scrupulous discussion of analyticity per se. In particular, we shall largely ignore the fact that all
propositions are not of subject-predicate form, as Leibniz himself
largely ignores it. None of these matters have any relevance to the
claim that Leibniz thought that all truths are analytic. An exposition
of analyticity that fits Leibniz's expressed views about truth and that
makes sense in the context of examples of truths like Leibniz's examples will suffice for our purposes.

Propositions are *analytic* whose truth depends upon and only
upon the meaning of the terms they contain. Generally the meanings
of terms are complex. In order to make meanings fully explicit, refor-
mulation of sentences is generally required. Such reformulations
substitute something like definitions for terms that have complex
meanings. In the case of analytic propositions this *analysis via* articulation of meanings ultimately makes the truth evident, displaying
it, for example, as resting on an identity whose denial would be
patently contradictory.

In an illustration that has become standard in modern discussions, the articulated meaning or definition "things that are both
men and unmarried" replaces the complex term "bachelors" in
analyzing the proposition.

(1) All bachelors are unmarried,

yielding,

(2) All things that are both men and unmarried are unmarried,

which rests on the identity

(3) What is unmarried is unmarried,

in the sense that to say that (2) is false is to assert that something is
both unmarried and not unmarried, which denies (3) and is, therefore, contradictory.[47]

Leibniz never uses the word "analytic" in this sense. As everyone
knows, the word "analytic" was first given the sense just sketched by
Kant. At the same time, Leibniz certainly does say that there are
truths which reduce to or rest on identities. He also often points out
that this foundation of such truths is not always evident and that it
requires analysis of the terms of a proposition to display the underly-

ing identity.[48] Perhaps his thinking in such passages is so close to our concept of analyticity that we can properly say that he is talking about the analyticity of propositions in our sense, although he does not use the word as we do. But just this much, far from showing that Leibniz takes *all* truths to be analytic, seems to establish the opposite. For Leibniz always very clearly distinguishes between truths that rely on the law of contradiction from *other* truths which need a further foundation and whose denials are possible and not at all contradictory. The consistency of Leibniz's distinction on this point is one of the reasons for which it is odd that many readers are satisfied to say that he makes all truths analytic.[49] The following is a particularly clear statement of Leibniz's; it is one of a number of statements with similar force:

> All existences excepting only the existence of God are contingent. The reason why something contingent exists [rather than another thing] is not to be sought in its definition [alone]. . . . Since there are infinite possibilities which, nonetheless, do not exist, the reason why this rather than that does exist ought not to be sought from definitions, otherwise not existing would imply a contradiction, and other things would not be possible.[50]

It is worth noting that, in Kant's initiating discussions and in all philosophical usage since Kant, "analytic" is essentially a contrastive concept, and the point of calling a proposition analytic is not fully intelligible without the correlative concept of "synthetic" propositions. Neither Kant nor any post-Kantian philosopher who uses the concepts analytic and synthetic has said that all truths are analytic. The contrast is always the basis for a dichotomous classification of truths. There are philosophical controversies concerning the viability of the analytic-synthetic distinction altogether, though philosophers do, for the most part, accept the distinction.[51] There are none who accept the distinction and then find that all true propositions fall into just one of the two available classes.

It is this extravagant opinion, that no philosopher would dream of holding himself, that is so commonly assigned to Leibniz. This reading of Leibniz requires, then, that we retrospectively apply to his thought an essentially contrastive concept that was introduced long after his death by Kant, and at the same time it requires us to suppose that Leibniz uses this contrastive concept noncontrastively and that he puts all truths on one side, though no other philosopher would do that. Once this interpretation is introduced, it turns out to be incompatible with almost everything that Leibniz said. This circumstance, instead of leading to the prompt rejection of the interpretation, or even to suspicions about it, has spawned various ingenious efforts to deal with Leibniz's inconsistencies, namely, those that the interpretation itself creates. The most outrageous plan for resolving these created difficulties is surely Russell's. Russell supposes that though Leibniz says that there are contingent truths, he does not *believe* that there are any, since Leibniz really thinks that all truths are analytic and, therefore, necessary. Russell finds that Leibniz was a fellow of poor character, lacking "moral elevation",[52] so he basely concealed his true views after discovering that they did not please Antoine Arnauld in 1686.[53] If Russell were right, we should have to think that Leibniz went on, after 1686, to write huge books and endless letters and articles, and thousands of fragments that no one saw but himself, in all of which he insincerely asserted that there are contingent truths only because he thought that this opinion would be more appealing to his royal patrons and religious authorities than his real belief that everything is necessary.

Other critics have not followed Russell in these accusations, but neither have they rejected the idea that for Leibniz all truths are analytic. Why not? One obvious reason hinges on the word "contains." Leibniz states in many places that if any proposition is true, then the predicate is *contained* in the subject of that proposition, or the subject *contains* the predicate. Furthermore, it is quite possible that Kant had in mind just this Leibnizean use of "contains" when he introduced the distinction between analytic and synthetic truths by saying that the predicate is contained in the subject of analytic truths, while it is not contained in the subject of synthetic truths which add something, as Kant puts it, that is not already thought in the subject concept. So we have two suggestive facts: first, Leibniz said that in all truths the predicate is contained in the subject, and, second, Kant said that if the predicate is contained in the subject, you have an analytic truth. Combining these we can get: Leibniz finds that all truths are analytic.

But this requires the additional premise that Leibniz and Kant mean the same thing when they speak of the predicate being contained in the subject of a proposition. How can that possibly be when

Leibniz makes it clear, again and again, that his "containment of the predicate in the subject" is compatible with the contingent status of a proposition? In the essay "On Necessary and Contingent Truths" Leibniz says

> Assertions are true of which the predicate is in the subject, so that in all true affirmative propositions, whether necessary or contingent, universal or singular, the notion of the predicate is *contained in some way* in the notion of the subject.[54]

Again, this citation is selected from a number of discussions which have the same force. I have added the emphasis "contained in some way" (*aliquo modo continetur*). What are the different ways in which the predicate might be contained? Leibniz clearly envisions two possibilities. In the case of necessary truths containment of the predicate in the subject is a matter of meaning, that is, containment is shown "ex definitione" or "per analysin terminorum." Only in these cases is the reason for the containment a "necessitating reason."[55] In the case of contingent propositions Leibniz says that there is no necessitating reason but only an "inclining reason" for the presence of the predicate in the notion of the subject.[56] Again, Leibniz distinguishes between predicates that are part of the essence of the subject and predicates that are in the subject but not part of the essence of the subject. Only propositions that ascribe essential predicates are necessary.

It seems to me beyond dispute that were Leibniz informed of Kant's conception of analytic and synthetic propositions, he would not say that he finds all truths analytic. His stated distinctions prepare for a much more plausible response. Analytic truths are those for which there is a necessitating reason for the inclusion of the predicate in the subject. These are propositions true by definition. They ascribe essential predicates. The denials of these are contradictory. There are other propositions which are synthetic. They are contingent propositions where the reason for the subject's containment of the predicate is not a necessitating reason. They are not shown true by appeal to the meanings of terms. They do not involve essential predicates of their subjects. And their denials are not contradictory.

That Kant's analytic statements are all necessary is a logical point at the most elementary level. Leibniz, who was, after all, a great logician, could not fail to notice that where the subject contains the predicate in Kant's sense, a proposition will be necessary, and its denial a contradiction. But in all the passages wherein he asserts his containment thesis, Leibniz also asserts that there are contingent as well as necessary propositions, and these differ "toto genere."[57] In one passage Leibniz actually seems to anticipate and reject the idea that his conception of contingent truths might, somehow, make them necessary along with ordinary necessities:

> If all propositions, even contingencies, are to be resolved into identical propositions, can we not conclude that they are all necessary? I answer, Not soundly.

Leibniz then explains that propositions of fact are all about existing things. What exists, a consequence of God's creation, is always an alternative to other possible existences. So there is a reason for what exists, but that something exists is not necessary. And he concludes:

> It must be said that in contingencies the predicate is by no means to be demonstrated from the notion of the subject; but rather a reason for it is given which does not necessitate but inclines.[58]

Furthermore, in many presentations of the containment thesis about all truths it is plain that Leibniz does not think he is asserting something controversial or even original in the least way. He intends this claim, rather, as an expression of a conception of truth shared by most philosophers.[59] He thinks it is Aristotle's conception of truth, as well as that of all the leading scholastics he can think of. But Leibniz does not propose that Aristotle and most scholastics held that all truths are necessary and that they can all be established from the analysis of meanings. Leibniz would recognize that as an extreme and unfamiliar view, while his containment thesis is presumably familiar and innocuous. In one passage Leibniz says, "[In a true proposition the predicate is contained in the subject] or I do not know what truth is."[60] This is just hyperbolic rhetoric for expressing the noncontroversial status of the containment thesis as Leibniz understands it.

It is not hard to state just what the containment thesis does mean as Leibniz intends it. It asserts only what might be expressed as follows: If 'S is P' is true, then, of course, P must actually qualify the subject S. That is, P must be a feature of that subject, for that is just what the sentence states. In other words, a list of all of the features of the subject S would *contain* the predicate P, for if P were not on that list, it could hardly be true to say 'S is P.'

Leibniz's thinking is also influenced by a conception which is now known as the "timelessness of truth." If an individual has some feature at some time, then the statement 'S is P' which expresses that fact is timelessly true. The statement does not become true when the individual comes to have the feature. This is not a mysterious doctrine if we think of the temporal qualification as tacitly included in the predicate. Then we get propositions such as "Mt. Etna erupts in 1983," which is always true, and not just in 1983. But consider "Mt. Etna erupts in 2003." If this is true, it is now true and at all times true, although we do not know that it is true. If it is true, then Leibniz will say that Mt. Etna (now and always) has the feature of erupting in 2003, although we are not smart enough to know that in advance. Further, erupting in 2003, just like erupting in 1983, is not an essential feature of Mt. Etna, if it is a feature. That means that if it is going to erupt in 2003, that is not a necessary truth, though it is, now, a truth. Understood in this way, the containment thesis is not entirely uncontroversial, but it is a plausible and very widely held view of truth. The containment thesis actually provides no support at all for the idea that Leibniz takes all truths to be analytic.

In addition to his views about containment of predicates in subjects, there are four Leibnizean doctrines that seem to press readers to the interpretation we are considering. These are (1) that for every truth an a priori proof is available in principle; (2) that God is able, because his mental powers are infinite, to reduce contingent propositions to identities and thus appreciate their truth, while for mentally weaker men a posteriori experience is the only source of knowledge of contingencies; (3) there is a complete concept for every individual, so that one who knows the concept would know everything that was, is, or will be true of that individual; and (4) an individual is a *species infima*, that is, a minimal species.

(1) In many passages and in various contexts Leibniz says that there is an a priori proof for all true propositions, although we are often unable to produce that a priori proof. Now, most philosophers of the twentieth century think that the feasibility of a priori proof is equivalent to, or is certainly a reliable mark of, necessary status. To prove some proposition a priori means, for us, to prove it without any appeal to the facts of the world, which are only discoverable a posteriori, or by experience. Again, we are now inclined to think that

if a proof does not need any appeal to the facts, it must rely wholly on analysis of concepts and meanings. That means, for us, that a proposition provable a priori will be an analytic truth and, therefore, necessary.

In considering Leibniz's ideas, however, this line of thought must be wholly set aside. It is simply an error to project into Leibniz's thought any restriction of a priori status to propositions that are necessary or defensible by appeal to meanings alone. God's policy of action; selection of the best, and man's policy; selection of the apparent best, are premises that Leibniz plainly admits in a priori proofs, but he regards these as contingent premises, and their contingency will be inherited by whatever is proved with their help. In fact, the contingency of all created existence alone guarantees the contingency of all matters of fact, even though a sufficient intelligence would be able to predict them, using God's selection of the best as a premise. Leibniz says:

> The first principle concerning existence is this proposition: God wants to choose the best. This proposition cannot be demonstrated; it is first of all propositions of fact, or the source of all contingent existence.[61]

The confinement of a priori to analytic truth is plainly wrong even for thinking about Kant, as his fundamental concept, synthetic a priori truth, testifies.

(2) Obviously we do not and cannot produce any of the a priori proofs for contingent facts that Leibniz says are possible in principle. The reason he gives for our failure is that the world is infinitely complicated, and each thing in it is related to everything else. An a priori proof of anything will have, as a consequence, to be an a priori proof of everything. It will have to take an infinity of factors into consideration. Our minds are clearly not up to such proofs. But an infinite mind, the mind of God, and only such a mind, could actually frame and grasp such proofs. This strand of speculation occurs frequently in Leibniz's writings, and it has contributed to the idea that Leibniz thinks that all truths are analytic, although we finite minds cannot appreciate the analyticity of what we discover through experience. Therefore we call these "contingent truths." Only God can understand these truths *as* analytic truths, but such they surely are.[62]

Leibniz frequently alludes to infinite analysis in mathematics. He likes to say that he appreciated the true character of contingencies when he placed them in the context of infinite mathematical analysis. Infinite analysis is the "radix contingentiae": the root of contingency. Again, he says that it takes a little flair for mathematics to grasp the nature of contingent truths, which are only resolvable, in some sense, at infinity, as curves meet their asymptotes at infinity, and an infinite-sided polygon becomes a circle. Contingent truths are often said to be like incommensurable ratios whose exact value is the sum of an infinite series of factors. And Leibniz actually seems insecure in this analogy because we finite minds are capable of summing such infinite series.[63]

Many of those who say that Leibniz makes all truth analytic are most encouraged by this appeal to infinite analysis. My guess is that such readers think that Leibniz means that we treat propositions as contingent because we cannot understand their necessity. These readers rightly note something that Leibniz surely does mean, namely, that what is only a posteriori to a finite mind may be a priori to an infinite one. They go on to the plausible but faulty extension: What is contingent to a finite mind may be necessary to an infinite one, and what is synthetic for us may be analytic for God. These extensions would only be legitimate if we could say that the infinite understanding that God is capable of is an understanding of meanings and definitions. Why should we think that? Of course, Leibniz does mean that an infinite analysis would be required to find all the predicates contained in a given substance-subject. But we have seen that the reasons for containment do not all give rise to necessary truths or analytic propositions. There is nothing in the idea of an infinity of predicates that tends to make them all essential predicates.

Leibniz sometimes says explicitly that infinite analysis of which only God is capable is needed to reduce contingent truths to identities. Can't we say that all identities are necessary? Identities come into the picture only via the notion of containment. If P is contained in S, then the identity underlying 'S is P' is expressible as 'S (which has P in it) is P', the identical part of which is 'What is P is P'. Let us agree that this is a necessary truth if anything is. What follows? If P is a contingent feature of S, then the identity is also statable as 'What is contingently P is contingently P'. But to point out that this identity, like all identities, is necessary does not in any way undercut the contingency of 'S is P'.

At times Leibniz did worry lest his view that all truths rest on identities make them all necessary. In a passage already quoted he asks, "If true propositions all reduce to identities are they not all necessary?" He then tries to dispel the appearance of necessity in a manner much like that I have just proposed. To say that there is an underlying identity only means that the predicate is contained in the subject. But the truth in question is necessary only if the containment is essential "ex notione subjecti" and not if there is a merely inclining reason for the containment, a reason "quae non necessitet."[64] The same understandable worry sometimes leads Leibniz to deny that contingent propositions really reduce to identities at all:

> . . . accordingly, in the case of contingencies, a connection [and rela-tion] of terms is given, though it cannot be reduced to the principle of contradiction or necessity through analysis into identities.[65]

But in this very passage Leibniz reasserts his idea that God's infinite analysis gives him a view of contingencies that we cannot share. It is, then, only a priori knowledge and not necessity or analyticity that infinite analysis yields.

It is likely that the same reflections underly Leibniz's misgivings about necessity in this passage:

> . . . I did not understand in what way the predicate can be contained in the subject, and yet not make the proposition necessary.[66]

Leibniz did not forget his distinction between necessitating and inclining reasons here. It is just because the containment thesis will always generate an identity that it so strongly suggests the necessity of the analyzed proposition to Leibniz and his readers. But, as we have seen, Leibniz would rather abandon the claim that an identity underlies every contingent truth than regard such truths as necessary.

The best support for the idea that Leibniz makes even contingent truths analytic may come from passages like this one:

> Truth is either necessary or contingent. Necessary truth can be known through a finite series of substitutions or through a commensurable coincidence [resolution to identity], contingent truth by infinite analysis, or through incommensurable coincidence. Necessary truth is that of which the truth is explicable; contingent, that of which the truth is inexplicable. A priori or apodictic demonstration is explication of truth.[67]

Leibniz never makes it entirely clear in just what way appeal to infinity is supposed to help us to understand contingency. In spite of the large number of passages in which he makes use of the analogy of incommensurability, he never makes it clear just how this analogy is to be understood either. Furthermore, his appeal to "substitutions" in passages like the one just cited sounds menacingly necessitarian. Be this as it may, we can be sure that Leibniz did not think that these analogies go to show that contingent propositions are really analytic. He surely does mean that we cannot complete some kind of analysis which God can complete, and this because the analysis in question is infinite. But to make a proposition analytic, Leibniz would have to say not only that its full analysis requires an infinite mind but also that that analysis is wholly conceptual and that the *substitutions* employed in the analysis are all of them definitional substitutions. Mere assertion that analyses are infinite does not imply that they are confined to conceptual matters. On the contrary, what God discovers through his infinite analysis is what we have to learn through experience. This prominently includes knowledge of causes of events and of free decisions, that is, of contingencies. In countless passages, including those we discussed in the first two parts of this essay, Leibniz makes it clear that God's foreknowledge is foreknowledge of contingent facts, of mechanically caused events, and of freely chosen actions. The apriority of God's foreknowledge is always distinguished from the necessity of what he knows. God cannot reduce actions and causes to definitions because they are not matters of definition.

Leibniz usually, perhaps invariably, combines his idea that God can make infinite analyses with the thought that God can know contingent truths a priori. The above passage ends saying that contingent truths are inexplicable by men and that by explicability is meant demonstrability a priori. This is the mystery about contingent truths that infinite analysis is to make intelligible. God's powers enable him to prove contingent propositions a priori, but that does not convert contingent truths into necessary or analytic propositions.

Here is what Leibniz really has in mind in his discussion of infinite analysis that makes possible a priori knowledge of facts. We men have enough understanding of the world to predict a few things like eclipses and next month's tides. The more knowledgeable and brilliant we are the more we can predict. Some of our predictions depend on our knowledge of our own future actions. We can predict that we will not run out of gas on a long trip because we know that we will stop and refuel when we run low. In these ways God is like us but infinitely wiser and more powerful. He has been able to predict everything from the beginning. "Everything" includes an infinite complexity of mechanically caused events and freely undertaken actions, and these are all contingent.[68] God knows all the contingent effects of mechanical causes and all the free decisions that agents will ever take. Everything is connected with everything else, so that the infinite truth of the world appears, from a particular point of view, in the complete truth about any individual. But this enormous truth contains a great deal that is irreducibly contingent.

God's knowledge is wholly a priori since he knows everything before he creates the world of which he has knowledge. He knows that this is the way things will turn out if he creates just such individuals subject to just such natural laws, and also creates such free men acting on such principles. That all this is knowledge of the actual world is a consequence of God's decision to create this "series of things." Here again we have a contingency. He creates as he does in light of a mental comparison with other possibilities, each of which is also infinitely complex. God might have created another world, or none. That would not be contradictory. But his creative action is contingent, and a great many of the things that happen in the world he created happen contingently. Perhaps we can say that for Leibniz anything that could be said to "happen" is contingent. For he describes necessary and essential truths about the world as conditional.[69]

(3) Leibniz regularly says that every individual has a "complete concept" and that all the truths, past, present, and future, about an individual could be read off from the complete concept. This gives rise to the thought that truths about individuals are conceptual truths, for does he not say expressly that they can be got out of concepts? Beyond this, Leibniz is a metaphysical *individualist*. The universe consists wholly of a multiplicity of entities that Leibniz calls substances. These are basic individuals whose existence manifests a true unity and independence. All truths about the created universe are truths about these substances. Again, this is an expression of Leibniz's nominalism. At his most theoretical Leibniz says that all substances are what he calls monads. His theory of monads is notoriously difficult to relate to discourse at the less abstract levels of physical science, psychology, and ethics. I think it is certain that Leibniz

himself never connected his *Monadology* with other universes of discourse in any definite way.[70] Nonetheless, Leibniz also allows discourse in which far less theoretical individuals such as persons and physical bodies are the subjects about which truths may be asserted. At both the most theoretical and the more practical levels of discourse he defends the idea that every individual has a complete concept, and he freely uses persons and blocks of marble as illustrations of individual things with complete concepts.[71] When Leibniz wrote to Arnauld saying that the entire history of the individual is contained in its complete concept, down to the minutest detail and once and for all, Arnauld found in this doctrine "a necessity more than fatal."[72] Thus, Arnauld may be the first of those who found in this opinion of Leibniz a philosophy that excludes all contingency. Readers who now say that Leibniz makes all truths analytic in connection with the complete-concept thesis are reasserting Arnauld's initial reaction.

The analyticity interpretation gets support here because we so naturally suppose that to speak about what is in a *concept* is to speak about meanings. If all truths about individual substances can be generated by knowledge of concepts, then they all come from meanings and are, therefore, analytic. This understanding is inadequate for reasons much like those we have already stated in the context of a priori proof and infinite analysis. Leibniz is using the term "concept" of a substance so that all features of a substance, and not merely essential, definitional, or necessary features, will appear in the concept. He uses the word "concept" to contrast with talk about the substance itself as an existant thing. The concept is the representation of the thing. The features of the concept follow the features of the thing and include contingent elements, if the thing has contingent features.

Of course, the concept of the individual is accessible to God before creation, so God is not merely forming a representation of an existant. This a priori accessibility of the concept is, again, an important part of the doctrine that encourages the analyticity thesis about Leibniz. Since the concept preexists the thing of which it is the concept, truths derived just from the concept must be conceptual truths. But, again, this is wrong. We finite minds can have concepts of things before they exist, and whether or not they later exist. We may have a complete concept (relatively speaking, of course) of a certain engine, and then we may build the engine that just fits that concept, or we may build another, or none, if other ideas suit us better. This is the way we should think of Leibniz's God, allowing the appropriate superiority of his power and wisdom. When we think in advance that the bearings we have designed for our engine will not last for more than one year of constant use, we envision a contingent feature of our engine. If we build the engine and are entirely right about the bearings, the fact that they wear out in less than a year does not become a kind of necessary truth. It is a contingent truth that we were able to foresee, so that it was part of our concept of this engine before the engine existed. To call it "a truth about an engine" presupposes that the engine is built. If we do not go on to build the engine, then all we have is a conditional truth. "If we build such an engine, and if the laws of nature are as we assert them to be, then the bearings of that engine will wear out in less than a year." This is a necessary truth, but as Leibniz himself says, its content is only of the form "Such a thing posited, such another thing is."[73]

We conclude that for God and for man the existence of concepts of things prior to the existence of the things of which they are concepts does not in any way imply that truths about the things, legible from the concepts, are necessary or analytic. In the absence of the existence of the thing such truths are not truths about individuals at all. With the existence, even the subsequent existence, nothing prevents them from being contingent truths.

(4) Leibniz sometimes says that an individual is a *species infima*.[74] That is, each substance is a least species, a species having only one member, namely, that individual substance itself. Now truths about the relation of species and subspecies are ordinarily truths based wholly on meanings within some scheme of classification. Let us assume in any case, that such is the status of assertions like "Cats are mammals." Let us assume that this and other truths like it are necessary and analytic truths. In the example we can see that being a member of the smaller class, cats, has as an essential requirement being in the larger class, mammals. If sentences about individuals could be assimilated to this pattern, they too would be necessary and analytic. It is as though the more defining qualifications one introduces in speaking of a species, the fewer will be the individuals that instantiate that species concept. Then Leibniz may seem to be

saying that the most articulate species concept, the ultimate definition of a subspecies, is always a concept so full that there is but one
individual that can satisfy that species concept. Such a concept will
specify everything about the single individual that is, under this
understanding, the member of a *species infima*.

This idea is plainly close to the complete-concept theory that we
have just considered. The remarks we made about that theory apply
equally to the notion of a *species infima*. Leibniz got the idea of a
species infima containing one individual out of scholastic thought.
The scholastics arrived at the concept in connection with the problem
of individuation. What is it that really makes one thing, one man,
for example, a different individual from another? According to a
powerful and plausible Aristotelian view the body is the ultimate and
decisive foundation for the individuality of things. But for scholastics
angels differ from men in that they do not have bodies. The idea that
each angel is a *species infima* is a scholastic solution to this problem.
It tries to accept the Aristotelian concept of individuation by ruling
that there can be only one bodiless entity of each conceptually distinct sort.[75]

Leibniz extends the idea of *species infima* to all individuals
whether or not they have bodies. He has in mind that no two individuals, such as two men, will have just the same bodily features,
nor just the same physical histories, etc. Therefore, classifications
based on subtle enough differences will yield classes containing only
one individual. But, as we saw, this will include classification with
respect to empirical and contingent features, and not merely with
respect to essential features. In fact, Leibniz's special objective here
is not complete concepts or a priori proofs but rather a vehicle for expression of his well-known view that no two individuals are exactly
alike, or that individuals never differ in number only.[76]

I have devoted a lot of detail to this point, that is, the idea that
all truths are analytic according to Leibniz, because it is an error that
is widespread and an error that, once made, leaves Leibniz's overall
thought in hopeless confusion and inconsistency. I think it can be
said that this misinterpretation is just based on inappropriate moder-
nizations of Leibniz's use of words such as "a priori," "concept," "containment," and "reduction to an identity." Confining ourselves to
Leibniz's senses of such expressions, none of his doctrines lend any
support to the popular misinterpretation.

4. Possibility and Possible Worlds

Leibniz often expresses his commitment to contingent truth by saying that not everything that is possible actually exists.[77] Spinoza and Hobbes are generally bracketed in his discussions as thinkers who erroneously eliminate contingency and equate what is possible and what is real.[78] If there were no unactualized possibilities, Leibniz says, it would be inappropriate to praise God for his creation,[79] and men could not be free and responsible for their actions.[80] To speak of human freedom presupposes that more than one possibility must be open to a man. To praise God presupposes that other worlds might have been created. This is the setting of the famous concept of *possible worlds*.

The thought of other possible worlds emphasizes a side of our reflections on contingency that easily generates puzzles and paradoxes. The recent great revival of discussions of possible worlds has not neglected to revive these paradoxes and puzzles.[81] The paradoxes turn on the idea of the *existence* of possible worlds. Suppose we agree that Leibniz is right about Spinoza. Then Leibniz asserts and Spinoza denies that there are possibilities beyond those that are actualities. But what can this mean? Both men know that what exists, exists, and what does not, does not. Leibniz says that *there are* further possibilities, and Spinoza that it is not the case that *there are* further possibilities. These perhaps inevitable expressions suggest that the difference is in some way a difference about *what there is*. To say that there are unrealized possibilities seems to be the same as to say that unrealized possibilities *exist* somehow. Of course, they do not exist in the way in which realized possibilities exist. But if Leibniz were to admit that these possibilities do not exist at all, that they do not exist in any sense, then what would be the difference between his view and Spinoza's? Generally, this kind of thinking has led many, and sometimes Leibniz among them, to think of a possible world as a kind of existent thing. Because it gives unrealized possible worlds some kind of ontological weight, I call this the ontological interpretation of possible worlds.

The temptations and advantages of the ontological interpretation can be illustrated in connection with Leibniz's discussions of the "problem of evil." Among the creatures of God are some, some men, for example, whose acts are vicious, whose characters are corrupt, and whose very constitution is deficient. How can an all-powerful and all-good God have produced such creatures? One view of Leibniz's solution to this problem is that God's creation does not include the fashioning of such deficient individuals at all because all individuals, as possibilities, exist eternally and, therefore, preexist all creative acts of God. A recent exposition states:

> Each substance has "always" subsisted, or, strictly speaking, has had a conceptual mode of being that lies outside of time altogether — *sub ratio possibilitatis*. Its total nature was determined, for its adequate and complete notion (including all its predicates save existence) was fixed. For this God is in no way responsible; it is an object of his understanding and no creature of his will.[82]

According to this line of thought, possibilities are completed essences which God knows about but does not make. Creation consists in admitting into actuality certain of these individuals who, actuality apart, are completely formed. In his policy for conferring actual existence on these individuals God sees to it that the best possible world becomes the actual world. This best possible world has some defective individuals in it but it is, on balance, better than any possible alternative. God did not construct these deficient individuals or their betters. He merely allowed them, so to speak, through the portals of actuality. I am not particularly concerned here with the success of this well-known formula for the absolution of God. I do want to stress that insofar as it does absolve him from the responsibility for having created deficient individuals, it gives those individuals, as mere possibilities, a certain considerable ontological standing. God is not responsible for these individuals because *they exist as possibilities* quite independently of him.

The ontological interpretation of possible worlds is especially clear in a passage at the end of the *Theodicée* where Leibniz adds a sequel to the dialogue of Lorenzo Valla that he has retold. The high priest Theodore is sent by Jupiter to be instructed by Pallas Athena so that he will understand how misery and corruption of some men is compatible with the greatness and goodness of God. The goddess meets Theodore on the steps of an immense palace of inconceivable brilliance. After first making him capable of receiving divine enlightenment, Athena tells him:

You see here the palace of destinies, of which I am the keeper. There are representations here, not only of everything that happens, but also of all that is possible; and Jupiter, having reviewed these representations before the beginning of the existing world, examined the possibilities for worlds, and made the choice of the best of all. . . . Thereupon, the goddess led Theodore into one of the apartments: when he was there, it was no longer an apartment, it was a world.[83]

In this forceful, entertaining, and figurative exploitation of the concept of possible worlds, unrealized possibilities are construed on the pattern of other worlds that one might visit or observe.[84].

The high-water mark of this realistic interpretation of possibility in Leibniz is probably his theory of *exigentia*. According to this view all possibilities contain a certain urge to exist. The actual world is the net effect of the strivings of individuals, many of which are incompatible with one another. The result is a world of maximal existence which we might think of on analogy with an ecological system wherein competing organisms fully exploit every possibility and exist in every ecological niche. Both Russell and Arthur Lovejoy point out that if Leibniz's theory of competing possibilities is taken literally, there appears to be no role at all for God in determining what exists.[85] This is precisely because the theory gives possibilities not only a kind of existence but also a certain activity that is independent of and precedes actuality.

Leibniz seems to have thought of the "urge to exist" of possibilities as at best a convenient metaphor. He usually speaks of unrealized possibilities as existing only as thoughts in the mind of God. In the *Theodicée* he says that the idea of a struggle for actual existence must really be understood as a conflict of "reasons in the perfect understanding of God," and at least once he expressly asserted that possible things, since they do not exist, can have no power to bring themselves into existence.[86] These views of possibility are deflationary in comparison with the ontological interpretation that makes possibilities into things that *are*. When Leibniz follows this ontologically restrained line of thought and speaks of possibilities that God considers before creation as "ideas," he means that something that is *just an idea* contrasts with things that exist in any sense at all. The fact that God recognizes that many different actualities *might arise*, depending upon what he freely decides to create, does not mean that anything already exists, as though ready for his "examination" in its fully formed state, merely leaving God to determine whether or not to license the full-blooded actuality of an already subsisting entity.[87]

Leibniz's writings and lifelong interest in the theory of combinations shed light on his thinking about possibility. In the *Ars Combinatoria* Leibniz relates his abstract development of a theory of combinations to truth by way of the reflection that a proposition is composed of a subject and a predicate and is, therefore, an instance of binary combination.

> It is, then, the business of inventive [combinatory] logic (as far as it concerns propositions) to solve this problem: (i) given a subject to find its predicates. (ii) given a predicate to find its subjects.[88]

From the point of view of combinations Leibniz is thinking of possible truths and not actual truths. That is, combinatory analysis will never enable us to see that the ascription of one predicate to a subject makes a true proposition and the ascription of another makes a false proposition. But if our language were adequate and complete enough, a merely combinatory procedure would generate all the statements about every subject that could possibly be true.

The idea of an adequate and complete language is itself problematic. Leibniz always supposes that adequacy will be enhanced by analysis and definitions that reduce complex predicates to their simpler and, ultimately, to their primitive constituents. The completeness of a language would require that the miscellany of subject terms of ordinary speech be replaced by terms representing the simple constituents of reality. This kind of project faces a large number of philosophical and technical difficulties. It is certainly a familiar project in twentieth-century philosophy. Ideas very much like those of Leibniz on the subject of possibility, ideal language, and combinatory analysis lie behind the modern development of truth-functional analysis, Russell's "logical atomism," the metaphysics and "picture-theory" of Wittgenstein's *Tractatus*, Rudolph Carnap's many versions of the theory of "state-descriptions," and the extensional semantics of quantification theory. Like Leibniz's schemes, a few of these recent projects for ideal languages have got beyond the programmatic stage. The scheme itself, however, enables us to grasp and evaluate Leibniz's thinking about possible worlds.

A drastically simplified model for the world will be helpful.

Suppose that the universe could only have two constituent substances in it apart from God. Suppose these substances are two dice and that names for each of them are the simple subject terms of our language. Suppose, further, that the only truth to be told about a die is what number of dots it shows. Then the simple predicates of the language will all be expressions like "shows a three" and "shows a six." Let us imagine that the whole history of the universe is just the outcome of one roll of the dice. The roll itself is not even a part of reality. Then all the truth there is about the universe would consist in saying what number of dots between one and six each of the dice shows. We can write this as a pair of numbers: for example, let the truth be that (5, 6), which is to be read "The first die shows a five and the second a six." In this representation the subject terms are indicated just by position in the pair. Leibniz's problem of the *Ars Combinatoria* would be this: find all the predicates of the first die. And the solution would be the set of all simple predicates:

{shows a one, shows a two,. . ., shows a six}.

All subjects of a given predicate, for instance, the predicate "shows a two," would be the set of all the subjects, or

{the first die, the second die}.

Though creation will be a trifling matter with this attenuated universe, God still has the job of determining which possible world shall come into existence. That means that God will determine which of the several outcomes for a roll of two dice shall be the actual universe. Being wise, God understands that the possible worlds are exhausted in the array of combinations:

$$(1,1)\ (1,2)\ (1,3)\ (1,4)\ (1,5)\ (1,6)$$
$$(2,1)\ (2,2)\ (2,3)\ (2,4)\ (2,5)\ (2,6)$$
$$(3,1)\ (3,2)\ (3,3)\ (3,4)\ (3,5)\ (3,6)$$
$$(4,1)\ (4,2)\ (4,3)\ (4,4)\ (4,5)\ (4,6)$$
$$(5,1)\ (5,2)\ (5,3)\ (5,4)\ (5,5)\ (5,6)$$
$$(6,1)\ (6,2)\ (6,3)\ (6,4)\ (6,5)\ (6,6).$$

Now we need something to distinguish the different possible worlds represented in this array in terms of value so as to make it thinkable in the framework of the analogy that God might judge one possible world better than another. Leibniz says that God combines things so as to produce a maximum of ordered variety. Let us say that the numerical total of dots on both dice measures the quantity of existence and that variety is represented only by evenness and oddness of the number of dots on each die. Under this stipulation the possible world (6,6) maximizes quantity but not variety, while (4,5) maximizes variety but not quantity. (5,6) offers a maximum of quantity with variety, so this may be our model for the best possible world.[89]

Were the universe as simple as this dice world, a mentality no more powerful than ours could survey possible worlds in advance as well as any divinity. We could know, as God would, that there are eleven possible totals of dots, ranging from two to twelve. There are fifteen worlds with sums less than seven and fifteen with sums more than seven. On the array these sets of fifteen possible worlds are displayed above and below, respectively, the diagonal going from the lower left to the upper right. The diagonal itself contains the six ways of getting a total of seven, which is more ways than there are for getting any other total. We could extend this set of analytical truths about the set of possible outcomes indefinitely. These truths about possible outcomes are all accessible to us prior to rolling the dice. Leibniz thinks of such intelligible considerations about possible worlds as themselves necessary truths, as indeed these are when considered as statements of possible arithmetical combinations. Should we point out to Leibniz that when these mathematical reflections are transferred to actual physical objects, they cease to be necessary truths? Real dice might be so constructed (for instance, they might be loaded) so that certain combinations will never come up. We might then say, for example, that it is not possible to roll a seven with a certain pair of dice. Still this would be a matter of hypothetical necessity according to Leibniz, depending on physical laws and conditions. The outcome (3,4) would not be contradictory, even for loaded dice. After all, God will decide the physical laws too, so He can make uninhibited use of combinatorially analyzed possibilities in connection with possible physical objects.

Thinking in terms of this simple model of the world and alternative possibilities, and in terms of our own real abilities to understand possibilities in advance, reduces our impulse to construe possible worlds as having any kind of existence at all apart from the one possible world which is *the world*. Our own thought and survey of possible outcomes of a roll of dice do not depend on thinking that those possibilities *somehow exist* with fully articulated status in advance of any rolling. No outcomes of rollings preexist the actual rolling in any sense whatever, and speech about possible outcomes only refers to what *may* happen *after rolling*. When Leibniz says that God considers a world or worlds in which Adam does not sin as well as worlds in which he does, he need mean by this nothing more than a vastly more complicated case logically quite like our reflection that in some rolls the first die comes up a one, and in others it does not. That these outcomes are open to intelligent survey does not mean that they must already exist in any sense at all.

In contemporary discussions of modal concepts in logic the ontologically weighty interpretation of possible worlds is currently defended by David Lewis. In his theory the ontological standing of all possible worlds is so considerable that "real" or "actual" cease to be ways of making fundamental distinctions between one possible world and all the others.[90] Lewis thinks that "actual" and "real" are *indexical* expressions like "here" and "now."[91] Any place at all is "here" for a person speaking from that place. One time is not fundamentally distinguished from others by being *now*. In a similar way there is an internal and an external use of "actual" in characterizing worlds. Of course, speaking within this possible world, we say that all the others are merely possible, while this one is actual. But the inhabitants of other possible worlds will inevitably make the same claim for the actuality of their world, and with the same justice. To say that other possible worlds are not actual does not diminish them in point of ontological standing any more than it diminishes the existence of places to say that they are not *here*. This ingenious, perhaps intuitively unconvincing, proposal is egalitarian about the existence of all possible worlds. Metaphysically speaking, they are all equally constituents of reality.

Possible worlds are all of them representations like the items in the array that represents thirty-six possible outcomes of one roll of a pair of dice. The real world is not a representation. It is the world. So, too, by our hypothesis there is but one roll of the dice. The real world cannot be identified with one of the items on the array, not even with the item that represents the world as it actually is. Lewis's theory about possible worlds succumbs, first, to the tempting thought that there are thirty-five items of one kind and one item of a different kind, thirty-five shadowy worlds and one full-blooded reality. On

this basis Lewis is able to propose that full-bloodedness or actuality
is perspectival. We have to judge, so Lewis thinks, from within one
of these thirty-six worlds. Naturally, the one we judge from will be
called "actual" and the others "merely possible." But we do not judge
from within one of these worlds, for none of them *is* the world. We
have, in the dice world, thirty-six *descriptions* and one world. No-
body lives in descriptions and must judge from such vantage points.
The thirty-six possibilities all deserve the old scholastic label "entia
rationis."

Leibniz makes use of this thought when he points out that we
have to think even of the actual world as a possible world and as contemplated by God.[92] We will be safe from ontological largesse as long
as we make all possible worlds alike and do not think of them as all
shadowy except one.

The most decisive argument against any ontological interpretation of possible worlds in the context of Leibniz's thinking is that it
undercuts the view of possibility that he defends. Leibniz himself
presents this argument. If possibilities were any kind of subsisting
things, intelligible because they are, somehow, *there* like Athena's
palace of destinies, to be inspected by God or man, then they would
have to be objects of a kind of experience rather than products of
reason and understanding. Inspection of possible worlds, were they
to exist in any way, would amount to a further source of a posteriori
knowledge. Theodore actually observes other worlds and explicitly
gains knowledge of them and of the comparison with his own world
by *experience*. And that is just what Jupiter has done in contemplating the possibilities prior to creation. But this figure gives us no reason to think that Leibniz actually inclines to the ontological interpretation of possibilities in the *Theodicée*. Athena herself calls the
contents of the palace "representations," and though Theodore *experiences* other possible events, this is described not as another reality
but "comme dans une representation de theatre."[93] In other words,
the items from which we learn about possibility are not other worlds
with a less robust kind of being, nor are they other worlds with the
same being as ours when viewed from within, as David Lewis proposes. They are not worlds at all but only representations. When
thinking about possibilities, we are comparing representations of
worlds with each other.

The fact that we make an actual object like the array of thirty-six possible dice worlds, or the palace of destinies of Athena, is an accidental feature of representation. Our representations could *be* all of them in imagination only. But whether the representations are real objects or only thoughts, the important point is that we do not have alternative worlds to compare, but only alternative representations, one of which, by hypothesis, represents the world as it is.

Leibniz makes the point in discussing the idea of a *"scientia media"* that if possibilities were to exist as inspectible things, then knowledge of them would be a posteriori. Such a middle science was proposed by Luis Molina, among others, as a device for resolving the tensions between the concepts of human freedom and predestination. The middle knowledge was supposed to be a kind of visionary appreciation of things accessible to God and constituting a third option between the absolute necessity of definitional and mathematical truth and the mere contingency of matters of fact which we learn in experience. Leibniz points out that if the notion of vision actually carries any weight in the concept of *"scientia media,"* the knowledge deemed accessible to God will be a posteriori knowledge:

> Thus the knowledge of God is not made up of a kind of vision, which is imperfect and *a posteriori*; but in understanding of causes, and *a priori*.[94]

This theme becomes immediately relevant to the thought of existing and inspectible possible worlds when Leibniz rejects the Molinist claim that God might see the future infallibly reflected in a great mirror.

> According to the advocates of the *scientia media*, God could not give a reason for his assertions, nor explain them to me. To someone who asks why he says that things will be thus, he would be able to say just that it is because he sees this event represented thus in that great mirror, posited among them, in which everything present, future, absolute or conditioned is exhibited. Such knowledge is wholly empirical, and it would not satisfy God himself because he would not know the reason for which this rather than that is represented in the mirror.[95]

A vision in a glass, no matter how accurate and trustworthy, is only another experience which cannot replace rational understanding. In the spirit of this conclusion we have to suppose that God's representations of other possible worlds have the features that they do *because* God understands how things would be related in those worlds. The same holds for the simpler human mind contemplating the simpler dice world. The array of thirty-six outcomes has the constituents that it does because we understand just what would be possible and we make the representations accordingly. Possible worlds are dependent upon our understanding, and not the other way around. And if other possible worlds did exist, somehow, and God could examine them, that would give him not reasoned knowledge but only a kind of empirical knowledge that is not available to us.

5. Freedom

Leibniz's understanding of freedom is dependent in many ways on his doctrines concerning contingency and possibility. Mechanism perennially challenges the claims of freedom. In the second part of this study we have seen Leibniz's proposals for the reconciliation of freedom and a ubiquitous mechanical causality covering all motions. The view that all truths are analytic which we have criticized in the third part would also contradict the view that men are free, and the rejection of that interpretation eliminates a general threat to Leibniz's doctrines. The theme of possible worlds, just considered in the fourth part, can also be interpreted in a way that creates a fundamental obstacle to freedom.

The thought that a man could have done something other than what he did do plainly requires that some other action was possible. Insofar as possible worlds are to offer a way of expressing our thoughts about possibility, we can say that where there is freedom, one action is done in the actual world and other actions in other possible worlds. But can we say that one and the same man exists in more than one possible world? Or is an individual confined to just one world so that other possible worlds could at best contain similar individuals faced with similar choices? If one and the same man cannot exist in more than one world, the prospect for freedom is dark. We shall apparently be forced to construe the idea of the freedom of one individual as equivalent to the idea of the behavior of more than one individual.

This is the problem of transworld identity of individuals. It arises in a clear form in Leibniz's exchanges with Arnauld, and it is much discussed in recent literature on identity and modal concepts.[96] Leibniz sometimes seems to imply that a true individual can exist in one possible world only. The thesis that there can be no transworld identity is defended at present, again by David Lewis among others. It is closely connected with the ontological interpretation of possible worlds just examined. If possible worlds *exist* in any sense at all, they seem to be, to that extent, like other places that one might visit, or at least places of which one might obtain news. Under any such conception each world will have its own population. At best one possible world may have an individual in it who more or less perfectly resembles, in history and features, an individual in another possible world. Even if such a similarity were perfect, an individual in one possible world cannot be the very individual that is in another world any more than a man born in New York can be the very same individual as an exactly similar man born in New Jersey.

We have repudiated the ontological interpretation of possible worlds, and we have argued that in his best thought Leibniz repudiates it too. If the prohibition on identity across possible worlds comes entirely from the ontological interpretation, we can expect that it will be removed when that interpretation is set aside. If alternative possible worlds are only representations of different systems and not existing systems of different entities, then it seems that possible worlds will contain different representations of one and the same individual. Freedom would, then, not be threatened.

When he received a sketch of the *Discourse of Metaphysics* from Leibniz in 1686, Arnauld found that the complete concept of the individual enunciated in article thirteen destroys the foundations of freedom and responsibility.[97]. The ensuing exchange on this point brought the problem of transworld identity to the surface. In that correspondence Leibniz uses the concept of possible worlds in arguments intended to overcome Arnauld's initially negative judgment. God knows all the things that Adam and all his descendants have freely done and all that they ever will do. He also knows all the things they might have done had they chosen to act differently, or were they going to choose differently in the future. This is part of God's knowledge of other possible worlds which he could have created. In other worlds Adam does different things. How does Leibniz think it possible to fit freedom for Adam and his progeny into this picture of God's knowledge and creation? There are two thoughts pertinent to this question, and the second of them hinges on transworld identity.

In the first place God can know in advance what a man will freely choose, so free agents do not present an obstacle to God's complete knowledge of the "series of things." It is this thought that is responsible for the rapid shift in point of view in the *Discourse* from the issue of determinism to the issue of foreknowledge.[98] God contemplates all possible worlds. Some of them have free agents in them, and some do not. Worlds with free creatures in them are better than worlds without freedom, so God will surely create one of them. This one is best of all (a judgment that requires knowledge of the actual series of things and of all possible series). But God does not produce the events of the actual world himself. They are produced by the causes that we rightly mention in explaining those events. Actions are really done for the reasons the agent has.

Here we find again the point of "On Nature Itself." Explanations have their footing in the world and not merely in its creator. By analogy, the pistons drive the crankshaft of an engine, and we cannot skip over or drop explanatory reference to the pistons and explain the motions of the crankshaft by appealing to the intentions or actions of the builder of the engine. So in the inanimate world it is forces that causes motions and not God. When a man acts freely, he, and not God, determines what he will do. This is the platform for Leibniz's defense of freedom and reconciliation of freedom with the complete concept of the individual and with God's knowledge. Though everything that I do belongs to my complete concept, many things belong contingently, and some because of what I freely choose to do.

> The connection of events, although it is certain, is not necessary, and . . . I am at liberty either to make the journey or not make the journey, for, although it is involved in my concept that I will make it, it is also involved that I will make it freely. And there is nothing in me of all that can be conceived *sub ratione generalitatis* . . . from which it can be deduced that I will make it necessarily.[99]

God's knowledge of what I will do is not the explanation for my free action. God knows my motives and he knows how I will assess my circumstances, and this is the basis of his knowledge of what I will freely do. God's knowledge no more impairs my freedom than does another man's knowledge of how I will vote impair my freedom to vote as I see fit.

Leibniz's second line of thought about the freedom of the individual in the correspondence with Arnauld is a good deal less secure
than the first line of thought. In the passage concerning a possible
journey that we have just quoted, Leibniz touches on the question of
the identity of individuals across possible worlds. In introducing the
possible journey as an illustration Arnauld had sought to distinguish
those facts about an individual without which he could not be the individual that he is from another range of facts which can vary without
affecting identity. Arnauld thinks that this distinction must be pressed
in opposition to Leibniz's claim that all the facts about an individual
are equally contained in the complete concept of that individual
which God is able to consult before creation. Thus, Arnauld says,
with echos of the Cartesian *cogito*:

> I am certain that, since I think, I, myself, exist. For I cannot think that
> I am not, nor that I am not myself. But I can think that I will make
> a certain voyage or not, while remaining entirely sure that neither the
> one nor the other will require that I am not myself.[100]

If we put this in the terminology of possible worlds, Arnauld is asserting that the very same individual can exist in more than one possible
world. In one possible world Arnauld makes a journey, and in another world the identical Arnauld does not make the journey. As we
have seen, this claim rules out the ontological interpretation of possible worlds.

In responding to this contention Leibniz comes very close to denying the possibility that the same man may be a constituent of more
than one possible world. In his earlier letters Leibniz had fallen into
use of the expression "possible Adams," and in reponse to the statement of Arnauld that we have just cited, he says that the notion of
multiple Adams has to be taken figuratively. When we think about
Adam from the point of view of a few salient characteristics—"that
he was the first man, put into the garden of enjoyment, and that
from his side God took a woman"[101]—we speak as though these few
characteristics determine the individual so that he will remain one
and the same substance whether he has or lacks other features. Different completions will be the various possible Adams, yet we speak
as though they will all be the same individual, differently completed.
This is what Leibniz says must be understood as a loose and meta-

phorical way of speaking. Rigorously speaking, a few salient characteristics do not determine an individual,

> . . . for there may be an infinity of Adams, that is to say, of possible
> persons [sharing these salient characteristics] who would nonetheless
> differ among themselves. . . . the nature of an individual should be
> complete and determined.[102]

If a man were to differ in any way at all from the actual Adam, in
his features, in his history, or in his relations to the rest of the
universe, then that man could not be Adam but, at most, another
possible man similar to Adam.

It seems to me that if he were to rely on this second line of
thought, Leibniz's reconciliation of freedom and the complete concept of an individual would surely fail. It is as though Leibniz is here
reducing the idea of two alternative courses of action available to a
free agent to the quite different idea of two very similar possible individuals, one of whom necessarily pursues one course, while the
other necessarily pursues the other course. If this result is allowed to
stand, it must be a severe disappointment to those who hoped to
analyze contingency in terms of possible worlds. We start by thinking
that I could take the journey, or I could not. It is up to me. Possible
world analysis then restates this as the fact that one possible world has
me taking the journey and another has me not taking it. But now the
ontological interpretation exerts its undesirable influence. It cannot
be true of one and the same individual that he takes a trip and does
not take that trip. So if these possible worlds are like existing things,
even with a shadowy existence, it will turn out that it cannot be me
that does not take the trip in another possible world, but, instead,
a man much like me. This is disappointing because the idea of freedom surely requires that one and the same individual may either perform or not perform a certain act. Freedom is rejected if we substitute
a conception of two different individuals, one of whom performs the
act, while the other does not. What another does can never be part
of the essence of *my* freedom.

Leibniz does not seem to appreciate fully the dangers implicit
in the denial of transworld identity. Yet even in these passages he
does not foreclose an understanding that will save both the complete-
concept notion and freedom. Thus, in the same context Leibniz considers the life of an individual up to a certain point in time and the

life of the same individual after that point. The crucial time is labeled
B. B is the time at which the individual does in fact perform some
free action such as setting out on a journey.[103] The line ABC then
represents the life history of the individual, and the issue of identity
and possibility focuses on the conditions for saying that the individual in the interval AB is the same as the individual in the interval BC.
Since there is a reason for everything, and no free action is a manifestation of arbitrariness or indifference, there was a reason prior to B
which explains why the journey is taken at B. Since the event at B
is a free action, the existence of a reason means that there is something about the agent's constitution, thought, perceptions, and assessment of his circumstances prior to B which would make it possible
to predict with complete certainty that he would make the journey.
It is in this sense that everything that he does is contained in the complete concept of the individual. But as we have stressed in part three,
the coercive reason for a free decision does not necessitate behavior.
The very idea of a course of action entails that other courses were
possible. The individual whose choice could be predicted by a sufficiently well-informed observer is, nonetheless, really choosing. This
too must be counted part of the complete concept of the individual.

The complete concept gives the impression of conflict with the
concept of free decision. But Leibniz means to include the fact that
he makes free decisions in the complete concept of an individual.
That he will make the free decision to take a journey is as much part
of the concept of a man as is the fact that he will take the journey.
We feel a conflict here that is reinforced by Leibniz's assertion that
an individual who does not make the trip cannot be the same individual. By the same token an individual who decides not to make
the trip cannot be the same individual. Then how can the decision
be free? If we set aside the ontological interpretation of possible
worlds, there is a way of putting together all of these ideas that recon-
ciles them all. This requires as the focal element the thought that a
man deciding what to do is, in the jargon of possible worlds, deciding
which of two possible worlds to bring about. Strictly speaking, there
is an infinite number of possible worlds in which I make the journey
and an infinite number of worlds in which I do not. The set of all
possible worlds is the union of these two sets. In a free action I determine that the actual world will fall into one or the other of these two
exhaustive sets of possibilities. In this respect Leibniz's conception of

human freedom is modeled in the creativity of God. God's work consists in determining which possible world will be real. He chooses a world which contains free agents. But that means that he does not *fully* determine which world will be real, for that is partly a consequence of all of the free decisions of all free agents. Every free act makes a difference as to what possible world is actual. We have seen that God knows just which world will be real, but that knowledge depends upon knowing how men will freely choose. This means no less than the thought that God's knowledge of the complete actual world depends upon his knowledge of our world-choosing actions as well as his own.

At the point of choice an individual can really do either of two things. If he does one, he makes himself and the world different from what it would have been had he done the other. In this sense, insofar as he is free, it is up to a man to determine which possible individual he is. The result of this decision, like all other features of an individual, contingent as well as necessary features, belongs to the complete concept of that individual. So we can say that though a man has a real choice, he will not be the same individual he would have been had he chosen differently. This does not at all require that there is, in some kind of existence or subsistence, another individual who does choose differently. The existence of such another would not help us to understand freedom. I determine what individual I will become not in the sense that there is a collection of individuals and I can become identical to just one of them. Rather, I can represent my future in different ways, and my action will determine which of these representations is a representation of the real world. Insofar as he means that when a man acts freely, he forecloses possibilities that would have made him a different man had they been realized, Leibniz is certainly right.

This ultimate reconciliation depends upon accepting the thought that Leibniz understands every free action as eliminating worlds from the roster of all possibilities. This interpretation would have men sharing in just the kind of creativity that Leibniz assigns to God. Men's power and knowledge remain insignificant in comparison with divine power and knowledge, but the essence of human action is otherwise quite a lot like divine action. In many passages in his writings this seems to be just the conception of human action that Leibniz does adopt. Thus:

[The rational spirit] is an image of divinity. The spirit not only has a perception of the works of God but is even capable of producing something which resembles them . . . our soul is architectonic in its voluntary actions. . . . In its realm and in the small world in which it is allowed to act, the soul imitates what God performs in the great world.[104]

NOTES

The following abbreviations are used in these notes:

G I–VII   Gerhardt, C.J., *Die Philosophische Schriften von G. W. Leibniz*, seven volumes, Berlin, 1885.

Grua I–II   Grua, Gaston, *G. W. Leibniz: Textes Inedits*, two volumes, Paris, 1948.

OF   Couturat, Louis, *G. W. Leibniz: Opuscules et Fragments Inedits*, Paris, 1903.

L   Loemker, Leroy, *Leibniz: Philosophical Papers and Letters*, second edition, Dordrecht, 1969.

M   Mason, H.T., *The Leibniz-Arnauld Correspondence*, Manchester 1967.

F   Frankfurt, H. G., editor, *Leibniz: Critical Essays*, Garden City, 1972.

I have translated the Latin citations from Couturat and Grua, of which there are no standard English translations, and the French from *Theodicée*, G VI. Other quotations in English translation only are from the works cited in the relevant notes.

1. See "A Brief Demonstration of a Notable Error of Descartes," L 297–302; also "Critical Thoughts on the General Part of the Principles of Descartes," especially Leibniz's comments on Part II, art. 4 and 36, L 392 and 393–95. Leibniz restates, summarizes, and refers to this issue in many of his articles and letters.

2. See Mach, E., *The Science of Mechanics*, McCormack, T. J., tr., La Salle, 1960, 360–5, and Papineau, D., "The *Vis Viva* Controversy," *Studies in the History and Philosophy of Science*, vol 8, 1977, 111–42.

3. *The Passions of the Soul*, Haldane and Ross, editors, *Descartes: Philosophical Works*, Cambridge, 1931, art. xxxv-vi, vol. I, 347–48.

4. See "On Nature Itself," L, 503.

5. *Principles of Philosophy*, art. lxiv, in Haldane and Ross, vol. I, 269.

6. The distinction between primary qualities (as those susceptible of mathematical characterization and thus objective) and secondary qualities (taken to include all sensuous qualities and to be subjective only) was first drawn by Galileo. The terminology "primary" and "secondary" was first used by Robert Boyle. The distinction plays a fundamental part in the philosophies of Descartes and Locke and has been retained by many thinkers up to the present. See, for example, Jackson, F., *Perception*, London, 1977, ch. 7.

7. See *Meditations*, "Replies to Objections," Haldane and Ross, vol. II, 253–54; and *Meditations*, VI, vol. I, 191.

8. *Principles of Philosophy*, Part II, art. xxxvi.

9. E. g., Letter to Mersenne, Adam and Tannery, *Oeuvres de Descartes,* Paris, vol. III, 648–49.

10. *Principles of Philosophy*, Part II, art. xliv–lii, Adam and Tannery, vol. VIII–1, 68–70.

11. "Critical Thoughts," L 398–402; and the note to Leibniz's comment on Part II, art. 53, G IV, 382–84.

12. "On Nature," L 505.

13. "On Nature," L 505; and Letter to DeVolder, L 516; see also, Naert, E., *Memoire et conscience de soi selon Leibniz*, Paris, 1961, 15–20.

14. Cassirer, E., *Leibniz's System in Seinen Wissenschaftlichen Grundlagen*, Marburg, 1902, Einleitung, art. 7, 90–102.

15. *Discourse on Method*, Anscombe and Geach, editors, *Descartes' Philosophical Writings*, London, 1954, 47.

16. *Principles of Philosophy,* Part IV, art. cciv, Haldane and Ross, vol. I, 300.

17. "But they who observe how many things regarding the magnet, fire, and the fabric of the whole world, are here deduced from a very small number of principles, although they consider that I had taken up these principles at random and without good grounds, they will yet acknowledge that it could hardly happen that so much could be coherent if they were false," *Principles of Philosophy*, 301. Here Descartes approximates the so–called hypotheticodeductive conception of theory formation and confirmation. The degree to which this kind of thinking appears in Descartes' ideas about scientific knowledge has been generally overlooked.

18. *Discourse on Metaphysics*, art. 10, L 308–9.

19. *Discourse*, art. 22, L 317–18.

20. *Meditations*, reply to objections, Haldane and Ross, 219.

21. "On Nature," L 505.

22. "On Nature," L 501.

23. L 498–508.

24. "On Nature," L 500.

25. "On Nature," L 501.

26. Boyle, R., *"Free Inquiry* etc.," 1692; see Loemker's account, L 498.

27. "On Nature," L 502.

28. "On Nature," L 504-5.

29. See chapter II above.

30. "On Nature," L 502.

31. "On Nature," L 503. The writer is Spinoza.

32. " . . . [I]f this world were only possible, the individual concept of a body in this world, containing certain movements as possibilities, would also contain our laws of motion (which are free decrees of God) but also as mere possibilities," from Leibniz's remarks on a letter of Arnauld, M 43.

33. *Discourse on Metaphysics,* art. 10, L 308–9.

34. See Hobbes' *Leviathan* Part I, ch. 1–3, and *De corpore,* Part IV, ch. 25.

35. See O'Shaugnessy, "Observation and the Will," *J. Phil,* 60, 1963.

36. See my "Teleological Reasoning," *J. Phil.,* 75, 1978.

37. For example, Grua 270–71. The distinction is also discussed in several letters of the Correspondence with Arnauld.

38. *Nouveaux Essais,* G V, 429.

39. M 43. See note 32 above.

40. See Clarke's fifth letter, addressed to art. 1–20 of Leibniz's previous letter, Alexander, H. G., editor, *The Leibniz-Clarke Correspondence,* Manchester, 1956, especially 98.

41. Leibniz's second letter to Clarke, art. 1, *Leibniz-Clarke Correspondence,* 16.

42. *Discourse on Metaphysics,* art. 5, L 305.

43. Montgomery, G., *Leibniz: Basic Writings,* LaSalle, 1902, 127.

44. See Russell, B., *The Philosophy of Leibniz,* London, 1902, ch. III, 25–30.

45. Louis Couturat played an especially important role in promoting this interpretation. See *La Logique de Leibniz,* Paris, 1901, ch. VI, sect. 5–18, 184–213. Summing up his detailed investigation, Couturat says, "En résumé, toutes verité est formellement ou virtuellement identique ou comme dira Kant, *analytique,* et par consequent doit pouvoir se demontrer *a priori* au moyen des definitions et du principe d'identité," 210. Couturat's book influenced Russell to change his interpretation from his 1902 exposition, according to which Leibniz makes existential propositions contingent, to the 1903 view that Leibniz did not really believe in contingency at all since he held that all truths are analytic. The prestige of Russell and Cout-

urat has been an enduring support for this interpretation. Among more recent writers the analyticity of all truth is ascribed to Leibniz by Fried, D., "Necessity and Contingency in Leibniz," *Phil. R.*, 87, 1978, 576; Wilson, M., "On Leibniz's Explication of Necessary Truth," in F 402; Lovejoy, A, "Plentitude and Sufficient Reason," *The Great Chain of Being*, Cambridge, Mass., 1936, as reprinted in F 295, 316, and 321; Hacking, I, "Individual Substance," F 138; Rescher, N., *Leibniz: An Introduction to his Philosophy*, Totowa, N.J., 1979, 23; and Nason, J.W., "Leibniz and the Logical Argument for Individual Substances," *Mind*, 1942, 201–2. Prominent dissidents are Broad, C.D., *Leibniz*, Cambridge, 1975, who recognizes the compatibility of the containment thesis and the complete concept with contingency; and Ishiguro, H., *Leibniz's Philosophy of Logic and Language*, Ithaca, N.Y., 1972, 15 and 120.

46. Quine, W.V., "Two Dogmas of Empiricism," in *From a Logical Point of View*, Cambridge, Mass., 1953, 20–46.

47. The limitation of this example to the subject-predicate propositional structure has no theoretical implications. Equally compelling illustrations could be constructed to fit any propositional form.

48. Grua 387.

49. OF 16–7 and 405; Grua 273.

50. "Omnes Existentiae excepta solius Dei Existentia sunt contingentes. Causa autem cur res aliqua contingens [prae alia] existat, non petitur ex [sola] eius definitione. . . . Cum enim infinita sint possibilia, quae tamen non existunt, ideo cur haec potius quam illa existant, ratio peti debet non ex definitione alioqui non existere implicaret contradictionem, et alia non essent possibilia." Grua 288.

51. See Strawson, P., and Grice, H., "In Defense of a Dogma," *Phil. R.*, 65, no. 2, 1956.

52. "Recent Work in the Philosophy of Leibniz," *Mind*, 1902, as reprinted in F 365.

53. "Recent Work."

54. "Verum est affirmatum, cuius praedicatum inest subjecto, itaque in omni Propositione vera affirmativa, necessaria vel contingente, universali vel singulari, notio praedicati *aliquo modo continetur* in notione subjecti." OF 16.

55. Grua 303; OF 405.

56. *Discourse on Metaphysics*, art. 13, L 310.

57. OF 18.

58. "Si omnes propositiones etiam contingentes resolvuntur in propositiones identicas, an non omnes necessariae sunt? Respondeo, non sane." ". . . dicendumque est in contingentibus non quidem demonstrari praedicatum ex notione subjecti; sed tantum eius rationem reddi, quae non necessitet sed inclinet." OF 405.

59. "First Truths," L 267.

60. Letter to Arnauld, M 63.

61. "Principium primum circa existentia est propositio haec: Deus vult eligere perfectissimum. Haec propositio demonstrari non potest; est omnium propositionum facti prima, seu origo omnis existentiae contingentiae." "Reflections sur Bellarmin," Grua 301.

62. See especially, Rescher, N., *The Philosophy of Leibniz*, Englewood, 1967, ch. II and III; and the same author's *Leibniz: An Introduction*, Totowa, N.J., 1979, ch. III and IV.

63. Parkinson, G. H. R., *Leibniz: Logical Papers*, Oxford, 1966. 77–78; OF 388 and 18.

64. OF 405.

65. "ita in contingentibus datur connexio [relatioque] terminorum sive veritas, etsi ea ad principium contradictionis sive necessitatis per analysin in identicas reduci nequeat." Grua 304; see also OF 388, 134.

66. "non intelligentem quomodo praedicatum subjecto inesse posset, nec tamen fieret necessaria." OF 18.

67. "Verum est vel necessarium vel contingens. Verum necessarium sciri potest per finitam seriem substitutionum seu per coincidentia commensurabilia, verum contingens per infinitam, seu per coincidentia incommensurabilia. Verum necessaria est cujus veritas est explicabilis; contingens cujus veritas est inexplicabilis. Probatio a priori seu [demonstratio] Apodixis est explicatio veritas." OF 408.

68. Letter to Arnauld, M 58.

69. *Nouveaux Essais*, G V, 428.

70. See, for example, the Correspondence with Des Bosses, L 596–616. Here Leibniz shows great flexibility, or ambiguity, on the connection between monads and the status of animals as unified beings. The much-discussed *vinculum substantiale* marks his insecurity concerning the adequacy of the theory that all true substances are monads.

71. M 42.

72. M 9.

73. *Nouveaux Essais*, G V, 428.

74. *Discourse on Metaphysics*, art. 9, L 308.

75. *Discourse*, art. 9, L 308.

76. This claim appears throughout Leibniz's writings. It makes up one of his arguments against atomism; it is a foundation for his relational theory of space and time; and it is a prominent dictum of the *Discourse on Metaphysics* and of the *Monadology*.

77. Grua 263.

78. Leibniz thinks that Spinoza and Hobbes held this erroneous view and that Descartes risks falling into it. See L 273 and *Theodicée*, G VI, 139.

79. *Theodicée*, G VI, 145.

80. Grua 270; and *Theodicée,* G VI, 122.

81. This revival has been stimulated in major part by the work of Saul Kripke, who made use of the concept of possible worlds in constructing a semantics for modal logic. For the revival of the paradoxes see the discussion of David Lewis's theory of possible worlds below.

82. Rescher, N., *Leibniz: An Introduction,* Totowa, N.J., 1979, 72.

83. G VI, 363.

84. Compare, "I argued against those misuses of the concept that regard possible worlds as something like distant planets, like our own surroundings but somehow existing in a different dimension, or that lead to spurious problems of 'transworld identification' "; Kripke, S., *Naming and Necessity,* Cambridge, Mass., 1980, 15.

85. For Lovejoy's view see F 327; for Russell's, F 378.

86. Grua 286; and *Theodicée,* G VI, 236.

87. This deflationary nonontological conception of possible worlds also seems to rule out the solution of the problem of evil that is imputed to Leibniz by Rescher and others. Nothing evil exists prior to the creation of the world. God's understanding that something evil *might* exist cannot be made to yield the idea that something evil *does* exist whether he does any creating or not.

88. Parkinson, G. H. R., *Leibniz: Logical Papers,* Oxford, 1966, 1–12; and Couturat, L., *La Logique de Leibniz,* Paris, 1901, ch. II, "La Combinatoire."

89. It is a defect of the simple dice world as a model for Leibniz's thinking that the best world can be achieved in either of two ways: (5,6) or (6,5). Strictly speaking Leibniz is absolutely committed to the view that there must be just one uniquely best possible world if God is to create anything.

90. Lewis, D., *Counterfactuals,* Cambridge, Mass., 1973, 84–91; and "Counterpart Theory and Quantified Modal Logic," *J. Phil.,* 1968, 65, 113–26.

91. *Counterfactuals,* 85–86.

92. Grua 270.

93. G VI, 363.

94. "Non ergo in quadam Visione consistit DEI scientia, quae imperfecta est et a posteriori; sed in cognitione causae et, a priori." OF 26.

95. "Secundum autores *scientiae mediae* non posset DEUS rationem reddere sui pronuntiati, nec mihi explicare. Hoc unum dicere poterit quaerenti cur ita futurum esse pronuntiet quod ita videat actum hunc representari in magno illo speculo, intra se posito, in quo omnia praesentia, futura, absoluta vel conditionata exhibentur. Quae scientia purè empirica est, nec DEO ipsi satisfaceret, quia rationum cur hoc potius quàm illud in speculo

repraesentetur, non intelligeret." OF 26.

96. See the works of Kripke and Lewis cited above and Chisholm, R., "Identity through Possible Worlds: Some Questions," and other essays in Loux, M., *The Actual and the Possible*, Ithaca, 1979.

97. Letter of Arnauld to Leibniz, M 9.

98. Articles 13–17, L 310–15.

99. M 58.

100. G II.

101. M 45.

102. M 45, and see also 60–61.

103. M 46.

104. *Principles of Nature and Grace,* art. 14, L 640.

V

Kant's Empiricism

According to Kant nature is the system of interconnected spatio-temporal objects and events comprising the total range of possible human experience, and nature is the subject matter of all human knowledge. At the same time nature is itself a product of the activity of the human cognitive constitution, and it would not exist at all were it not for human mental activities. The mind creates nature. This is a summary expression of a radical subjectivist tendency in Kant's thought. He says that we are *affected* by an unknown and unknowable reality, and this provides a *raw material* that excites the operation of our various faculties. In particular, it activates the sensitive aspect of our cognitive constitution which organizes the input as a system of "intuitions" in space and time, and it also awakens the conceptualizing aspect of our mental makeup which works up intuitions into representations of objects and thus gives rise to conscious experience and to the realm of objects of such experience. All of the objects with which experience can ever acquaint us must be found in this spatiotemporal world of perceptual experience. Even philosophical knowledge as expressed in principles like the principle of universal causality is only knowledge about the empirical world of possible experience. Kant never tires of warning us against interpreting such metaphysical principles as are accessible to us as truths about reality outside the mind-imposed conditions of possible experience. His Transcendental Dialectic is a catalog of erroneous theories produced by philosophers who have made the very mistake that he so urgently requires us to avoid.

This is radical subjectivity because the only reality we get to know, on Kant's theory, even though it is called "nature" and is the subject matter of all science, is not a reality that is independent of our existence as subjects of experience, and not independent of the occurrence of our thinking processes as subjects. The content of our experience cannot be characterized at all without ineliminable reference to contributions that we make in working up raw materials into a unified and comprehensible system of objects of experience. The objects we get to know would not exist at all, they would be *nothing*, in Kant's own explicit and dramatic way of putting it, without our mental activities. That is, the very mental activities that go into our getting to know about the existence and character of objects of experience help to create those objects and to determine their character. Without our thought nothing would be caused by anything else, nothing would be prior to or later than anything else, or simultaneous with anything else either. For space and time and causality are among the features of empirical things that owe their standing entirely to the contribution of the knowing subject. Of course, the things that originally set in motion all of this creativity of the mind would exist even though we did not exist. But these are, as Kant calls them, *things as they are in themselves*, and we can never know anything at all about them. Things in themselves are never objects of our experience, and the failure to realize that we can know nothing about them is the greatest source of error in metaphysics according to Kant.

I think that the magnitude and the daring of the claim that the mind itself fabricates the world it experiences has always been one of the reasons for great interest in Kant's philosophy. At the same time, it is generally believed, and I believe also, not only that Kant was one of the great original figures of philosophical thought, but that his philosophy contains insights of permanent value, insights from which we can learn, and which make the arduous penetration of his obscurity and his inconsistency worthwhile. It is his thinking about experience, objects of experience, and consciousness, that is, it is his radical and unattractive subjectivist theory, that also embodies his most valuable permanent contributions. It is of these contributions that P.F. Strawson speaks, in his wonderful book on Kant, saying that Kant made "very great and novel gains in epistemology, so great and so novel that, nearly two hundred years after they were made, they have still not been fully absorbed into the philosophical consciousness."[1] What I have to say here is organized with a view to showing how this permanent and large contribution of Kant's thinking can be approached in the setting of an explicit doctrine whose subjectivism appears so extravagant.

I have already said that Kant holds that all human knowledge, apart from appreciation of merely formal truths of logic, has for its subject matter the realm of possible experience, which is the perceivable natural world. This much is in itself appealing to empiricists like all of us because it is a powerful empiricist commitment. Kant is indeed an empiricist of sorts.

We can think of empiricism as a doctrine concerning knowledge or as a doctrine concerning reality. As a theory of knowledge, empiricism is the view that all knowledge claims rest ultimately on appeal to perceptual experience. As a theory of reality, empiricism is the view that the world accessible to us in sense experience *is* reality. Kant's thinking has a major antiempiricist component corresponding to each of these two conceptions of empiricism. First, there is his theory of synthetic a priori knowledge, that is, the claim that we do possess factual knowledge about the world which is not justifiable by appeal to experience. So Kant thinks that there is knowledge which is not empirical knowledge. Second, there is Kant's doctrine of the *thing-in-itself*, that is, a reality which we never do, and cannot possibly, encounter in experience. So Kant thinks that there is reality which is not empirical reality.

Both of these central themes of Kant's philosophy are crucially connected with his subjectivism. The theory of synthetic a priori knowledge is connected with subjectivism in that the constitutive role of the mind in forming the spatiotemporal world is the foundation of Kant's explanation for our possession of synthetic a priori knowledge. Kant is persuaded by Hume's analyses that no necessary propositions and no universal propositions can be given a rational justification if the admissible foundation for such justification is limited to experience. Experience cannot prove that in the future it will not itself overthrow any universal generalization that we find supported today. And any factual proposition defended by appeal to experience can hardly be necessary, since further experience might always show it false. Kant accepts this much from Hume. He does not follow Hume in simply abandoning the task of justification of our necessary and universal beliefs. He does not fall back, as Hume does, on mere naturalistic *explanation* rather than *justification* of our possession of such beliefs. How can we simply abandon justification here? What leads Hume to his famous skepticism is precisely what sets the fundamental question for Kant. If knowledge of scientific law cannot, and if knowledge of causal necessity cannot, be justified by experience, then Hume says we do not really have any such knowledge. Kant agrees that such knowledge cannot come from experience, so it must be a priori. It is not merely *analytic* knowledge, that is, these known truths do not reduce to formal and barren identities, so it is *synthetic* knowledge. But we do have such knowledge. It is absurd to suppose that scientific and mathematical understanding, the greatest achievement of human reason, is in fact no achievement at all but, rather, a collection of rationally unsupported beliefs with which nature happens to endow us. Thus, for Kant the question cannot be whether we have synthetic a priori knowledge but only "How is synthetic a priori knowledge possible?"

Many philosophers before Kant thought that man has some inner source of knowledge or other. What is special about Kant's view on this point is precisely the empiricist element in it. What we know on the basis of our constitutional resources are, for Kant, truths about the world of experience even though they are not truths derived from the world of experience. It is beliefs about the world of experience that Hume's skepticism undermines. The general disparagement of perception in rationalist thought led to the idea of siphoning away the perceptual as the locus of secondary qualities and mere *phenomena*. Rationalists thought that scientific grasp was attainable only when an intrinsically misleading perceptual picture of reality was replaced by mathematical representation. Kant rejects both the skepticism engendered by radical empiricism and the downgrading of perceptual reality by the rationalists. The world of which mathematical science is a true representation is the world of objects in space and time. That is the realm of perception.

The second major antiempiricist theme in Kant's thought, the concept of the thing-in-itself, is also directly connected with his subjective theory of the constitution of the natural world. That there must be another reality apart from the one that is created in the course of our attainment of conscious experience is a fundamental feature of Kant's theory from the outset. Although the end product of the activities of our mental constitution would not exist without those activities, and although this end product exhausts the range of scientific investigation, the subject is not also asserted to be the source of the initial input upon which these lavish creative powers are to operate. Kant's notion of affection by things is patterned on the anal-

ogy of perception. This is only an analogy, however. To say that we
are affected by outer reality is not just an extremely abstract way of
saying that we perceive things. The objects we encounter in perception, according to Kant, are produced by our mental faculties working on a raw input which first awakens their creative potential. We
cannot suppose that Kant is referring to objects of perception as the
items that originally affect us. He cannot be telling us that the input
that awakens our faculties comes from the finished product that their
activity creates. It must be reality independent of our thinking that
provides the original source of affection out of which we construct objects of experience. We know, for example, that these objects all exist
in space and time. But this is because the raw material of the initial
encounter with outer things is subjected to the *forms of our sensibility*. Space and time, according to Kant, are those forms, and they
constitute a framework provided by the subject upon which the materials of receptivity are deployed. The original sources of this affection are not spatiotemporal things at all.

Thus, the idea of a second reality composed of things in themselves is a fundamental part of the theory of nature that ascribes it
to the creative activities of the knowing subject. This is reflected from
the start in Kant's use of the word "appearances" (*Erscheinungen*")
as a general term of reference for the constituents of the world of
possible experience. There would be no point in calling the items encountered in experience "appearances" without a correlative reality
that is not merely empirical. There must be things-in-themselves
even though we cannot get to know anything about them.

Another deeper aspect of the relationship between Kant's subjectivism and his conception of things-in-themselves is illuminated
by comparing Kant's position with Berkeley's idealism. Early reviews
of the *Critique of Pure Reason* were disappointing and rather shock-
ing to Kant because they bracketed his views with Berkeley's idealistic
philosophy. The attitude of those who saw an affinity with Berkeley
is not any mystery. Berkeley, too, rejected the theory of secondary
qualities and insisted that the reality we encounter in our perceptual
experience is the only reality we come to know. Furthermore, in his
way Berkeley makes the empirical world depend for its very existence
on the mental activities that we naively think of as giving us access
to it. Is that not a view like Kant's? It is not, in the first instance,

because for Kant perceptual experience is founded upon an affection by a nonmental reality even though the object of which we ultimately become conscious is not that nonmental reality. For Berkeley there is no reality apart from empirical reality, and that means apart from the content of consciousness. Kant never entertained such a view and was legitimately alarmed when his ideas were taken to endorse it. At the same time this distinction which was so crucial to Kant tends to shrink in significance just because Kant holds that we do not and cannot know anything about this nonempirical reality. His theory then seems quite like Berkeley's with the difference that Kant adds a gratuitous commitment to a wholly unknowable reality.

I want to use the difference between Berkeley's and Kant's subjectivism as the motif for a first effort of rethinking Kant's thoughts in a way that captures what is valuable in them. I said that the thing-in-itself is the core of the difference, but the fact is that though Kant mentions it, he does not emphasize the thing-in-itself when he argues at length against the viewpoint of idealists and distinguishes his position from theirs. Instead, Kant tries repeatedly to formulate a surrogate distinction between subjective and objective, although both sides of the distinctions he introduces inevitably appeal to empirical reality, that is, to the reality that is thoroughly undermined by the subjectivism of his overall view. In the *Prolegomena,* for example, Kant offers a distinction between "judgments of perception" and "judgments of experience." If I judge that the room feels warm to me, the correctness of this judgment of perception requires nothing more than my own perceptual state. In a judgment of experience, however, I judge that the room is warm, and if I am right, an objective quality exists in the object of my experience. Therefore, my judgment is objective and generates predictions about the experience of others which are not entailed by assertions limited to my perceptual states. This distinction is supposed to divide public intersubjective knowledge from mere private appreciation of one's own mental states. Kant tries to make the distinction within the realm of natural objects of experience, all of which are products of our own constitution as subjects of experience.

In the second edition passage entitled "The Refutation of Idealism" and in the Paralogisms dealing with spurious philosophies of mind, Kant makes similar and more complex efforts to distinguish between a level of subjective experience and a level of objective fact, again without relinquishing any of the overall subjectivism of the thesis of the mind-dependence of nature. Kant organizes his views with reference to a philosophy of mind which he rightly takes to be held in common by many philosophers of both rationalist and empiricist schools, and which he regards as the foundation of various species of idealistic philosophy. The definitive and most influential articulation of this philosophy of mind is Descartes'. Descartes' scrupulous pursuit of indubitability led him to a revolutionary conception of the conscious mind and its immediate objects. This conception has dominated philosophy and determined the schedule of philosophical problems since the time of Descartes. Kant, or course, shares this inheritance. It is prominently reflected in his notion of "representations" as immediate objects of consciousness. Kant also recognizes fundamental limitations and illusions of the Cartesian philosophy of mind. He rejects outright the essential premise that as conscious subjects we are in direct touch only with the private contents of our minds, and that all other realities are at best subject matter for relatively tenuous hypotheses. A line from Hume's *Treatise* is a fine statement of this Cartesian premise and an indication of its power over philosophers of all schools: " 'tis universally allowed by philosophers, and is besides pretty obvious of itself, that nothing is ever really present with the mind but its impressions and ideas, and that external objects become known to us only by those perceptions they occasion."[2] This is the view that engenders idealism. It does so when arguments for the existence of extramental realities are left problematic or are flatly ruled out, as they are by Hume and Berkeley respectively. If we cannot get beyond our ideas, beyond "perishing" mental existences, as Hume calls them, with which we are in direct contact, then perhaps those perishing ideas *are* reality, and nothing beyond and in addition to such mental things exists at all.

This epistemological starting point, shared by Descartes, the classical empiricist tradition, and so many later thinkers, does not offer a minimally coherent account of conscious experience according to Kant. We cannot start with the idea of a conscious subject surveying wholly self-contained and ephemeral materials, such as Hume's perishing impressions and ideas. The missing ingredient necessary for the coherence of this viewpoint is the enduring conscious subject for whom the transitory contents are objects of consciousness. For we are not *given* any *self* except as one among other objects of experience.

Experiences of a self are just experiences of "empirical self-consciousness," and they are, as such, together with their content, as transitory as other experienced contents. We do not experience our selves as an enduring content that goes with all the other transitory contents. The empiricists actually share elements of this insight with Kant, but they do not pursue it to the end. Berkeley recognized that the concept of a perceiver, a thinking self for which ideas are conscious contents, could not be simply another idea. So Berkeley posited the *notion* of "spirits" to fill in for the missing idea. To Hume this account of a needed owner of impressions and ideas was not only unconvincing but also incompatible with Berkeley's own brilliant demolition of the corresponding concept of a material substance as the needed owner of sensible qualities. Paralleling Berkeley's repudiation of material substance, Hume repudiated mental substance. The only reality to which experience attests is the reality of the conscious contents of experience. Thus, "when I enter most intimately into what I call *myself* . . . I never can catch *myself* at any time without a perception, and never can observe anything but the perception."[3] This is much the view that Kant expresses when he limits knowledge of the self to empirical self-consciousness. Transcendental self-consciousness (or apperception), the principle of the necessary ownership of all my experiences by a single subject, corresponds to nothing that I experience and is, therefore, reducible to the barren analytic formula "All my experiences are mine." An "abiding self" contemplating hypotheses that might account for its fleeting conscious states is not a part of any epistemological starting point to which we are entitled. An abiding self is not given, and our idea of an abiding self is itself something that needs to be accounted for.

Kant's solution to the problem posed by a starting point that lacks a given subject of experience is more or less dictated by the problem. The stability and unity of experience does not come from an antecedently given enduring subject. Therefore, the antecedent existence of enduring objects of experience must provide the foundation of stability and unity.

Kant expresses this saying that there must be a "permanent" in perception. The content of experience must support the thought that the same object is encountered again, and, thus, the object must endure unperceived in the interval between perceptual encounters. Then the sameness of the object of perception can introduce the fundamental stability which the absence of any given sameness of the subject leaves wanting. For this, objects of perception must be independent of our perception of them. Kant reads this independence as the necessary existence of enduring objects in space. Space is the presupposed region for the existence of unperceived things which, a fortiori, cannot be found in the given temporal sequence of our perceptions. The concept of an enduring self as an accompaniment of experiences is itself derivative and depends upon the continuity provided by episodically perceived but continuously existing spatial objects. Kant thus solves the problem of the external world by refusing to allow it to arise and rules out all solipsistic philosophies and all the conceptions of mind that give rise to the theories he collects under the pejorative title "rational psychology." Perceived objects in space must exist unperceived, our acquaintance with them must be direct and no mere question of inference or hypothesis, and they must not depend upon our perception of them for their existence.

The core of Kant's profound contribution to metaphysics and epistemology is to be found in these views about the concept of experience, the subject and the object of experience, consciousness and self-consciousness. It is in just these areas that much remains to be learned from Kant, for just these views have "still not been fully absorbed into the philosophical consciousness" as Strawson says. I cannot try to restate these views here in a way that satisfies us and conforms to current philosophical perspectives and usage. I will address the much more modest question of the compatibility of this promising view of experience with the pervasive subjectivism that we find in Kant's conception of the empirical world. For notwithstanding his anti-idealist arguments for the independent existence in space of immediate objects of consciousness, Kant never retreats from his contention that space is itself subjective and that perceived objects exist "only in our faculty of representation." Here, as in the contrast between judgments of perception and judgments of experience, Kant tries to substitute a distinction *within* subjectively constituted nature for a distinction *between* subjective experiences and objective realities. How can Kant have supposed that his anti-idealist views could be consistent with his assertion that the mind makes nature? How can we find these strands of Kant's thinking compatible? If we are to regard his opposition to idealism and the philosophies of mind that engender solipsistic problems as part of his permanent contribution, we need a way of looking at Kant's subjectivism that mitigates its seeming irretrievable unattractiveness.

I want to look again at the premise that makes Kant's theory seem so extravagantly subjective. The continuously existing spatio-temporal world of perceivable objects is our own creation. The a priori knowledge we have of it is explicable precisely because we have made this system of things ourselves, and that is why we are in a position to say what the fundamental principles of its structure must be. Given this understanding, all our knowledge, and not merely synthetic a priori knowledge, must be regarded as knowledge of a mere construction, a world that is a creature of our thought and, therefore, a world that deserves to be called *imaginary*. This is why Kant's subjectivism seems to collide with his refutation of idealism. In his refutation he insists that immediate acquaintance with independent objects is essential if we are to have *experience* and not just *imagination* of outer things. How can this distinction move us if Kant presents the whole of possible experience together with all objects in space and time as products of our own minds which exist only in us? It appears that we are asked to distinguish between reality and imagination in a context which is all imagination to begin with.

It is imagination that carries the burden at crucial junctures in Kant's own construction. Imagination is at the heart of memory and all synthesis. Imagination for Kant is the capacity to think a nongiven object. All the mental activities upon which conscious recognition of objects depends involve appeal to something not presently given. Imagination enables us to conceive the existence of objects unperceived and to appreciate the continuous existence of what is experienced intermittently. Imagination is Kant's fundamental tool for the construction of a stable world out of transient receptions of raw material. Thus, that stable world is an imaginary world.

I have intentionally pressed Kant's subjectivism to the limit, reading it as the view that the world is a figment of the imagination. I mean to show how very close Kant's view is, even in this extreme form, to another passage of thought about experience which can be presented so as not to seem extreme at all but, on the contrary, so as to seem quite commonsensical. This view does not promote a despairing *ignorabimus* concerning things-in-themselves, nor does it generate Humean skepticism concerning the empirical world. Finally, this view is quite like the thoughts that Kant presents, and sometimes it seems to be none other than just Kant's thought.

This alternative interpretation can be expressed within the framework of a rough empiricism that endorses the general idea of a perceptual foundation for knowledge while remaining noncommittal on the analysis of perception and all other matters of detail, crucial though they must be in the long run. One thing is certain for any such empiricism: the perceptual experience upon which our knowledge is thought to depend is *episodic*. Our visual experiences, for example, start and stop as we open and close our eyes. The content of visual experience shifts gradually and abruptly depending upon our movement, and the movement of obstructions to vision, and upon what it is that happens to be visible. Tactual impressions require contact and are interrupted or broken by broken contact. There are comparable discontinuities affecting the other perceptual modes. Sleep ends experience altogether, and awakening restores it with new content. This is the character of our experience. It is for this episodic character that Hume said that impressions and ideas, the only things truly "present with the mind," are perishing existences. Episodic character is not a disappointing or regrettable fact about perceptual experience. It is not feasible at all to suppose that experience of all the things we perceive would be better if it were more continuous, or that our perceptual experiences would be more helpful to us if they coincided in duration with their objects.

In saying that we are empiricists we mean that we take this mass of episodic experience to be the only foundation we have for knowledge of the world. That world of which we do get to have knowledge does not have an episodic character, and its constituents are not perishing things as all of our experiences certainly are. On the basis of intermittent and relatively chaotic visual, auditory, and tactual experiences we get to know a stable world of things that has permanent existence globally and of which prominent local constituents are relatively enduring things. These enduring things are not given.

I state rough empiricism in this way in order to suggest Kant's conception of *representation*. Kant says that appearances exist only in our faculty of representation, and this strikes us as a hopelessly subjective conception, giving nature the status of an imagined world. But in one way Kant only means that objects are never the *given* content of any perceptual experience, and that such content is all that ever is given. Properly viewed, this is undoubtedly correct. The given content of a perceptual experience is, for example, a view of a bridge. The bridge itself is not given. It is this view that perishes should the viewer close his eyes. The bridge does not perish. The view, not the bridge, is, as Kant says, necessarily locatable in time with respect to all other mental contents of the subject. One might say, speaking of the view, that part of the bridge is obscured by an office building. This sort of thing is true of the given content, but not of the enduring object. This content and not a stable object is what is given. Such reflections will always eliminate the possibility that the content of an experience might be an object in nature.

Our thinking is complicated by the fact that we can only describe the given content of experience in terms of objects which are not given in the experience. This is Kant's view. Only when quite a bit of collecting, comparing, abstracting, in short, a lot of *synthesis* has taken place can we have an idea of an object of perceptual experience such as a bridge. Only then can we describe anything as "a view of a bridge." All description, being irreducibly comparative, necessarily goes beyond the immediately given and alludes to a range of related contents. Furthermore, consciousness of perceptual experience is itself dependent upon the same synthesis that makes description possible. Consciousness presupposes that experiences involve recognition. So, in order that experiences be conscious at all, they must be recognized as experiences of this or that, and that means just that they must fit descriptions framed in terms of objects of experience. Therefore, it seems that we can only describe our experiences in terms of a picture of stable objects that *we form* on the basis of episodic and perishing experienced contents. Intrinsically, that is, apart from all comparison, the given is indescribable, for description *is* comparative. So we can describe the given only in terms of the nongiven. This dark-sounding formulation means that to describe our experience at all we have to say things like "I can see part of the bridge from here," although the bridge itself is not given for it does not perish, and the bridge is not in itself partly obstructed, and so on. After we have attained consciousness and can describe our experiences in the language of objects, it remains the case that what is truly given is not objects but always perishing views, or representations.

Empiricists generally concede nowadays that we can devise no language of empirical description short of the so-called material-object language in which descriptive terms fit, in the first instance, relatively durable public objects. This is certainly part of what Kant means in arguing for permanence as part of our necessary conception of objects perceived. That is the argument that Kant depends on in opposing subjective idealism and the Cartesian starting point in epistemology. It remains to be seen whether this conception of permanence in *immediate* objects of perception is compatible with the subjective tendency of Kant's own commitment to the transience of the given in experience. So far we have seen that Kant shares this commitment with all roughly empiricist viewpoints.

The known world of permanent existence is not what is given. Certainly from the point of view of empirical learning theory it must be supposed to take some doing on the part of any organism to get to recognize what it is in experience that betokens objects of continuing existence. But we do succeed here, and when we do, we have a picture of a stable empirical world of which our experiences are transitory representations. We speakers can describe our experiences precisely by characterizing them as experiences of that stable world. The natural philosophical question here is What is the status and the validity of the conception of the stable world to which we attain? Sticking to the factual level which is itself undercut by skeptical speculation, we all tend to think that the picture we have of the stable material world is something like an automatic interpretation we make of our episodic experience quite early in life. What I want to emphasize is that however it is formed, it must *be formed*, for it is something like a picture of the world and not the world itself which we come to possess. What is given, when we have matured and learned a bit, is still a transient content. The attainment of the level of conscious description gives us two things to talk about. One is the now-describable experiential episodes themselves, and the other is the picture of the world that we form on the basis of those episodes. We form the picture. Doing so is coming to understand our experience. As a picture it exists only in our thinking, and without our thinking processes this picture of the world would not exist.

At this point I think it looks as though Kant's subjectivism will inevitably follow, and it will not be compatible with the objective claims of his refutation of idealism. Kant thinks, and it seems that we shall have to follow him, that one kind of request for objectivity is inevitably going to be disappointed. Suppose we ask, How does our picture of a stable world compare with reality? Is it a good representation? Or does it fall short? When he is at his most subjective, Kant thinks, first, that these questions cannot possibly be answered and, second, that the fact that we cannot answer them has something to do with the limited character of merely human cognitive capabilities. For have we not agreed, as empiricists, that the accessibility of the world *consists* in our possession of a picture of it in terms of which we describe and interpret the ephemeral given? We are in no position to compare reality with our picture, as though both the world and our picture of it were available for comparison. The closest we get to reality is the picture. There is no comparing to be done. At the same time Kant continues in the conviction that just such a comparison would have to be made in order to justify any claim that the picture we have in our minds is not just something created by us but is also a valid indication of things as they exist apart from our experience and our capacity to create conscious pictures in terms of which fleeting impressions are interpretable.

We have only our picture of the world of stable objects, and we cannot compare the picture with the world itself, for we only know the world insofar as we have this picture. Kant ordinarily reads this as entailing a limited subjective horizon for human knowledge. But no such discouraging conclusion actually follows from the character of our experience and our conception of the world based on experience. Subjectivism here is an intellectual illusion to which Kant and many other philosophers are susceptible. Things must be represented if they are to be known, and representation does lead to knowledge of things and not to knowledge of itself. Kant is sometimes partially aware of this himself, and that is why he never abandons the idea that the needed distinction between subjective and objective must be formulable within the framework of the assumption that stable objects are "thought" by us but never given. In the *Prolegomena*, for example, Kant says that intuition must represent objects since "the properties of things in themselves cannot migrate from those things into my faculty of representation."[4] Thus, to say that we must represent things is just to say that the things we get to know cannot themselves enter our minds. This is hardly a limitation or a reason for any discouraged subjectivism. The idea that our knowledge is drastically limited requires the further thought of a contrasting cognition of reality that does not involve representation. If we could go beyond mere representation, or strike through the veil of appearances and, thus, encounter reality itself, then our knowledge would be unfiltered by subjective mediation. It is this thought that supports subjectivist conclusions. But this thought is very implausible when explicitly stated and examined. Surely it is only because we are able to represent the world that we are able to get to know anything about it at all. Representation is a necessary means to knowledge, not an obstacle. We noted above that the episodic and perspectival character of perceptual experience cannot be thought a regrettable feature of it. Essential properties of experiences can never be properties of objects, and essential properties of objects can never be properties of experiences. This is as it should be. Objects could not possibly be given. They cannot migrate into our minds, as Kant says. We have to see the world *from somewhere*. But an object does not exist from somewhere. The world does not start and stop, but how could we expect that our experience of it might be other than transient? A continuous experience of everything at once, from nowhere in particular, would not be experience at all. Exactly what is required is transient experience (in which objects are not given) which we come to recognize as experience *of* objects.

Kant loses sight of these relations because he always thinks in terms of an alternative mental constitution, superior to the human, namely, the mind of God. In the seventeenth and eighteenth centuries philosophers still commonly adverted to God's thinking, not merely as part of a theological commitment but also as a convenient vehicle for expressing views about necessity and objectivity. The greatest philosophers thought it profitable to argue about what God might have done; and what He could not have done; and whether He might have created the universe earlier than He did; and whether He perceives the world; and what sufficient reasons He has for creating as He does. Along with its other functions, the idea of the mentality of God operates in Kant's thought to make our human intellectual undertakings seem comparatively inadequate. This encourages Kant to read the necessary role of representation in knowledge as a limitation and a falling-short of theoretical possibilities. For example, Kant says that *human* intuition is sensuous, meaning that *we* have to be affected, and thus representations have to be engendered in us. These representations and not the affecting reality are given. God's in-

tuition would not suffer these limitations. God knows reality without
having to be affected. He does not really have to look down through
the clouds or wait for a propitious moment for his apprehension of
things. He does not, then, rely on representations as we must. The
idea of this kind of mentality is just what makes our apprehension
of reality seem disappointing.

Consider Kant's conception of space and time in this light. Men
have to apprehend things from somewhere and at some time. Since
a thing must be viewed from somewhere if it is going to be viewed
at all, its being somewhere relative to a man's viewpoint is a necessary
condition for its intellectual accessibility to him. But this is a consequence of the fact that men must rely on representations. If we did
not have to take a look in order to know reality, as God does not, it
would not have to be somewhere in order to be known. If we knew
everything without bothering with a sequence of transient experiences, interrelatable in time, and, therefore, surveyable by memory
and understanding, then time would be all at once for us. There
would be no time. These are precarious speculations. The idea of the
mind of God helped Kant to feel supported by thoughts on the mar-
gin of intelligibility like these. God does not have to create a picture
and then face the unanswerable question of its adequacy. He grasps
things as they are in themselves, without a perspective and without
imposing subjective conditions. Further, while human intuition is
passive and receptive, and only our *understanding* is active and creative, God's intuition is called "creative intuition" by Kant, suggest-
ing the theory of Malebranche inherited by Berkeley that God's thought
of reality is the same as his sustaining creation of it. Naturally, God
does not have to acquire and collect subjective views of things, retaining old ones for the sake of comparison and eventually for the construction of descriptions cast in terms of abstracted empirical concepts. But this is just what man must do. This fanciful thinking about
divine cognition prevents Kant from recognizing the potential of his
own theory, not as a quasi-factual account of our mental faculties,
but as an exploration of the very concepts of cognition and experience. If we do reinterpret his thoughts as philosophical analyses of
these concepts, then they do not have to carry nearly the burden of
unattractive subjectivism that Kant himself ordinarily presents along
with his best insights.

Verbal expression is a form of representation and a helpful model
for the relationship of representation and reality. Consider proposi-

tional expressions as our pictures of the world. To contemplate the world at all we have to frame propositions. To believe anything we have to assent to propositions. To know anything is to assent to a proposition in a context wherein other complex conditions are satisfied. It looks as if our knowledge will always be mediated by propositional expression, and this looms as an obstacle to some fancied unmediated objectivity. Are propositions, then, an unavoidable distorting lens, imposed by our needs, through which we have to approach reality? We are tempted here to complain about a logical feature of the perspective of any knowing subject as if it were a factual obstacle to human knowledge. Propositionality makes thought possible. We cannot put a natural object in the place of a propositional subject. A structure of words makes it possible to say something. A structure of objects says nothing. Therefore a structure of objects does not say anything that might be true, or believed, or known.

Still we come back to Kant's question If all we have is the proposition, then how do we know it is true? Kant often thinks that the fact of the matter is that we do not. Our picture of the world goes no further than the systematic interconnectedness of our thoughts, for it can go no further. Then Kant leans toward something like a coherence theory of truth. Scientific knowledge is the coherence of appearances. But his thought about perception and his refutation of idealism pave the way for something better than this. As empiricists we ought to answer the question How do we know that propositions are true? by appeal to experience. Of course, when we have attained consciousness, and our experiences have become describable, we cannot literally follow the "plain historical method" Locke envisioned. We cannot retrace our epistemological steps back to the unsynthesized and indescribable given. But we are entitled to call attention to simple situations where "I see it" is the only right answer to give to questions like "How do you know that the mail has arrived?" This is a good answer, one that Kant's understanding makes available for epistemology. For does he not say that enduring objects in space must be the immediate objects of perceptual consciousness?

Idealism is the thesis that the objects of consciousness are all mental things, that is, that they are all ideas. Ideas are dependent upon thought for their existence. But Kant argues that the things of which we are conscious in perception are not mental things but objects, independent of our thought, that exist in space. These are the immediate and not the inferred objects of perceptual experience. Of course, this is inconsistent with the Kantian claim that there are no spatial things apart from our mental activities. To say that objects are "independent" has to mean that they exist *in themselves*. It is the comparison of human with divine apprehension of things that encourages Kant to make space and time systems of purely subjective relations, and not just systems of relations, following Leibniz. If we drop the rhetoric of the limitations of mere human faculties, we are free to characterize the objects of consciousness in perception as spatiotemporal objects, while conceding that such objects are never given. The given is always a perishing content. As such, the given is not an object of consciousness at all. Synthesis of the given, that is, integration and learning which results in a conception of a stable world of objects is required for all recognition, description, and consciousness. When we attain consciousness we can recognize an experience as a view of a bridge. Only thus recognizable can experience be conscious at all. The experience retains the perishing and perspectival features of a representation. That is its subjectivity. But when a perceiver does see a bridge, for all the subjectivity of his experience, the object of which he is conscious is a bridge and not a representation.

To say that objects are not given is to say that objects do not migrate into our thought, as Kant puts it. Upon reflection, this cannot be a shortcoming of our thought. Objects could not migrate into God's thought either. We can and do become conscious *of* objects. That we do is a presupposition of consciousness in general according to Kant. That means that self-consciousness and consciousness of our representations as such are conceptually dependent upon our success in attaining consciousness of enduring independent objects. As objects of consciousness the status of mental things, of ideas, is derivative. This ordering of things is quite the reverse of idealism. It is at the center of Kant's most valuable philosophical insights.

NOTES

1. *The Bounds of Sense*, London, 1966, 29.
2. Selby-Bigge, editor, London, 1888, 67.
3. The same, 252.
4. Section 9.

VI

Ambiguities in Kant's Treatment
of Space

1. Introduction

One of the sources of persistent obscurity in the philosophy of
Kant is the fact that he introduces a double standard for dealing with
questions about what there is. In the *Critique of Pure Reason*[1] this
appears first in the culminating assertion of the Transcendental Aesthetic: the assertion of the "empirical reality and transcendental
ideality of space and time." To say that space and time are empirically
real means that the things that figure in our experience are spatiotemporal things. These are the things found in the commonsense
world of perception and the things that make up the subject matter
of all scientific investigation. All of these empirical realities exist in
space and time. But to say that space and time are transcendentally
ideal means that they do not characterize things *as they are in themselves*, as opposed to things *as they appear in our experience*. Things
apart from our experience and independent of our mental activities
are not spatiotemporal things. Vis-à-vis things as they are in themselves, space and time are not anything real at all. In the realm of
things as they are nothing corresponds to our ideas of space and time,
and these realities do not exist in space and time. "It is solely from
the human standpoint that we can speak of space, of extended things,
etc." (A 26, B 42). Time, "in itself, apart from the subject, is nothing"
(A 35, B 51).

One may suspect at the outset that the device that Kant introduces here for treating questions about what there is may be too
powerful for any legitimate use. It looks as though Kant avails himself of a means for having it both ways at crucial junctures. Faced with
the destructive claims of skeptics and idealists, Kant is a staunch

realist. The objects of perception are real things. They constitute a causally connected, spatiotemporal system of material objects which Kant calls "nature," and our knowledge of these objects is objective knowledge. When he is pursuing this realism, Kant likes to label entities envisioned by others that fall outside the sphere of possible experience mere "Hirngespinst" and "Gedankendingen." But when Kant's thoughts of human morality and freedom seem to be threatened by this all-too-causal empirical reality, he is prepared to downgrade it, to emphasize that these empirical "objects" are *only* appearances, to reprimand "stubborn insistence" on their reality (A 537, B 565), and to rest his conception of man and the human situation on a further reality that underlies and is more fundamental than appearance.

As a parallel for "the empirical world" of things we can perceive and study scientifically, Kant uses the expression "the intelligible world" for the realm of things-in-themselves. But in the *Critique* and all later works Kant consistently asserts that we cannot know anything whatever about the intelligible world — an odd sort of intelligibility! Before the *Critique*, in his *Inaugural Dissertation*, for example, Kant accepted a traditional concept of an intelligible world as opposed to a world of perception, and he believed, in the spirit of Plato and the rationalists, that we could have knowledge of nonsensible reality. In his mature writing Kant repudiated the claim to know the nonsensible, while retaining the designation "intelligible," although it is only fitting in the context of the earlier view. The single surviving theme from his earlier position is Kant's occasional speculative suggestion that a creature whose intuition (mode of receptivity) is nonsensible might actually know things-in-themselves and that God may know things-in-themselves without anything like sense experience.

Two kinds of reality, empirical and transcendental, risk generating two systems of truths, one for each reality. Our complete and permanent ignorance of things-in-themselves, in Kant's thinking, conveniently avoids the possibility of conflict between these two systems of truths. The unknowability of transcendental reality "makes room for faith" in Kant's own words. But in this connection, too, the duality of the empirical and the transcendental, or knowable and unknowable reality, seems too convenient to be legitimate. An unfriendly critic can read Kant's doctrine as an admission that the faith that defends "God, Freedom, and Immortality" operates only by relegating them to a region where nothing can tend against them since nothing can be known at all. At the same time the seeming robustness of empirical realism also relies on the utter unknowability of things-in-themselves in the sense that, if we could know anything at all about things-in-themselves, we would immediately recognize their ontological primacy and the derivative and figmentary status of appearances. The veil of appearances seems to be more than that in Kant's system, one might argue, only because it is all that we can know.

Should we reject the dual standard of reality, the merely empirical reality of objects of experience, and the unknowability of things as they are apart from how they appear to us? Or is there some fundamental truth in Kant's realism which is not hopelessly undercut by his transcendental idealism? These questions go to the heart of Kant's system. In trying to answer them we will find that the concept of space plays a particularly prominent role.

2. Outer Sense and Idealism

Kant's efforts to distinguish his views from the ideas of earlier thinkers such as Descartes or Hume bring his conception of outer sense to the fore. Kant often relies entirely on the fact that he endorses both inner and outer receptivity, while the "problematic and dogmatic idealists," as he classifies them, accept inner receptivity but not outer. In the beginning of the Aesthetic he defines outer intuition or outer sense as a capacity "to represent to ourselves objects as outside us and all without exception in space" (A 22, B 37). In contrast, in inner intuition the mind "intuits itself or its inner state" (A 23, B 37). Here Kant quite plainly thinks that "outside us," where we locate what is available to outer sense, means outside the mind, where located things will not be mental things. Inner sense, just as plainly, has only mental things like thoughts and ideas for its objects.

Kant thinks that the Cartesian ordering of these matters, inherited by the empiricists, involves a reduction of receptivity to inner sense alone.

> They have no expectation of being able to prove apodeictically the absolute reality of space; for they are confronted by idealism, which teaches that the reality of outer objects does not allow of strict proof.

On the other hand, the reality of the object of our inner sense (the reality of myself and my state) is, [they argue,] immediately evident through consciousness. [A 38, B 55]

Kant goes on to say that the Cartesian-empiricist fails to note that the object of outer sense in space is just as accessible to us as the object of inner sense.

In his interpretation of the tradition preceding him Kant is surely right. For Descartes spatial reality, the realm of extended substance, contrasts at the most fundamental level possible with the realm of mental things. Extension does not think, and the mind is not extended. To this distinction Descartes very definitely adds the view that spatial reality is never *given*. It is not, as Kant would put it, intuited. In Descartes' system, space is identical with matter. The existence of a spatial realm is the existence of extended substance. This existence is viewed by Descartes as something that must be argued for. Descartes never contemplates arguing for the existence of our own conscious states, thoughts, and ideas. The point of the *cogito* in this context is precisely to show the impossibility of thinking of my own mental states as something for which I could stand in need of an argument. Stated in terms of "intuition," for Descartes the mental and inner is intuited, while the nonmental, outer, and spatial is not intuited but is a matter of relatively tenuous hypothesis. For Hume, too, "impressions and ideas," both of which are mental things, are the only things "really present with the mind,"[2] while the existence of extended bodily things is only recognized with the help of naturally implanted, though rationally unsupported, beliefs. In the case of Berkeley the given does not include anything outside the mind, for, indeed, there are no extramental realities at all.

Thus, the Cartesian-empiricist's conception of consciousness is very much what Kant calls simply inner sense. Kant gives us a whole mental faculty, namely, outer sense, beyond any cognitive equipment assigned us by the idealist tradition. The outer in Kant's system is given in intuition just as the inner is given in intuition. And the outer is not the mental.

It is not surprising that Kant thinks that his acceptance of outer sense sufficiently distinguishes his view from any form of idealism. His theory of outer intuition also explains why he is so unconcerned about egocentric and skeptical problems which inevitably make up the first order of business from the Cartesian viewpoint. These problems will not arise if we find nonmental objects in space among what is immediately given. In the Cartesian-empiricist tradition we can say that the problem of outer reality is the problem of the existence of spatial things to correspond to our ideas of spatial things, ideas which are not themselves spatial things. "The problem of the external world" means the world of spatially locatable things all of which are, unlike any idea, external to the mind. In Kant's scheme spatial things are given. They are given to outer sense, so that the problem of the external world cannot be put in the usual way at all. Kant's empirical realism is the assertion that objects in space are given.

Sometimes Kant calls the opposed view "empirical idealism." Just as transcendental idealism means that spatial things are only ideas and nothing real in the sphere of things as they are in themselves, empirical idealism means that contents of our conscious experience of spatial things consist merely in ideas of spatial things and offer nothing at all in the way of actually existing spatial objects. The idealist view that objects of experience are *nothing* real in space is "problematic" in Hume, in that Hume thinks that there *may* by outer objects as well as ideas, and dogmatic in Berkeley, who thinks that there *cannot possibly* be outer objects as well as ideas. In Kant's thinking we are not limited to a foundation of ideas of spatial things any more than we are limited to a foundation of ideas of mental things. Both are present to us as immediately as anything can be. Naturally Kant found it hard to accept early criticisms that bracketed his theory with Berkeley's. Berkeley denies more explicitly than anyone else the immediacy of spatial things outside the mind, and then he goes on to deny the existence of spatial things outside the mind.

Upon the least examination, however, Kant's empirical realism turns out to be a fragile thing. Although outer sense represents things "as outside us and all without exception in space," Kant says, again and again, throughout the *Critique*, that space exists only "in us," that, like time, space would be nothing apart from the human cognitive constitution. Spatial appearances exist only "in the faculty of representations," (A 104), and "all objects with which we can occupy ourselves, are one and all in me" (A 129). The mind absorbs spatial objects in this prominent Kantian claim. The innerness and mind-dependence of *all* objects seem to set at nothing the thought that Kant has distinguished his position from that of the Cartesian-empiricist.

When we have come a good way into the *Critique*, to the Paralogisms wherein Kant explains the illusions to which rationalist philosophy of mind is susceptible, he says:

> The expression "outside us" is unavoidably ambiguous in meaning, sometimes signifying what as *a thing in itself* exists apart from us, and sometimes what belongs solely to outer experience. [A 373]

The view so clearly put here contradicts the claim that the theory of outer sense separates Kant's philosophy from all the forms of idealism that Descartes' account of mind and perception generates. Kant tells us here that outer appearances do not exist "apart from us." What can this mean if not that they do not exist outside our minds and thoughts? The relevant problem that the Cartesian tradition seemed to face might be put in the question "Are there spatial things which exist apart from us, that is, apart from our thoughts and representations of spatial things?" Of course, Descartes, Berkeley, and Hume all know that within our thought we find ideas of spatial things and that these ideas differ from ideas of things which are not spatial. In mounting a proof of the existence of extended reality Descartes is responding to the fact that ideas of spatial things do not exist apart from us, while spatial things, if any there be, do exist apart from us.

The whole Kantian theory asserting the necessary existence (if experience is to be possible) of causally connected and enduring empirical objects, the theory secured with such energy and subtlety in the Analytic half of the *Critique*, seems to be thrown away here when Kant says that none of these realities are anything at all outside our own thinking. This collapse of the pretensions of outer sense reminds us that Kant sometimes confines his opposition to idealism to a very different line of thought. This alternative opposition merely stresses that Kant accepts, while idealists deny or doubt, the existence of things as they are in themselves in addition to appearances of objects of experience. Arguing in this vein, Kant places no weight at all on outer sense, as though he realizes that in his system outer sense is simply not *outer* enough to reach any nonmental realities that may exist apart from us.

In the section of the *Critique* entitled "The Ground of the Distinction of All Objects in General into Phenomena and Noumena," that is, into appearances and things as they are in themselves, Kant goes so far as to reduce the concept of a reality beyond that of appearances to the status of a "merely negative concept" (A 254, B 309). By this he means that the idea of noumena is simply the idea of realities that are *not* known in experience. Since objects of experience are all the objects of which we can have any knowledge, noumena, if there are any, are just objects of which we have no knowledge. Kant goes on to call the very concept of such further, wholly unknown, realities a "problematic concept" and a "limiting concept" (A 255, B 311), and he seems to imply that we cannot get quite as far as the unqualified assertion that there are any such noumena. The concept of a further kind of being beyond appearances only clearly marks the end of the realm of objects of whose existence we are sure, namely, the mind-dependent objects constituting the empirical world. Kant is saying that we think of mind-dependent realities *as appearances* of real entities other than themselves, but perhaps there is no other reality, in which case appearances are not really appearances, but instead they are the only kinds of things that there are apart from the minds which intuit these things. Is this not exactly Berkeley's view? The idea that, for the things immediately present to the mind, *esse* is *percipi* is the idea that we have no right to think of these things as appearances. Berkeley's ontology is limited to the ideas present to minds and the minds to which those ideas are present. If we are forced to interpret Kant as surrendering the true outerness of appearances in favor of a counterfeit outerness of space which exists only in our minds, then his whole metaphysics must appear an enormous disappointment, and all of the famous and difficult arguments of the first half of the *Critique* must seem a waste of effort.

3. Transcendental Aesthetic

In the hope of salvaging as much as possible from this threatening disappointment let us examine in more detail the main doctrines of the Transcendental Aesthetic which I identify as follows: (a) the metaphysical expositions of space and time, (b) the transcendental expositions, (c) the view that space and time are *forms* of outer and inner sense respectively, and (d) their asserted transcendental ideality.

The opening section of the Aesthetic is concerned with the definition of "intuition" (*Anschauung*) and related concepts that underlie Kant's controlling distinction between receptivity and spontaneity, that is, between the functions of intuition and those of understanding and reason. There follow immediately separate and parallel discussions of space and time. In each case a four-point *metaphysical exposition* of the concept is supposed to be followed by a *transcendental exposition*, but the passages are marred by Kant's curious failure to adhere to the distinction between these two points of view, even though the distinction seems to have been invented by him precisely for the purpose of facilitating this very discussion. The four metaphysical points are that space, or time, is (1) not an empirical concept, (2) an a priori and necessary concept, (3) a singular rather than a discursive concept, and (4) a concept of something infinite.

The expository confusion in both discussions consists in Kant's inserting the transcendental considerations between the second and third metaphysical points and then only partially correcting the disorder in passages that follow and in changes in the second edition. The actual reason for this, I believe, is that Kant wants to make the transcendental points in the context of the premises relevant to them. These premises are the first two metaphysical points and only those two. In a later passage Kant himself explains the arrangement saying that he wanted to save space. But the confused ordering does not save any space unless Kant means that, with any other organization, he would have had to restate the needed metaphysical views in order to connect them with the transcendental exposition which would be separated from them.

In the instances of both space and time the four metaphysical points are assertions for which no arguments are given. Perhaps by a metaphysical *exposition* Kant means an account that ought to be accessible to any highly intelligent and philosophically mature common sense. He seems to expect that the statement of the claims will suffice for their acceptance. This is not entirely unreasonable in that there is much to be said for the four points.

The first point, considering only space for the moment, is that space is not an empirical concept. Kant says that the concept of space is presupposed for rather than derived from experience. To see what Kant has in mind it is useful to refer to another similar point that Kant often makes later in the *Critique*. Unlike ordinary empirical objects, space is not itself perceived. So space is not a concept like the concept *ocean* or *box*. These are empirical concepts which we possess because we encounter such things as oceans and boxes in our perceptual experience. Of course, space might be an empirical concept, although not an object of perception, if it figured in hypotheses belonging to an explanatory theory, in the way in which the concept of a gravitational field figures in theories that explain the perceived motion of objects. Kant's second metaphysical point rules out this kind of theoretical status for the concept of space. Space is necessary for any outer experience at all, while theoretical objects are doubly contingent and never necessary. Theoretical objects are contingent, first, because the facts which they are introduced to explain are contingent facts. But theoretical objects have a second kind of contingency beyond the contingency of the facts they explain. For theoretical objects may always be repudiated in favor of other theoretical commitments that explain the same facts even better. The status of space is nothing like this because, according to Kant, there could not be any facts of outer intuition without space.

Kant expresses the necessity of space, saying that we can think space *empty*, but we cannot think it *away*. The inhibition on thinking space away is related to the fact that space is not something we detect by perceiving it or experiencing it. Things that we do detect by perceiving them, things like oceans and boxes, we can think of as empty (oceans empty of fish and boxes empty of apples, respectively), and we can also think such things away, that is, think a universe without oceans or boxes among its constituents. Now thinking space empty is simply thinking away *all* of the constituents of the outer universe. Since space is not one of these, we have nothing to bring under the heading of thinking away space itself. There is nothing else that might disappear from the outer beyond the things that appear in it, and space is not one of these things. Kant reads the fact that we perceive things in space and that space is not threatened by disappearance as the necessity of space.

The two other metaphysical points are of less importance to our present interests. That space is not a discursive concept, as the concepts *ocean* and *box* are, means that it is the idea of an individual. There is just one space in which all outer things are located. The plural "spaces" indicates only parts of space and not instances of space, while oceans and boxes are instances, not parts. This is a very important assertion since it is the foundation of the unity and uniqueness of the spatiotemporal universe and, thus, of the connectability in principle of all objects of possible experience. The final claim, the infinity of space, we can pass over without comment here.

The metaphysical expositions are reflections on the concepts of space and time which do not depend on any special commitments or on any characteristically Kantian critical or transcendental arguments. The transcendental expositions, which are loosely derived from the metaphysical, plunge us at once into specifically Kantian doctrine as well as into considerable obscurity. From the nonempirical yet necessary status of space and time the transcendental expositions purport to explain how it is that we possess knowledge in geometry (in the case of space) and knowledge of a much more vaguely indicated body of more or less mathematical doctrine (in the case of time). The explanation is more implied than stated, and it makes minimal sense only in the context of views about necessary truth, mathematics, and experience which are not themselves discussed in the Aesthetic, although they have been sketched in the introduction to the *Critique*.

The root idea is that no necessary truth can be justified on a foundation of empirical evidence. Kant takes this to have been established definitively by Hume. If we learned about space empirically, as we learn about boxes and oceans, no knowledge of space could amount to necessary truth. But knowledge of space is geometry, and geometry is a body of necessary truth. The discussion here in the Aesthetic makes no effort to explain how truths about space are actually reached but rests content with the general thought that since our idea of space is not derived empirically, propositions about the structure of space can also be expected to be nonempirical. Kant always takes it for granted that we do possess knowledge in mathematics and that the mathematical propositions we know are synthetic (rather than analytic) and necessary (which requires that they be a priori). The tenor of Kant's thought is illuminated by a comment he makes on Hume's view that belief in strictly universal and necessary propositions is not rationally justifiable: "[Hume] would never have been guilty of this statement so destructive of pure philosophy, for he would have recognized that according to his arguments pure mathematics would also not be possible; and from such an assertion his good sense would have saved him" (B 20). Here Kant shows his conviction that we must find some explanation for necessity in mathematical knowledge since we do possess such knowledge, and he also reveals his rather sketchy knowledge of Hume's opinions. For concerning geometry Hume did extend his skepticism to mathematics in the *Treatise of Human Nature*, and he said that theorems of geometry are only approximations: "As the ultimate standard of these figures is derived from nothing but the senses and imagination, 'tis absurd to speak of any perfection beyond what these faculties can judge of; since the true perfection of anything consists in its conformity to its standard."[3]

The transcendental expositions of space and time constitute an answer early in the *Critique* to one form of the great motivating question "How is synthetic a priori knowledge possible?" The answer that explains how synthetic a priori mathematical knowledge is possible is, however, only a sketch or a promise of an answer the full version of which depends not only on the thought that space and time are necessary and a priori concepts but also on the claim that there are what Kant calls "a priori manifolds" of space and time and "a priori syntheses" of these manifolds in the course of which the objects of mathematical truths are "constructed," in Kant's terminology.

It is only because space and time are recognizable as forms of outer and inner sense that Kant is able to assert their transcendental ideality. For this ideality means that things as they are in themselves are not spatiotemporal things. On the surface of it such a claim contradicts the general impossibility of knowledge of things as they are in themselves. In the absence of the identification of space and time as forms, Kant could at best assert that we do not know whether or not things as they are in themselves are characterizable in spatial or temporal terms. The relevance of the formal status of space can be illustrated in analogies. Imagine an illiterate who learns to read only telegrams. At one stage he has come to understand that the words printed on the telegram make up a verbal message received somehow from a distant person. But at this stage he interprets every word on the form as part of the message, including, for example, the words "Western Union." He will have to learn that these words are imposed by the form and are not part of the content. It would be absurd for this reader to wonder, after learning the status of "Western Union," whether there might be another "Western Union" which is part of the content of every message *as it is in itself*. Of course, we might think that anything might be part of the hidden content of a message. But no part of the content can have just the role and meaning that the words "Western Union" have on the telegram blank because that meaning and role contrast with content by definition.

Such an analogy is imperfect in that "Western Union" is part of the telegram form on which the matter is organized, but it is not a necessary part, while according to Kant space and time are necessary forms for the organization of the matter that we receive in intuition. The essential contrast of form and content is preserved in the analogy. Once we have *identified* space and time as forms, it is absurd to suppose that these concepts might also characterize the unknown source of intuitive inputs. Therefore, this identification of space and time relieves the appearance of contradiction in the assertion that unknowable things-in-themselves are not in space and time.

All of this depends on understanding in what sense we might think of space and time as forms. The word "form," which is the same in Kant's German discussion, appeals to the contrast between matter and form that goes back to Greek thought. Kant says that space is "nothing other than simply the form of all appearances of outer sense." The traditional contrast is filled out when Kant identifies sensation as the matter of such appearances. According to the traditional distinction an individual existing thing has to have both form and matter. Matter cannot exist without form, that is, without being anything in particular, and form cannot exist, Platonism apart, without being the form of some matter. Kant's conception of an appearance conforms, at least superficially, to this pattern. As far as outer sense is concerned, the matter of an appearance consists of sensible qualities such as color and texture, which fill formal elements such as surfaces and volumes and so constitute perceivable objects of some magnitude.

We saw that the pretension of Kant's empirical realism seems to collapse with the absorption of space by the mind. This absorption, in turn, is clearly traceable to the claims of the Aesthetic. Space is identified as the form of outer sense and, furthermore, as a form imposed by us. This identification "internalizes" space, and it is necessary for the transcendental exposition. This understanding of space is required for Kant's explanation of our possession of synthetic a priori knowledge in geometry. Therefore, space, the imposed form of outer things, cannot be used to secure the distinction between Kant's views and the idealists'. We shall now consider the possibility that the matter of outer sense might play this role.

4. The Construction of Spatial Objects

In expressing his opposition to idealism Kant's appeal to the accessibility of objects of outer sense is so clear and emphatic that it is hard to think of it as simply a mistake. No doubt the force of the Cartesian contrast between the spatial, extended, and material world and the conscious unextended mind inclines him to express his thought about the nonmental outer in terms of spatiality. There is certainly something wrong with this mode of expression. Kant, however, did not simply fail to notice that the mind-imposed status of space is incompatible with the employment of space as the mark of the non-mental existence of things *apart from us*. Is it possible that he rests his rejection of idealism, not on the form of objects of outer sense, but on their matter; not on space, but on sensation?

The matter of outer appearance is its sensuous aspect. This is what Kant calls *sensation* (Empfindung). Sensation makes up the stuff of which spatial organization is the required form. This statement has to be replaced by a much more theoretical understanding of sensations and their relationship to perceivable objects. Our receptive faculty gives sensations a spatial location. But we cannot think of this receptivity as literally operating on received sensible qualities. We cannot suppose, for example, that it is a feature of our receptivity to assign a color sensation to a place, because Kant states very clearly that, prior to any synthesizing activity, individual sensations do not have any extension at all. Sensible qualities such as color are the sorts of things of which we can be conscious as the perceivable features of an object, as the color of a surface, for example. As such, sensible features themselves are the product of synthesis, in this case, of a kind of aggregating activity operating on unextended sensations which have been located in the same region. Only the resulting aggregate deserves to be described in color language. The unextended content of a single sensation is located but is not perceivable. This is the claim of the Axioms of Intuition according to which all objects of experience are extended magnitudes and, therefore, aggregates, the least constituents of which are not perceivable.

We are treating a major side of Kant's thinking which has come to be an embarrassment to modern admirers of Kant. The machinery of the mind, the transcendental psychology, in which Kant tries to depict the actual procedures whereby raw materials are transformed into a world of experience, is a "wholly fictional subject matter," as P. F. Strawson described it. If anything is acceptable in this Kantian enterprise, it will certainly have to be drastically redescribed in some way that gets away from the idiom of quasimechanical speculation.

At the same time, however little is retained of this account of the mind making nature, no understanding of what is best in Kant's thought is possible if these speculations are simply ignored. Neglect encourages, in particular, a mistaken interpretation of the terms of Kant's theories which tends to place them in a spuriously direct relationship to commonsense concepts.

According to Kant unknown things as they are in themselves *affect* us, and unextended sensations are engendered as a consequence. In the process our receptive constitution deploys these sensations in space. The various combinatory powers that Kant ascribes to the human mind under the title of powers of *synthesis* survey these located sensations and assemble objects from them. These are perceivable objects, and they, rather than their theoretical constituent sensations, are the first items accessible to consciousness. There are no objects of consciousness more primitive than perceivable objects. Many of the important claims of the Analytic come from the idea that any conscious experience at all, and any self-consciousness, is conditioned by the completion of this mental construction of objects of perception. The ultimate constituents for the construction of objects with perceivable features are sensations, but they do not have perceivable features. The term "sensation" in eighteenth-century philosophical parlance is ordinarily used for qualities apprehended, such as heat and color. Kant's constituents are called sensations only in virtue of the extended perceivable things which have sensible qualities and which are supposed to be *made* out of sensations.

This style of thought, prominent throughout the *Critique*, becomes easier to understand when we see it in the context of the thought of Leibniz, who exerted a decisive influence on Kant in just these theories of mental construction. The whole format for the construction of a scientific world of phenomena out of elements of which we are not conscious is taken over from Leibniz's account of apperception. Conscious experience results, for Leibniz, from the aggregation of innumerable unconscious *petites perceptions*. The motion of the sea is perceived as a roar only because the mind must aggregate the infinite events which make up the motion of the water, each one of which is itself silent, and the mind perceives only the aggregate (confusedly, without distinguishing the constituent events) as sound. For Leibniz the spatiotemporal character of things is *phenomenal*, that is, it reflects not the reality of the things experienced but the conditions the mind imposes in the process of experiencing anything at all. So underlying realities are unextended, but to be perceived, they are represented in aggregates that produce the perspectival spatiotemporal subject matter of human experience and knowledge. So for Leibniz phenomenal reality is not a valueless illusion. *Phenomena bene fundata* offer a kind of surrogate for metaphysical reality and truth. As in Kant, phenomena are the locus of all scientific thought. The elements which are related in our best thought do correspond globally to reality, although there is no one-to-one correspondence of appearance and reality. The ambiguous evaluation of phenomenal reality in Kant's system and the theory of transcendental ideality have their roots in Leibniz's thinking.

We have sketched Kant's idea of the construction of empirical objects out of sensations. We are now in a position to address Kant's idea of the constructions the mind makes in the pure or a priori manifolds of space and time. Kant says that "transcendental logic" differs from ordinary or general logic in that it has its own subject matter, an a priori subject matter, to which the basic combinatory forms of general logic are applied. The a priori manifolds of space and time make up this self-contained field of application for transcendental logic (A 55, B 79).

The concept of these a priori manifolds can be understood in terms of what we have said about sensation. Kant says that our receptivity includes a location-assigning procedure which places sensations in space where they are ready for synthesis into perceivable spatial objects. Pure space, or the a priori manifold of outer sense, is just the idea of the system of locations by themselves, without any sensations assigned to them. Perhaps there is a big difference between a location-assigning system and a system of locations to which things can be assigned. In virtue of the former Kant speaks of space as the form of outer intuition, while only in virtue of the latter can he speak of space itself as an intuition, and an a priori intuition at that. Kant plainly believes that he is entitled to the transition from the former to the latter, but there is little or no mention of this issue in the *Critique*.

Here we should see the Kantian position as an attempt at a compromise between the conceptions of space defended by Leibniz and by Newton. Newton insisted on an absolute container space which would exist whether or not there were any spatial things to be found anywhere in space. In the *Correspondence* with Clarke Leibniz repudiated this on roughly verificationist grounds, and he asserted that space is a system of relations between coexistent entities. There would be no space were there to be no things spatially related. Kant was attracted by the Leibnizian account, but he remained convinced that something like absolute space is conceptually indispensable because of a curious argument about incongruent counterparts.[4] Congruent objects are those that have the same shape and the same dimensions. Two such figures can occupy the same space. When superimposed they fit each other exactly. Two gloves of a pair are close to congruence, but they cannot occupy the same space because of the left-hand orientation of the one and the right-hand orientation of the other. Since the internal spatial relations of the parts of each glove are the same, it appears that were Leibniz right about space, there would be no difference at all between a universe consisting only of a left-hand glove and a universe consisting of a right-hand glove of the same dimensions. All relations between coexisting things would be the same in each universe. Kant is intuitively convinced that Leibniz's theory of space makes it impossible to represent a difference that would be real here. The problem is solved by the existence of absolute space, since the two gloves would have different relations to absolute space and would necessarily fill different regions of it.

In Kant's system the whole discussion of the status of space is brought within the domain of appearances. Things located in space are, first, sensations, and, second, material objects. Is there space in the absence of spatial things? There is not in the sense that space is transcendentally ideal and does not exist apart from the outer sense which is a component of our cognitive constitution. But space does exist apart from spatial things in the sense in which outer sense offers a system of places which is independent of the fact that sensations are arranged in that system. This means that the impossibility of thinking space away carries an implication for the thing-like character of space itself which goes beyond the metaphysical exposition, which is compatible with Leibniz's theory. Newton thought that we need an absolute container space in order to distinguish absolute and relative motion. Analogously, Kant thinks that we require such a space in order to solve the problem of incongruent counterparts. Therefore, although he makes space phenomenal as Leibniz did, Kant's a priori space with neither sensations nor objects in it functions as absolute space, within Kant's thinking, just as absolute space outside the mind functions in Newton's.

This commitment to absolute space allows Kant to think of the location-assigning aspect of outer sense as an a priori system of locations. "[S]pace and time are represented a priori not merely as *forms* of sensible intuition, but as themselves *intuitions* which contain a manifold" (B 160). We can think of pure space as something like an armature on which sensations are organized. The chief doctrines of the transcendental logic and, prominently, the Principles result from the consideration of the powers of combination that men possess applied to these empty but a priori manifolds. The Axioms, Anticipations, Analogies, and Postulates are said to be a priori laws of nature. They are supposed to hold for the empirical realm because empirical objects are the result of applying the very same constructive powers to the same manifolds of space and time, but when these manifolds are filled with sensation. The structural laws which result from the application of combinatory creativity to empty space are true of the empty proto-objects constructed of empty locations. Therefore, they are also automatically true when these locations are assigned sensations with the combining procedures unchanged.

In the simplest case, that is, the Axioms of Intuition, we are to understand that the laws of extended magnitude are generated along with the extended objects of which they are true. This is achieved when the pure manifold of nonempirical space is synthesized so that empty points are assembled into empty regions, surfaces, and volumes. Since the empirical manifold results simply from filling the same locations with sensation, the same geometrical laws will hold for empirical and pure space. Geometrically describable objects arise from the aggregation of locations. This is the detailed story that lies behind the transcendental exposition of space in the Aesthetic. Whether the constructed objects are empirically full or empty makes no difference to their geometrical properties.

5. Sensation and the Objectivity of Outer Sense

We saw that space, as the region of outer things, collapsed back into the mind because space is only a mind-imposed form and spatiality does not characterize things as they are in themselves, or even sensations, apart from the location-assigning propensities of our own minds. Since the outerness of space is all in the mind, Kant's system seems to be no improvement on the perennial idealistic weaknesses of the Cartesian-empiricist outlook. But we have raised the question whether Kant intended spatiality to be the aspect of outer appearances that carried the crucial burden of realism. We have examined Kant's conception of sensation, space, and objects with a view to determining whether or not sensation, the matter of outer objects, might be the needed support for Kant's anti-idealist assertions. Kant never says that sensation is imposed by us, or that the mind makes sensations. If he meant sensation to carry the burden of realism, it would be understandable that Kant should frequently assert, as he does, both that outer sense refutes idealism and that space exists only in us, and that he should assert both in the same context of discussion. There is much in favor of this interpretation, although, as we shall see, it cannot be the whole of his thought about the connection of outer sense and mind-independent reality.

In a revealing passage just prior to the Transcendental Deduction of the Categories Kant says:

> There are only two possible ways in which synthetic representations and their objects can establish connection, obtain necessary relation to one another, and, as it were, meet one another. Either the object alone must make the representation possible, or the representation alone must make the object possible. In the former case, the relation is only empirical, and the representation is never possible a priori. This is true of appearances, as regards that element in them which belongs to sensation. In the latter case, representation itself does not produce its object in so far as *existence* is concerned, for we are not speaking here of its causality by means of the will. Nonetheless, the representation is a priori determinant of the object, if it be the case that only through the representation is it possible to know anything *as an object*. [A 92]

This passage has implications for the meaning of Kant's entire transcendental philosophy. According to the Cartesian-empiricist way of thinking, our knowledge of external things, if we have any, is based on the fact that those external things cause our representations. Kant would say that within that framework of metaphysical thought these philosophers have supposed that spatially extended objects are mind-independent entities that "make possible" our representations. The revolutionary character of his thought is that Kant will say that sometimes the dependence runs the other way, so that our representation makes possible the object. At its most idealistic this amounts to a reductive phenomenalism in the manner of Berkeley. The idea of empirical objects of perception is simply the idea of groups and patterns among transient subjective experiences. But in the passage just quoted Kant expresses a far less idealistic view and expressly denies the reduction of objects to representations.

Within the passage there are two themes that we will consider separately. First Kant says that the empirical part of representation, that is, sensation, is "made possible" by the object. In other words, with respect to sensation Kant's view resembles the Cartesian-empiricist line of thought. Something outside the mind is responsible for the sensation. The object in question is certainly the thing-in-itself. This is the mind-independent reality that affects us and engenders sensations. The sensation is a representation, and, as such, it is called a "modification of our receptive faculty," and it is, in consequence, also something in us and in the mind. But these original representations are not the product of our own creative faculties. They are received. They would not exist at all were it not for things as they are in themselves. We will treat this relation between sensations and reality immediately in assessing the appeal to sensation as the chief support of realism.

The second theme of the quoted passage will become important at the end of our discussion. This is Kant's statement that even in those contexts where it is right to say that the representation *makes possible* its object, we should think, not that this means that representations produce objects in point of existence (*dem Dasein nach*), but only that the representation makes it possible for us to know realities *as objects*. In other words, Kant repudiates any scheme which would try to reduce objects of representations to representations themselves, as radical phenomenalism, for example, reduces material objects to sense data. We are never to say that an object of knowledge is nothing more than our representations and the patterns detectable among them. Kant's phenomenalism does not account for the existence of objects known but only for their objecthood in our knowledge. In other words, we are constitutionally disposed to represent realities independent of our minds as objects of perception. All of the characteristics of objects of perception have an irreducible mind-dependence. But it is still independent reality that has become an object for us. The scheme of representation does not create the object that it represents. In the last analysis it is things as they are in themselves that are represented in experience of spatial objects. In experience independent reality is represented as a system of stable objects of perception in causal interconnection with one another. There are a great many passages in which Kant expresses a phenomenalism far more radical than this. For the present let us return to the more limited claim about the character of sensation.

How should we understand the question "Does the object make the representation possible, or does the representation make the object possible?" Let us call this the *priority* question. In itself it seems to presuppose a distinction between representations and objects, while this presupposition is one of the things at issue in the confrontation of realism and idealism. Kant's term *"Vorstellung"*[5] is broader than anything the English word "representation" naturally suggests. It is meant to cover not only perceptual contents but also all intuitions, pure and empirical. Elementary sensations which are not conscious contents are nonetheless representations. Furthermore, all concepts, pure and empirical, are representations. Even concepts which are defective precisely in failing to represent anything, such as the Ideas of Reason, are representations. It is important to appreciate the abstractness of Kant's usage here because it reveals his willingness to speak of representations whether or not they represent anything and whether or not they are conscious items that represent something to anyone. In the context of the priority question Kant is thinking of representations as contents of perceptual experience like the ideas of Locke, Berkeley, and Hume, but he is also including elementary unextended sensations which are not conscious and have no role at all in the empiricist tradition. These, as we said, come into Kant's picture from Leibniz's concept of *petites perceptions.*

Kant means us to think that it is idealists like Berkeley who hold that representations make possible objects. Berkeley says that an object like a cherry is a bundle of ideas of sense, including some red ideas, some round ideas, and some sweet ideas. There are cherries only in that we have such ideas in such bundles. When Kant himself addresses the priority question, his thinking focuses on elementary sensations and their origin, because even red ideas are a product of synthetic activity. Elementary sensations are the ones which objects plainly make possible. What objects? Here Kant must mean the things-in-themselves that engender sensations by affecting us. So it is, indeed, Kant's doctrine of sensation and not his theory of spatiality that opposes idealism.

The obscurity that darkens this opinion comes from the fact that Kant thinks that these very same sensations do make possible objects, namely, empirical objects. The procedures of combinatory synthesis which we have sketched operate by assembling perceivable objects out of elementary sensations. So sensations both make possible objects and are made possible by objects, and in different contexts Kant gives both answers to the priority question.

We confront here one of the confusions in Kant's thought that comes from his dual standard for questions about reality. There are empirical objects and transcendental things-in-themselves. Sensations are made possible by things-in-themselves, and sensations make possible empirical objects. At times Kant encourages us to think of things in space as the locus of nonmental being, and he defines inner sense as access to mental things. This is Descartes' opinion, but if it is also Kant's, then his theory seems to coincide with idealism. The allegedly nonmental spatial world is a construct from representations (sensations). When he asserts his realism, Kant forgets or repudiates the suggestion that spatial things are nonmental, and he counts objects in space as representations along with sensations. They are all mind-dependent realities, and Kant asks of this whole class of things, Do they make possible mind-independent objects? He decides for realism in answering this question. Of course, sensations make objects of perception in space possible, but then they are just appearances. As appearances, they represent realities which are not just appearances. In our spatial representations realities which are not representations or appearances become objects for us. "Through the representation it is possible to know anything *as an object*."

The underlying difficulty of the dual realities is compounded by ambiguities in the concept of representation. Consider again Berkeley's understanding of the nature of a cherry. We should not really describe Berkeley's bundle theory of perceived objects as the view that representations make possible (or make) objects. The term "representation" is out of place in this description. An element in a bundle does not *represent* the bundle anymore than a brick represents a wall of which it is an element. The idealist theory really amounts to a renunciation of "representation" as a concept suitable for ideas of sense. The point of idealism is that there is nothing nonmental for mental items to represent. An analogous but restricted point holds for Kant's phenomenalism. The construction of perceivable objects out of spatially deployed sensations by our faculties does not generate an account of objects of perception within which we can say that sensations *represent* perceived objects in space. But Kant does like to say that "we represent objects as outside us and all without exception in space." Using such phrases, he allows himself to think of representations as items having spatial objects which they represent. But Kant constructs spatial objects out of elements found in the manifold of outer sense. So it is quite misleading for him to suggest that those elements represent spatial objects. In the history of reductive phenomenalism this illicit use of "representation" frequently lends plausibility to otherwise unpalatable accounts. As long as the concept of representation is illicitly retained, the harshness of the reduction is softened. For the concept implies that there is still a difference between representations and objects of just the sort that the reduction intends to deny.

We have said that representations make possible empirical objects and are made possible by transcendental objects. If we delete the implication, which Kant frequently allows himself, that inner elements represent constructed objects in space, on the ground that this is an illicit use of "represent," a univocal and relatively clear anti-idealist line of thought emerges, and it is, I believe, a major part of what Kant did want to say on this topic.

What the Cartesian-empiricist tradition calls objects in space are simply complex representations according to Kant. The processes envisioned in the Analytic try to describe how we form such representations. If we ask how it is that spatial things have the status of representations of anything, we must say, in Kant's thought, that they *inherit* this status from their constituent sensations. So the representational character of perceptual experience is traceable to sensation. Sensation is the proper foundation for realism.

This way of reading Kant's treatment of the priority question may seem to fall short of his expressed views in two ways. First, Kant habitually speaks of perceived objects in space *as objects* and seldom *as representations*, and much of the Analytic itself is dominated by a usage of "object" in which it is obviously spatial things that are objects and not things-in-themselves. Second, the priority question, we said, presupposes a distinction between representations and objects.

If we interpret the objects of which the priority question inquires as transcendental objects, Kant's *ignorabimus* will imply that we have no means at all for making good this distinction. If spatial objects are just representations, we have no further objects to play the role of things represented.

Concerning the first of these reservations, Kant is certainly entitled to speak of objects of perception and empirical objects and objects in space. We could not plausibly propose that he should only speak of empirical, perceptual, and spatial *representations*. But all these things are objects only because we think about them, and make judgments about them, and investigate them scientifically. Conscious contents involve objects and not merely representations because these contents figure as the subject matter of thought.

> Objects are given to us by means of sensibility; they are *thought* through the understanding. . . . But all thought must, directly or indirectly, by way of certain characters, relate ultimately to intuitions, and therefore, with us, to sensibility [sensible representations], because in no other way can an object be given to us. [A 19, B 33]

In other words, mind-independent reality becomes an object for us by engendering sensations and thence empirical representations. Then these representations also become objects of thought, and thought about them is thought about reality precisely because it is traceable to these sensations.

Reflection on the second reservation bears out this understanding. Since Kant holds that we can know nothing about things-in-themselves (and sometimes goes so far as to put in doubt the thought that there are any), we are tempted to think, and Kant is also tempted to think, that he means that empirical realities are the only ones that can figure at all in our philosophical account of things. There is no question, for Kant, of getting beyond the empirical object. This "going beyond appearance" is the issue for the old Cartesian-empiricist outlook. Mathematical characterizations, for example, manage to penetrate to things as they are apart from our experience. Mathematical thinking, it seems, enables us to get at, and not merely to represent, reality. But this is no part of Kant's scheme. For Kant, getting at reality *is representing it*. We cannot make a comparison of represented and unrepresented reality. In consequence, we should not interpret the priority question as presupposing that we can make such a comparison. Unrepresented reality cannot be compared with anything, because being represented is the condition for figuring in any comparison we can make.

In his relationship to the idealist problems generated by the Cartesian philosophy of mind Kant is actually the champion of the concept of representation. The idealist renounces representation by denying reality to anything but the mental content itself. There is nothing to be represented. The nonidealist within the Cartesian tradition also rejects the idea of representation in his aspiration to get beyond appearances so as to compare unrepresented reality with our ideas of it. The great Cartesian question of the "resemblance" of ideas and their objects expresses this aspiration. This dream survives in Kant's conviction that God knows reality without representing it, without being affected by it, and without experiencing it. In the case of men Kant grasps, at least most of the time, the thought that representation is the vehicle of knowledge of the represented, not a barrier which once interposed makes possible only knowledge of the representation itself.

Kant wants to allow space to be absorbed by the mind and, at the same time, to single out outer sense as the uncompromised connection with things that exist *apart* from *us*. Inner sense involves an element of sensation too, but there is no mind-independent entity represented here, because inner sense is the mind's receptivity to itself. If we construe inner sense as the mind, as thing-in-itself, affecting itself and giving rise to appearances of itself and its state, we remain in the realm of the mental. Outer sense starts outside the mental, not because its representations are spatial, but because sensations of outer sense have their origin in nonmental independent reality.

That sensation is the essential link to the extramental explains Kant's statement in the Schematism; "Reality, in the pure concept of understanding, is that which corresponds to sensation in general" (A 143, B 182). And in the Paralogisms Kant can say, in the context of the assertion that sensation is the sole input for perception, "Perception exhibits the reality of something in space, and in the absence of perception no power of imagination can invent and produce that something. It is sensation, therefore, that indicates a reality in space or time, according as it is related to the one or to the other mode of sensible intuition" (A 373-4). And a few lines later, "Space is the representation of a mere possibility of coexistence, perception is the representation of a reality" (A 374).

6. Primary and Secondary Qualities

Kant's distinction between the formal and material ingredients of empirical intuition is his inventive reworking of the traditional distinction between primary and secondary qualities. One of the reasons for which it is hard to appreciate Kant's reliance on sensation rather than space for the basic connection of thinking to the nonmental is that Kant reverses the traditional evaluation of primary and secondary. Primary qualities, for the tradition initiated by Galileo and perfected in the articulation of Locke's *Essay*, are those which accept mathematical and prominently geometrical or spatial characterization. It is in respect of primary qualities that our ideas resemble things and correctly represent a mind-independent reality. Our ideas of secondary qualities involve sensible characteristics like color and heat. These are literally features of our ideas, that is, of mental things, but they have no footing at all in nonmental outer reality.

The distinction between primary and secondary qualities is at the core of post-Renaissance philosophy because it explains the success of mathematical science and the failure of the earlier scholastic-Aristotelian program which relied upon a relatively naive interpretation of perceptual experience. The demotion of the sensuous to the status of wholly subjective appearance fitted the growing understanding of the physics and physiology of perception. The objectivity assigned to the mathematically representable side of experience fitted the notion that mathematics is the "language of the book of nature," with the help of which we penetrate the veil of misleading sensuous representation to a true conception of outer reality. When Kant trades this distinction between qualities for a distinction between form and matter, he discards much of the explanatory benefit of the post-Renaissance view. The aspect of our representations that accept mathematical representation become transcendentally ideal for Kant. Spatial characteristics—figure, magnitude, and motion—are no longer attributes of mind-independent reality for Kant. They exist only from our point of view. The sensuous component, in contrast, downgraded by the tradition, is the indispensable link to things that affect us in Kant's account.

Each component of this reversal of the evaluation of the sensible and the mathematical has to be qualified. Kant offers a new security for extension-dependent qualities which remain the locus of mathematical description for him. But the new security is an a priori foundation dependent on our cognitive constitution. Numerical and geometrical representation ceases to be thought of as intellectual penetration that gets beyond appearance. Since things-in-themselves are not spatiotemporal, mathematical propositions do not fit them. On the side of the sensible Kant continues to think of sensation as an effect in us and does not assert any resemblance between inner and outer in terms of sensible features. But sensations are the foundation of objectivity in the sense that they are the matter of all objects for us, and they would not exist but for the influence of things outside us. No such claim is made for the mathematical aspect of representations. So Kant is able to say that space represents only "possible coexistence," while perception does represent reality because perception contains empirical intuition or sensation (A 374). We can say, then, that the synthesized, nonempirical, proto-objects, the geometrical objects of the Axioms of Intuition, are not representations *of anything*. But empirical appearances are representations that must have their object. They derive this status from sensation.

One can recognize patterns of thought from both Descartes and Leibniz subjected to imaginative permutations by Kant in this context. According to Descartes' conception of "confused" as opposed to "distinct" ideas we are disposed to mistake the sensuous mental effect for the extended outer cause. Thus we project sensuous content, which is immediately intuited but not extended, onto space, which is extended but not intuited. Descartes thinks this projection is an understandable human error. He explains our disposition to this error by saying that we use the sensuous qualities as clues to the harmfulness and utility of things in the spatial environment. This disposition contributes to self-preservation, and its effect is enhanced by the fact that we think of the clues as features of, and not merely effects of, the objects. In this, Descartes supposes, as Kant does, that essentially unextended things (Descartes' sensuous ideas and Kant's sensations) are projected into space by us and then thought by us to characterize regions and surfaces. The great difference lies not in the concept of the projection of the unextended into space but only in the legitimacy of the projection. Descartes and any other subjectivist on secondary qualities must say that color characterizes nothing that is actually extended, since the locus of color is the mind where there is nothing extended. For Kant the same projection is not an error but an aspect of cognitive functioning which issues in a constructed perceivable object.

Like Kant, Leibniz, too, has it that an essentially nonspatial reality is represented spatially by the human mind. Reality is itself not spatial in two senses for Leibniz. First, space is only a system of relations and never anything like a container for things, and, second, this system of relations belongs only to representations or phenomena and not to things independently of the fact that they are mentally represented. Leibniz was never attracted at all by the Cartesian method of doubt and the solipsistic starting point that it fosters. He refuses to enter upon the epistemological enterprise on which Descartes wagers everything. Instead Leibniz offers an overall metaphysical account which is to be accepted if it does justice to all of our experience and thought. He does not try to show how this account might be reached by any reflective man in the face of the most extreme skepticism.

Within Leibniz's account the ultimate explanation for the fittingness of our thought to reality is preestablished harmony. Everyone finds this unsatisfying, and Kant expresses his dissatisfaction, saying that Leibniz "intellectualized the senses." Perception is just confused thought for Leibniz, and all thought is a self-contained activity of the mind. There is no original input traceable to our being affected by things, because in the last analysis we are not affected by anything, according to Leibniz, but only programmed in advance to have the mental contents that we do have.

No doubt Kant inherits from Leibniz a starting point alien from the Cartesian-empiricist egocentrism and solipsism. It is no part of Kant's plan to doubt whether represenatations are really representations and then to overcome this doubt. Kant's acceptance of the Cartesian view that we are affected by the things that we represent is a repudiation of Leibniz's reliance on harmony as the ultimate foundation of knowledge. Like Leibniz, Kant understands the spatial images of conscious perception as the aggregation by the mind of items which are not themselves extended. But like Descartes, Kant thinks that these items are effects of outer realities. Against Descartes, with whom he shares the notion of perceptual images as effects of outer realities, Kant thinks that our idea of color requires that extended things be colored things. Mere ideas will never make color intelligible without receptivity. Only because spatial things can actually have sensible features is it the case that "Perception *exhibits* the reality of something in space, and, in the absence of perception, no power of imagination can invent or produce that something." This is related to the view that Hume expressed in saying that all ideas are copies of impressions. Though it is found in spatial things, color is subjective in Kant's view, as it is for the standard theory of secondary qualities.

In this setting of the views of predecessors Kant's reordering emerges naturally. There is some objective influence on our faculty of receptivity that is responsible for the existence and representational character of outer intuitions. In order to think of outer reality consciously we make spatial pictures by assembling essentially unextended sensations which have been assigned places in the mind-imposed system of locations. These pictures, in virtue of their empirical content (sensation), represent reality outside the mind *as* objects in space. Spatial pictures as assembled objects really have surfaces and their surfaces are really colored. Color is an emergent feature which arises in the synthesis of a multitude of sensations which have been assigned to locations near one another. Thus, color stands for, and represents, the outer thing without resembling it, while the spatial features neither stand for nor resemble any reality. In some ways this concept of space is like the psychological concept of a visual field. Geometrical features of things come from the features of mind-imposed space and play no part in the relation of objects of perception to things outside the mind. This fits nicely Kant's claim that geometry is necessary and a priori, and yet geometrical truths are true of empirical objects. Space is the region of all possible objects ("possible coexistence"), and when space is filled with sensation, synthesis generates apprehendable structures (empirical objects) out of deployed sensations. That these representations represent the nonmental is due entirely to the contained sensations. The mathematical knowledge we have of such objects is, as Kant says, only a question of getting out what we have put in ourselves. It is secondary qualities that are responsible for the fact that experience reaches beyond merely mental realities, while primary qualities betoken nothing mind-independent.

7. The Spatial and the Temporal

Were sensation all there is to connection with things outside the mind, space would be just as mental as time is. Spatial things would be mental representations of nonmental realities, and temporal things would be mental representations of mental realities. This pleasant symmetry is not tenable. It is contradicted by the fact that Kant clearly requires that spatial representations be *subjected to time* in order to become participants in the activities of the mind. Some of the essential doctrines of the *Critique* depend, first, on the thought that spatiality per se makes representations unfit for mental status, and, second, it is precisely the spatiality of spatial representations that renders them fit vehicles for securing the concept of anything *enduring* at all, even of minds as enduring conscious subjects.

Kant segregates the spatial and the temporal with startling rigor. All readers follow him easily when he confines inner mental objects to a temporal order and allows spatial distinctions no footing in the mind. This satisfies a widely shared intuitive conviction that thoughts are not located anywhere and that ideas do not displace any spatial occupant. Kant's confinement of the mental to time is part of the common ground of his inner sense and Cartesian consciousness. But Kant's exclusion of time from the objects of outer sense, which are subjected to space and space alone, is not attuned to any widely

(A)   (B)

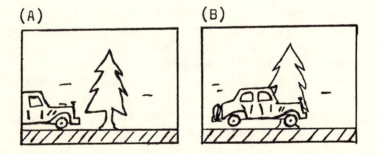

shared philosophical presumption. As a result, readers of Kant sometimes suppose that he does not mean to exclude temporality from the
outer. It is often said that Kant means to say that all inner things are
subject to time and all outer things to space and time. And this seems
a needed reading lest Kant be thought to leave no conceptual room
for change in the outer world at all. Such an understanding, however,
conflicts with very simple and clear statements in the *Critique* such
as this one: "Time cannot be outwardly intuited anymore than space
can be intuited as something in us" (A 23, B 37). Can one hope that
even such direct assertions are open to interpretation or overridden
by other considerations? We certainly must say that Kant's ultimate
view is that material objects both fill space and endure in time. In
his thinking, then, the spatial and the temporal are wedded. The
point, however, is that they need to be wedded. No object of outer
intuition, considered in itself, is something that exists in time.

As a first approximation for the understanding of this perplex-
ing view, we can point out that time is not essential in the realm of
the extended, whether or not time, as a matter of fact, applies to
things in that realm. The fact is that as conscious subjects we confront
an outer world in which there is change. Since this is so, we have to
deploy temporal concepts in describing that world. But this is an empirical fact. It is conceivable that we might have found an outer reality in which there is no change whatever. Under such circumstances
change would be confined to the domain of our conscious survey of
this wholly static reality. It would not be necessary to ascribe time to
both the inner and the outer. Our first thought, then, is that time
is not absolutely necessary for the very idea of the outer as space is
absolutely necessary.

(C)

(D)

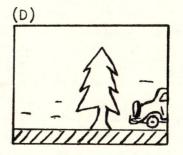

The thought of a changeless spatial world leads to a further speculation, and one that is a lot closer to Kant's actual view of space and time. It seems theoretically possible to deny that there is any change in the actual world and to assert that the spatial world we do experience is a static world. All the apparent temporal distinctions in the outer world will have to be recast as temporal distinctions that apply only in the mental world of experiences. For example, we may think of the sequence of images A–D, in the figure, as the content of consecutive visual experiences of a subject. The natural interpretation of such a sequence assigns change, and therefore time, to both the outer and the inner. The subject's inner experience changes as the outer car passes the tree. But we are not forced to interpret A–D as consecutive viewings of the same outer region, namely, one in which changes are taking place. We could think of it instead as consecutive viewings of four different regions of a wholly static space. If we think of the images A–D as consecutive frames of a motion picture film, then the viewing of the film realizes the possibility of the second interpretation, that is, consecutive experiences of four different static arrays. This analogy ignores the real motion involved in the manipulation of the film. When we view a film we create the illusion of change in the object by arranging to witness related but unchanging objects in a special temporal order. In principle we could think of our ordinary experience of the world as conforming to this pattern. Therefore, the ascription of time to the outer is an expendable convenience.

We made informal use here of the distinction between the thing seen and the visual experience of that thing. Kant, too, recognizes such a distinction. He frequently says that apprehension of the manifold of intuition is always successive, whether or not the manifold itself is successive (inner) or simultaneous (outer). The perception of a line, however short, (an example Kant likes) involves a synthesis which is necessarily successive. The allusion to synthesis in this opinion reminds us that outer sense does not reveal a world in which the question "Are there really changes here, or not?" naturally arises. Due to outer sense we have a range of intuitions. There are a multiplicity of individual representations of outer things. For the description of these representations spatial terms are needed and temporal terms are not. Nothing happens in one representation. The ordinary world is not something simply given to outer sense. The world is constructed by our synthetic powers (the understanding) operating on material provided by receptivity. In Kant's terms the restriction of temporality to the inner means that all the temporal distinctions used in thinking of the ordinary world are traceable to synthesis and none to outer receptivity.

Kant often speaks of the products of the synthetic powers of the mind as objects of outer sense. For example, a line is an object of outer intuition. This seems unproblematic because a line *is* a static thing. Its synthesis, however, is successive and involves time. Strictly speaking, nothing complex is merely intuited. Even the least complexity is ascribed to synthesis. Combinatory activity—assembling, integrating, collating, comparing, retaining, retrieving, reproducing, and, in general, synthesizing—is all mental activity. Kant often says that we are not conscious of these operations, and some are even "concealed in the depths of the soul," but this merely emphasizes that he does think of them as mental processes. No one thinks otherwise. It is inevitable, in Kant's system, that these activities be temporal activities, and any materials involved in these activities must be in time in order to be accessible for synthesis.

It is for this reason that Kant confines the Schematism to consideration of the temporality of intuition. The job of the Schematism is to bridge the gulf between the Categories as pure concepts of understanding and the empirical sensibility that offers human beings matter for experience. The Categories are developed from the forms of judgment identified in formal logic. Although the transcendental deduction of the Categories is supposed to guarantee that any reality we are able to experience will conform to these pure concepts, the deduction does not reduce the merely formal and logical significance of the Categories. Any rational creature will have experience in conformity with just these twelve Categories, in Kant's view, but this might have a wholly different meaning for creatures whose receptivity is not spatial and temporal as our receptivity is. So the Schematism interprets the Categories for beings with sensible and spatiotemporal intuitions. But Kant seems to ignore the spatial altogether, so that in the Schematism, as he describes it, the Categories are subjected to a temporal condition. Some readers have supposed that he might have offered a spatial as well as a temporal Schematism for the Categories. This is not correct. The Categories are the pure forms that are available for the combination of materials provided by receptivity. Combination is not intelligible without time. As Kant says, synthesis is always successive, whether or not the manifold is successive or simultaneous. Thus Kant calls time the form of all appearances whether inner or outer. In this view Kant distinguishes appearances, which presuppose synthesis, from intuitions, which do not. Outer intuitions have to be rerepresented as mental experiences in order to enter into any combinatory activity. For example, the apprehension of a cube offers an object of outer sense that has spatial features such as being cube-shaped and no temporal features. It is the visual experience of the cube and not the cube itself that enters into mental activities. When spatial things are rerepresented, they trade in their spatial character for a new mental character. The visual experience of a cube is not a cube-shaped experience. It is a datable event related in time to all other events in the mind.

If outer sense is not directly available for synthesis, this is just another way of saying that we cannot have any immediate or noninferential knowledge of outer things. The raw materials of knowledge all have to be representations in inner sense. But if this is so, then in what sense are there any data of outer sense at all? It seems that Kant's outer sense has become something like the outer world for the Cartesian-empiricist. It is a hypothetical source of some of the data we really do have, namely, the things present to the mind and available for synthesis. How else can we interpret the fact that in Kant's scheme items that actually possess spatial features cannot enter into mental processes or consciousness. They have to be *subjected* to time. Kant has internalized the problem of the external world. In order to figure in mental activities, representations must be temporal representations. When it comes to the supposed data of outer sense, so often touted as immediate, it turns out that subjection to time amounts to rerepresentation. As Kemp-Smith put it, appearances in space are not really representations at all: "They are objects of representation, not representation itself."[6]

No spatial thing can exist as a subjective state. At most a representation of a spatial thing, a representation which does not itself have spatial features, can truly exist in the mind. But the great problem with this is that the spatial is now cut off from both the inner and mental and from the metaphysically outer. From the perspective of the inner, spatial representations are objects that have to be rerepresented in time in order to belong to thought and to the empirical world the mind constructs. From the perspective of things as they are in themselves spatial representations are mere appearances. Spatial reality threatens to become empirically ideal as well as being transcendentally ideal.

This instability in the status of the spatial sheds light on some difficulties in interpreting Kant. Faced with the demand for a distinction between the subjective and the objective, Kant repeatedly formulates distinctions that seem to fall entirely on the subjective side. For example, his contrast between judgments of perception and judgments of experience, drawn in the *Prolegomena*, operates in a realm that is all appearance. In the Analogies he purports to distinguish the temporal order of our experience and the temporal order in the object. But the only object under consideration is outer appearance and not mind-independent reality. Such passages result from the fact that Kant treats outer intuition as a source of input for inner intuition. Then, relative to inner representations, the outer becomes a system of represented objects. Thus he is able to treat outer appearances as if they offered independent objects about which a world of facts could be ascertained.

When he is thinking this way, Kant's conception of the mind retreats to inner sense, to the traditional Cartesian consciousness which has to develop knowledge of spatial things through immediate contact with inner representations (ideas) of spatial objects. This thought contradicts the claim on which much depends, in the Paralogisms, for example, that inner and outer sense are symmetrical, and both are immediate, and objects are *given* to both. In a footnote which strengthens the newly composed "Refutation of Idealism," the preface to the second edition of the *Critique* explicitly asserts that the "permanent" which must be found in perception "Cannot be an intuition in me" (B xxxix), for intuitions in me have only the status of ephemeral representations. Here Kant seems to promote the object of outer sense, the object of perception, to mind-independent reality, and simultaneously to reduce our knowledge of it from the direct intuition claimed earlier to something mediated and inferential.

We will miss what is important for Kant's thought here if we treat these passages as mere slips into the Cartesian point of view. The thought that what is *permanent* "cannot be an intuition in me" points to an entirely different significance for the inaccessibility of representations of outer sense to both consciousness and synthesis. Why is it that the permanent cannot be identified with any intuition? Plainly, the answer is that anything truly mental, any subjective state, is essentially transient. The fact that time is the form of the mental guarantees that everything purely mental has, as Hume expressed it, "a perishing existence." Nothing mental could possibly be permanent because impermanence is the form of mental things. Mere temporal existence is impermanence.

We have now discovered the deeper Kantian motivation for the sharp segregation of the temporal and the spatial. Kant's thought of the outer has to satisfy two demands that seem to conflict with one another. On the one hand, he would like the outer to be intuited and thus immediately accessible like any other intuition. And this is required for the transcendental ideality of space. On the other hand, he wants the outer as merely spatial, to be exempted from the ever-vanishing essence of inner things and mental things, even though the price of this exemption is separation from mental activities and consciousness. The inaccessibility of the spatial and its tendency to become something independent of the mind is a consequence of a powerful demand of Kant's theory and is no mere slip. The defect of the Cartesian-empiricist perspective is that it envisions a starting point for philosophical reflection consisting of a conscious mind confronted by data, all of which are perishing mental contents. Something outside the destructive scope of temporality must be provided in order to account for the idea of the subject himself. No concept of consciousness is intelligible which starts from a framework limited to mental things.

The demand for something not subject to the ravages of time, and therefore not mental, is the point of Kant's central argument concerning apperception and personal identity. Any conception of mental activity presupposes that the materials involved be accessible to one subject of consciousness. The possibility of learning, discriminating, recognizing, remembering, and forming concepts requires that the data be data for one subject. But inner sense does not reveal any such "abiding self."

Berkeley earlier noted that we have no *idea* of the subject of experience, and he provided the "notion" of a *spirit* to make up for the missing idea. Hume, too, recognized that we have no experience of the self. Refusing to introduce an ad hoc surrogate like Berkeley's *spirit*, Hume tried to reduce the subject of experience to the content of experience in his bundle theory of the subject. This amounted to an extension to mental substances of Berkeley's bundle theory of spatial substances. This is the gist of the history of the problem of the unity of apperception up to Kant. Kant takes the bundle theory of personal identity to be the *reductio ad absurdum* of the Cartesian-empiricist program, which tries to derive everything from the purely mental, purely inner, and purely temporal.

Kant insists on a substantial foundation for the unity of the subject of experience outside the various experiences of that subject. The great Kantian contribution here is the recognition that the subject could not possibly be *given* in experience. Hume said that when he looked within in order to find himself, he found instead only another perception (perishing mental content). Kant understands that this is inevitable. Suppose we found a common element in all our conscious experience, and we inclined to think of this ubiquitous element as our own abiding self. This would have to be an error. Kant sees that no such element in experience could be the foundation of the connectedness of experiences that makes them all contents for one subject. On the contrary, experiences stand in just the same need of connectedness to one another and presence to a common subject whether or not they have a common element of any kind. The very idea that I could note a common element in my experiences presupposes that I, as a single subject, have all those different experiences, so that I might note a common element among them. The common element, if there were one, could not be the reason for the fact that all the experiences containing the common element are *mine*. We have to look outside the realm of conscious contents to find a foundation for the unity of consciousness.

The nontemporal spatial object of outer sense offers a foundation for permanence because it is not an essentially perishing object. Of course, the spatial object is not the sought-for subject of experience. But the nontemporal outer object provides the minimal conceptual framework for the idea of the endurance of the subject. Enduring things in space introduce the "determinate time" within which the endurance of the subject can be thought.

> For in what we entitle "soul" everything is in continual flux and there is nothing abiding except (if we must so express outselves) the "I," which is simple solely because its representation has no content. [A 381]

> So long, therefore, as we do not go beyond mere thinking we are without the necessary condition for applying the concept of substance,

that is, of a self-subsistent subject, to the self as a thinking being. [B 413]

Now consciousness [of my existence] in time is necessarily bound up with consciousness of the [condition of the] possibility of this time determination; and it is therefore necessarily bound up with the existence of things outside me, as the condition of the time determination. [B 276]

Endurance does not contradict the essential character of things that are outside thought. This is the positive benefit of the Kantian treatment of space as inaccessible to immediate consciousness. The subject cannot be intuited, nor can it be constructed out of the flux of intuited contents. It has a stability borrowed from the endurance of outer things.

A natural objection to Kant's circuitous reasoning about the subject of experience might run as follows: Consciousness, he says, reveals no enduring substantial subject. It also reveals no enduring substantial object. The given, construed as the totality of materials that the mind does have to work with, entirely consists of perishing contents. When Kant claims that the outer enduring object is required for the possibility of an inner enduring subject, it seems that he merely assumes the possibility of the one in order to provide a conceptual foundation for the other. Why does he not just assume the existence of the substantial subject and confess that his procedure is really no more realistic than that of Berkeley?

The essential difference between the inner and the outer is supposed to furnish the Kantian response to this objection. For no assumption that Kant could make within an ontology limited to inner objects could possibly be efficacious just because it is the essence of the inner to be perishing and insubstantial. Nothing mental endures because time is the form of the mental. So there can be no question of assuming the endurance of something mental. Furthermore, this opinion is not an arbitrary dogma. That the contents of consciousness are essentially transient is indisputable phenomenology.

The temporal is the realm of all contents of consciousness, so it looks as if we have to posit something nontemporal in order to introduce the least stability in our thought of ourselves and the world. But Kant would like to say that we do not have to posit anything because perception acquaints us with the spatial and with things that have permanent existence in space. The first Analogy of Experience asserts that our experience is necessarily of enduring substances. To the extent that the discussion is not entirely phenomenalistic and reductive, Kant seems to identify the enduring component of what is perceived with matter and to assimilate the assertion of the Analogy to the conservation of matter. This is explicitly Kant's view in the parallel discussion of the *Metaphysische Anfangsgründe*.[7] But there is another side of the idea of permanence that is less theoretical and sweeping and, perhaps, more attractive.

Permanence requires, at a minimum, that the temporal parameters of the object perceived be extended beyond those of the perception of the object. Thus, the idea of permanence *is* the idea of the existence of objects unperceived. It is this conception of permanence that furthers Kant's realism. Commitment to permanence in perception is the idea that our perceptions are *of* relatively stable objects which endure through gaps in our episodic experiences. Permanence expresses categorical opposition to the thesis that *esse* is *percipi*.

We have seen that the very advantage of nontemporality carries with it the disadvantage of separation from consciousness and the need for rerepresentation. If we forget about this problem for the moment, as Kant seems to, the prospects for his theory are good. Time comes into the picture of spatial reality only via experience. As a rerepresentation, an experience of a spatial thing has a date, that is, a place in the sequence of all mental contents of a subject. Nothing merely conceptual obstructs the possibility that an identical outer thing could be experienced at two different times. This is just what cannot happen with inner objects. I can experience again today the object that I experienced yesterday, but I cannot have the experience I had yesterday again today. At best I can have a qualitatively identical experience, never the numerically identical experience. For objects of inner sense, the date, that is, place in temporal sequence, is part of the principle of individuation. Therefore, if experiences have different dates, they are, ipso facto, different experiences. The enduring existence of things in space does not contradict the very essence of spatial existence, while to speak of the enduring existence of things that exist only in time does contradict the essence of such temporal things.

Once concepts of spatial enduring objects are given footing, we are able to speak, as Kant says, of "determinate time." The outer object exists when we perceive it. It endures between our perceptions of it. A clock is a reperceivable object with the help of which the time

between perceptual experiences is measured. The whole spatial world
is a generalized clock. It makes time determinate in the sense that it
makes it possible to say at just what time our inner experiences occur.
The endurance of the self that must accompany all experiences is
registered in the objective temporal order of outer things. The dates
of objects in clock time place the whole inner sequence of experiences
of objects in an objective context. This is Kant's completion of his
argument on apperception. Outer things are essential for the temporal continuity of the subject of experience.

This argument appears in various relatively obscure formulations in the Transcendental Deduction, in the Paralogisms, and in
the Refutation of Idealism. I have rehearsed it here in order to emphasize the strategic importance for Kant of the inaccessibility of the
spatial from immediate consciousness. Immediately accessible contents are essentially transient. In Kant's most theoretical thinking,
transience, like permanence, is pressed to the limit. Permanence means
conservation of matter *forever,* and transience means that mental
things are all new *at each instant.* The least endurance that goes beyond the instantaneous depends upon the powers of synthesis and
entails a mode of existence that is not possible within the mind itself.
Perhaps these extremes of permanence and transience are not necessary for Kant's objectives. They seem to come from a Leibnizian style
of thinking about parts and wholes and infinites that is familiar in
the "Inaugural Dissertation" and in the Antinomies. In any case, the
general line of thought is crucial to Kant's philosophy as a whole. To
say this is not to say that he offers a consistent account of the inner
and the outer, the spatial and the mental, so that his main conten-
tions can be contemplated within the equilibrium of a coherent and
plausible system of concepts. There are inconsistencies which cannot
be removed while remaining faithful to Kant's overall thought because they lie too deep, and Kant's awareness of them is too slight.
Nonetheless, the basis of a generally Kantian reconstruction of most
of what he says does seem to be possible.

8. A Sketch for the Consistent Kantian

We saw at the beginning of this essay that spatiality seems to
be equivalent to the locus of extramental existence in Kant's initial

definition of outer sense in the Aesthetic. This interpretation gave way to an inner and mental status for space in light of the asserted transcendental ideality of space and the idealist tendency of the claim that space is only *in us*. The complete collapse of Kantian realism then seemed to be avoidable only if we could understand outer sensation rather than spatiality as the irreducible connection with mind-independent things. Whether or not sensation supplies an adequate foundation for Kant's realism, however, it is clear that the main arguments of the *Critique of Pure Reason* require that spatiality carry with it an immunity from the transience of all things of which time is the form. This brings to the fore once again the identification of space with the region of nonmental existence.

Failure to resolve strains here leaves Kant seeming to assert that space is neither the metaphysically outer, since it is only appearance, nor mental, since it is not subject to the form of time. A satisfactory reconstruction must start from the fact that this pressure for an intermediate status that will bridge the gulf between the mind and the world arises quite naturally. Some such bridge is, indeed, just what is needed to overcome the solipsistic viewpoint and attendant skepticism and idealism. At the same time we obviously cannot leave space in an entirely unprovided-for limbo between appearance and reality.

The concept of representation must do most of the gap-closing work. Although he is the champion of representation against the challenge of idealist reductions, Kant frequently yields to the idealist thought that representations amount to a sort of impregnable epistemological shield that perfectly protects an ever-virginal reality from the assaults of enquirers. Every passionate investigation is repelled coldly, and all aspiring lovers of truth only get to know their own fantasies. There is something wrong here. Representations are involved in all efforts to know anything. But this does not mean that representations block knowledge from the outset by substituting a surrogate object. The idealist line about representation can be combated, in part, by shifting to use of the verb instead of the noun. We represent reality as a stable system of relatively stable material objects. It is *reality* that we thus represent. We do not represent our own representations as such a system. And, in any case, our representations certainly do not compose such a system. Our representation of the world is, itself, a thing of the mind, and it has concepts and propositions and images for constituents, not relatively stable material objects in space. If we resolve to defend Kant's philosophy and we are asked, "Is reality spatiotemporal?" we should not answer, as Kant himself often answers, "Empirical reality is spatiotemporal, but mind-independent reality is not." That reply goes with the idea that our representations are spatiotemporal and all we know about are our representations. The right answer should be, "We represent reality as a spatiotemporal system." This answer does not change the subject and insist on speaking only about representations. It is a guarded answer, but not a negative answer about mind-independent reality. For the question "Is reality spatiotemporal?" the answer "So we represent it" is a form of affirmative answer. Its force is very close to that of "We certainly think so."

If we accept this reading of the relationship between representation and reality, what are we to make of Kant's claims that space is only an imposed form and that space is transcendentally ideal? The idea that space is a form comes from Leibniz's analysis rejecting thinghood for space. Formal status makes space a principle for the organization of simultaneous existants and denies that space would be anything were there no such existants to be organized. This much does not impair the objectivity of space. If space is a system of relationships among simultaneously existing outer things, then spatial representation is representation of the outer. Spatial things will be outer things, though space itself is not one of them. This seemed to be Kant's view in the Metaphysical Exposition of space. It is only because Kant also thinks of space as a form *imposed by us* that the spatial tends to become subjective and ideal.

Why does Kant think that space is imposed by us and is not a system of relations in which things would stand even if we did not represent them at all? There are two reasons for this. First, this conception enables him to explain some synthetic a priori knowledge, as we saw in discussion of the Transcendental Exposition. I will simply pass over this presumed benefit of the ideality of space and will not consider here whether anything of that benefit could be retained if space were not regarded as an imposed system of relations. However this is decided, we cannot suppose that Kant flatly asserts that space is imposed simply because that will enable him to explain our knowledge of geometry and its application to the world. He must have reasons for thinking that this status is independently plausible. I want to call attention to a set of convictions that operate in the background of Kant's thinking, and sometimes in the foreground. For example:

> Those who take space and time for some real and absolutely necessary fastening as it were of all possible substances and states do not think that anything else is required in order to conceive how to a number of existing things there applies a certain original relation as the primitive condition of possible influxes and the principle of the essential form of the universe. [Even if we grant it as much reality and necessity as we can, space] . . . only represents the intuitively given possibility of universal coordination. [The question remains] . . . what is the principle upon which this relation of all substances rests, a relation which when seen intuitively is called space. [*Inaug. Diss.*, 16]

Here Kant is saying that we cannot simply accept space as the order in which simultaneous existents stand. That existents stand in any order, that they are related to one another in any way, requires an explanation beyond their mere existence. "Simply because of their subsistence they are not necessarily related to anything else" (Ibid., 17). Things must already form a whole or a universe in order to stand in any relations, even spatial relations. The imposed character of space comes out of these thoughts without reference to the explanatory fruitfulness of the idea of mind-imposed space vis-à-vis geometrical knowledge.

To give as much definition as possible to these elusive thoughts, let us consider reality without worrying at all about representation or knowledge for the moment. We can conveniently take God's point of view, remembering that it is one with which Leibniz and Kant sometimes seem to have a certain familiarity. Suppose God creates a planet. It will have all the contents and characteristics that he has put into it. There will already be spatial relationships between the parts of the planet, but the planet itself will not be anywhere in space, for there is nothing with which it is coordinated. Now let God create another planet. He need not first create more space so that there will be room for another planet. The fact that it does not need creating is a reflection of the nonthing-like status of space and of its necessary availability. Let us imagine that God makes the second planet larger and warmer than the first. As soon as there is more than one thing, in addition to the properties that each thing has, there will also be

a multiplicity of relations between things. All the relations seem to
have a secondary significance from the point of view of ontology and
creation. They do not place any demands on the creative powers of
God at all. A planet will not have the features it does have unless
God actively puts those features into it in his creation of it. But the
relations do not require anything beyond the creation of the individuals with their features. In creating the second planet God does
exactly what he would have done had he created it first. And then
it is, automatically so to speak, somewhere with respect to the first
planet, larger than the first, and warmer than the first. The thought
that relations obtain without being created is part of the Leibnizian
claim that relations are not real.

In order to connect this with our reconstruction of Kant's thinking, we have to add the thought that relations, and the ones constituting space in particular, have their existence only in representation.
To illustrate this we can pursue our story of creation. In what sense
is one planet larger than the other or located somewhere with respect
to the other? Each planet is itself. It has all its properties. It exists exactly as it would if the other planet did not exist at all (ignoring some
physics). From the point of view of the planet *in itself*, if we could
speak of such a thing, "larger than" or "located . . . with respect to"
do not enter into its existence at all. Of course God will know that
one planet has a certain size and the other a certain size. God will
know that one of these is greater than the other. This is because the
planets are assembled into a universe in God's thought. That they
manage to stand as constituents of anything is mediated by thought.

The idea that relations are imposed is the idea that they only obtain in the context of a surveying intellect or consciousness which provides a connection among things that would otherwise simply not
stand in any relations at all, even though the several things were to
exist. This pattern of thought is clearly visible in Kant's transcendental psychology. In the absence of a mind whose survey relates them
planets would stand in unrelated isolation much like the isolation
and wholesale disconnectedness that Kant ascribes to elements of the
unsynthesized manifolds of intuition. Kant's demand for synthesis is
not a matter of supposing that the mind will not appreciate the relationships between spatial things (that they form a triangle, for example) without synthesis. On the contrary, they do not form a triangle
or anything else until they are synthesized, although receptivity alone
assigns them location. Unsynthesized elements of intuition are simply

not related to one another at all, apart from the fact that synthesis can relate them. The perceivable features that they have as geometrical configurations have being as a consequence of synthesis. In this context, in the transcendental psychology, Kant is thinking of both elementary intuitions that need to be related and of complex intuitions that represent related things as mental items and not outer realities. But this thought clearly instantiates the pattern that relativizes relations to a surveying mind.

Quite apart from the issue of the mental status of spatial things that Kant asserts in his theory of the mental construction of spatial objects out of located but unextended sensations, his claim that the several constituents of a spatial thing only stand in spatial relations as a consequence of synthesis is not valid within the terms of Kant's own discussion. The fact that things are *in space* at all is ascribed to receptivity which gives a location to the original intuitions of outer sense. Kant says that all magnitude comes from synthesis. But the mere concept of location cannot be divorced from that of spatial relations in the way in which Kant requires. We may think with Kant that no ultimate original sensation is colored or otherwise sensuous and that the perceivability of the sensuous element in perception comes from a mental aggregation of many unperceived constituents. We cannot, however, altogether abandon the idea that the locations to which sensations are assigned in receptivity are near and remote from one another prior to synthesis. To withdraw this idea is to drain the meaning from "location" altogether. Plainly a certain manifold can be synthesized and perceived as a yellow surface only because many sensations with locations near one another have similar representational character, even though we are not conscious of that character on a sensation-by-sensation basis. The whole doctrine that traces geometry to receptivity would be lost if we could not say that the results of a synthesis were significantly determined in advance by the relations between the locations to which the several synthesized sensations are assigned. There is, then, a plain sense in which synthesis does not create objects with geometrical features out of mere collections of unrelated sensations. At most, synthesis discovers the geometrical features of preexisting systems of sensations. Borrowing Kant's own phrase, we should say that the spatial object is not produced by the synthesis insofar as its existence is concerned ("dem Dasein nach," A 92) but that the function of synthesis is only to make it possible for us to know spatial things as objects.

Once we give up the idea that space is imposed by us, we can restate the main themes of Kant while allowing that spatial things are independent of the mind. The mind contains only representations of spatial things. This is not a disaster now that we have got clear of the thought that knowledge by means of representations must be just knowledge of those representations. Our representations embrace our thought of the universe as a system of spatiotemporal, causally interconnected, material objects whose existence does not depend on our thought. Kant surely wants to make available the anti-idealist result of this externalization of the spatial. In the Paralogisms, for example, Kant says that each subject has his own private time and that private times are only commensurable with one another through the public time of spatial existence. Were space mental, it would be as private as time and would offer no exit from egocentrism. The crucial arguments of the *Critique* that we have outlined will be rescued by this understanding, since those arguments require that space be nonmental, while our spatial representations have their place in the sequence of subjective states.

Whether this reconstruction involves the retraction of the familiar Kantian claim that things-in-themselves are unknown is still not clear, but perhaps it now seems far less important. Our perceptual knowledge is all conditioned by complex relationships that obtain between ourselves and the things we perceive. As empiricists we believe that all our knowledge is based on perceptual knowledge. If we mean by knowledge of things-in-themselves knowledge that does not depend on any relations in which we stand to what we know, then we have no knowledge of things-in-themselves. Is there something from which we are, therefore, barred?

What are atomic theory, molecular biology, and radio astronomy telling us if not about how things are in themselves, as opposed to how things appear? If this sort of thing is not knowledge of things-in-themselves, then the demand for such knowledge seems like the demand to know what things would look like if there were no creatures with eyes. There may survive enough of a feeling that there could be some kind of divine, wholly nonrelational grasp of reality to support the idea that there is something that we cannot know in principle, because our knowledge depends on relations. But I prefer Kant's thought that the concept of a noumenon is only a negative and limiting concept and not the concept of an unknowable reality at all.

NOTES

1. Quotations from the *Critique of Pure Reason* are from the translation of Norman Kemp-Smith; those from Kant's "Inaugural Dissertation" are from the translation of G. B. Kerferd.

2. *Treatise of Human Nature*, I, ii, 6.

3. *Treatise of Human Nature*, I, ii, 4.

4. This argument plays a significant role in Kant's thinking about space throughout his mature work. See "Von dem Ersten Grunde des Unterschiedes der Gegenden im Raume," (1768), Preussischen Akademie Ausgabe, Berlin, 1905, II, 381; the "Inaugural Dissertation," (1770), section 15; and the *Prolegomena*, (1783), section 13.

5. Rudolf Eisler gives "representatio" as the overall signification of "Vorstellung," but his discussion includes sensation, perception, knowledge, and both empirical concepts and pure concepts, ideas and notions as species of the genus "Vorstellung" for Kant. See *Kant Lexikon*, Berlin, 1930, 588.

6. *A Commentary to Kant's 'Critique of Pure Reason,'* New York, 1930, 295.

7. Drittes Hauptstuck, Lehrsatz 2, Akademie Ausgabe, Berlin, 1903, IV, 541.

Index

Adams, possible, 167
aesthetic, transcendental, 204ff
Albert of Saxony, 44
Alquié, F., 59n
analytic-synthetic, 183
analytic propositions, 143
analyticity
  a priori proof and, 148f
  contingency and, 139ff
  of all truths, 175n, 176n
  Leibniz and, 139–56
apperception, transcendental, 187
Aquinas, 29, 58n, 59n, 60n, 62
Aristotle, 15, 38, 39, 42, 58n, 64, 65,
  76, 77, 95, 96, 97, 98, 114,
  118, 147
Arnauld, A., 33, 145, 154, 167, 169,
  175n, 177n, 179n
attributes
  and substances, 81ff
  infinite attributes of God, 86ff
Augustine, 28, 58n, 62
Austin, J. L., 19
automata, 47
averroism, 78
Ayer, A. J., 16, 19

behaviorism, 19–21
Bennett, J. A., 121n
Berkeley, G., 16, 18, 80, 96, 105,
  184, 185, 187, 195, 201, 202,
  203, 204, 214, 217, 218, 232,
  234
Boyle, R., 132, 174n. 175n
Buridan, J., 44
Burman, F., 55

Cabala, 96
Carnap, R., 19, 160, 174n

causality
  causa sui, 63, 72
  Spinoza's theory of, 71ff
Chisholm, R., 16, 179n
Clarke, S., 24n, 141, 175n
cogito, 1, 10f, 27
complete concept of the individual,
  154
consciousness, 45, 114ff
conservation of energy, 123, 124
conservation laws, 138
containment of predicate in subject,
  146ff, 156
Couturat, L., 175n
Cusa, Nicolas of, 59n

de Launay, Abbé, 36
Des Bosses, 177n
Descartes, R., 1, 26–60, 64, 65, 66,
  68, 74, 77, 78f, 88, 91, 93, 96,
  97, 99, 100, 101, 102, 106,
  114, 120n, 123, 124, 125, 126,
  127, 128, 129, 132, 134, 173n,
  174n, 177n, 186, 200, 203, 218,
  223, 225
  analogy of pilot and ship, 31
  geometrical physics of, 125
  on perception, 12f
  on the rejection of the psychologi-
    cal in physics, 38
  scientific explanation for, 128
DeVolder, 174n
Dewey, J., 19
doubt, method of, 16, 27

Elizabeth, Princess, 33, 36
empiricism, 1–25
  as epistemology and as metaphysics,
    182f

in Kant, 180ff
evil, problem of, 128
exigentia, 159

final causes, 40, 42
foreknowledge, God's, 152f
form
    and formal cause, 96
    and matter, 38, 65
    the soul as, 65
formaliter, versus eminenter, 99f
Freud, S., 61
Fried, D., 176n

Galileo, 5, 174n, 222
Garber, D., 24n
Gassendi, P., 32, 61
Gibieuf, Father, 33
Gilson, E., 35, 58n
God's existence, proof of, 10, 29
Gouhier, H., 60n
gravity, 39, 42f
    and teleology, 40
Grice, H. P., 176n
Gueroult, M., 83, 120n

Hacking, I., 176n
Hampshire, S., 62
Hegel, G. F., 71, 74
Hobbes, T., 32, 61
Hume, D., 16, 18, 80, 81, 182, 186,
    187, 200, 207, 213, 232n
hypothetico-deductive method (in
    Descartes), 4

idealism, subjective, 188f
    transcendental idealism vs. em-
        pirical realism, 202
    transcendental idealism vs. trans-
        cendental realism, 198
incongruent counterparts, 213
individuation, 77, 92
inertia, 38
intelligible world, 199
intentional species, 51
interaction of mind and body, 34,
    49–51, 55

Ishiguro, H., 176n

judgments of perception vs experience,
    185, 231

Kant, I., 7, 13, 14, 18, 23, 74, 105,
    143, 144, 145, 146, 147, 149n,
    182–243
    applicability of geometry to empiri-
        cal objects, 214
    concept of God's mental processes,
        194ff
    construction of objects of percep-
        tion, 211
    idealism according to, 184, 202
    concept of imagination, 189
    perspectivalism of, 190
    concept of representations, 190
    subjectivity for, 180ff
    concept of synthesis, 191
Kemp-Smith, N., 230
Kripke, S., 23, 178n, 179n

Latta, R., 59n
Leibniz, G. W., 2, 3, 6, 7, 8, 13, 14,
    16, 46, 59n, 66, 68, 75, 83, 84,
    85, 96, 106, 123–81, 211, 213,
    217, 223, 224
    agency according to, 134ff
    correspondence with Clarke, 3, 212
    existence and contingency for, 144
    human action on the pattern of
        divine, 172f
    incompleteness of matter, 127
    mechanism reconciled with agency,
        135ff
    nature according to, 131ff
    opposition to indifference, 140
    theory of truth, 147
Lewis, C. I., 16
Lewis, D., 163, 164, 167, 178n, 179n
Locke, J., 16, 17, 19, 174n, 217,
    222
Lovejoy, A., 159, 176n, 178n
Lucretius, 61

Mach, E., 19, 173n
Maimonides, 96

Malebranche, N., 66, 80, 170n, 195
mass, 193
mechanism vs. nature, 131ff
mechanism, bodily, 46–48
Mersenne, M., 33, 37, 174n
metaphysical exposition, meaning of,
    205
Meyer, L., 69
Mill, J. S., 19
modes, 81ff
Molina, L., 165
Moore, G. E., 19, 76
More, H., 66
motion
    and the will, 138
    continuation for Descartes, 130ff
    instantaneous, 126
    natural, 39
    quantity of, 123,

Naert, E., 174n
Nason, J. W., 176n
necessitating vs. inclining reasons, 146
necessity
    for Hume and Kant compared, 182
    hypothetical vs. metaphysical, 139
    infinite analysis and, 150, 152
    and deductive explanation, 140

occasionalism, 51, 79–80, 81, 96, 133,
    136
O'Shaugnessy, B., 175n
outer sense, 200ff
    relation to the nonmental, 200

Papineau, D., 173n
Parkinson, G. H. R., 177n, 178n
perception
    causal understanding of, 6–7
    empiricist theories of, 17
    metaphysics of, 113ff
perceptual consciousness, objects of,
    15–16
perishing mental contents, 186, 232
permanence in perception, 187, 231,
    235
petites perceptions, 211, 217
phenomena bene fundata, 68, 211f

phenomenalism, 8
    in Leibniz and Kant, 9, 14
    origin of, in Descartes, 8–9

Quine, W. V., 19, 176n

Randall, J. H., 121n
realism, empirical, vs, transcendental
    idealism, 198, 220
refutation of idealism, 23, 185, 231
Regius, 31
Reid, T., 18
representation, 195f, 218f, 237
    and object, 214ff
    vs. reality, 193, 238
Rescher, N., 176n, 177n, 178n
res extensa, 125
Rorty, R., 19
Russell, B., 7, 16, 18, 19, 20, 21, 22,
    60n, 145, 159, 175n, 178n

scientia media, 165, 178n
secondary qualities, 124, 183
    versus primary, 222ff
Sellars, W., 19
sensation, 209ff
    and objects of sense, 214ff
    and reality, 219
    as the matter of objects of outer
        sense, 210
Shirley, S., 121n
Smart, J. C. C., 22
Snell, 130
soul as a form, 30, 40
space, 198ff
    and endurance, 188
    as substance, 66
    in us, 188, 202f
    metaphysical vs. transcendental ex-
        position of, 206
    necessity of, 206
    uniqueness of, 204–5
space and time
    as forms, 208
    expositions of, 205
    subjectivity of, 198
species infima, 148, 155, 156
Spinoza, B., 2, 3, 8, 16, 61–122,

121n, 157, 175n, 177n
causality and representation, 114–18
consciousness according to, 105ff
containment of effect in cause, 117f
extension and thought (instability of the parallelism), 92–93
external things, knowledge of, 103ff
finitude according to, 67–68
form according to, 81
idealism, Spinoza's tendency toward, 95
ideas according to, 100ff
ideas of outer things problematic for, 108ff
imagination according to, 69–70
knowledge of the body in, 105
incorporative epistemology, 119
physiology of perception in, 102ff
rejection of dualism, 77
doctrine of substance, 62ff
substance and causality, 76
thought as an attribute, 88ff
time according to, 70–71
understanding of perception, 111ff
Strawson, P. F., 176n, 181, 188, 210
substance, 30
created, 87

infinite, 75
substantial form, 37, 38–41, 129
vs. accidental form, 41
synthesis, and time, 228f
synthetic a priori in mathematics, 207f

teleology, 6, 40, 129–30, 136f
things in themselves, 99, 183f, 221, 242
time
and contingency, 67
and schematism, 229
categories subject to temporal conditions, 229
definition of, 235–36
determination grounded in outer objects, 233f
in outer intuition, 226ff
Tschirnhausen, E. von, 86, 88–92

Valla, Lorenzo, 158
vinculum substantiale, 177n
vis viva, 123

Wilson, M., 176n
Wittgenstein, L., 22
Wolfson, H., 96, 120n, 122n